The Lamb's Book of Life

Scriptural references are based on
the New International Version
and the King James Version.

All Scripture quotations, unless otherwise noted, are taken from The Holy Bible, New International Version (North American Edition), copyright © 1973, 1978, 1984 by the International Bible Society. Used by permission of Zondervan Publishing House. Italics and brackets used in quotations from Scripture have been inserted by the author. Cover art adapted from © Brenda Carson | Dreamstime.com & © Valery Antipin | Dreamstime.com with alterations.

ISBN 978-0-9668099-6-1

Wake Up America Seminars, Inc.
P.O. Box 273
Bellbrook, Ohio 45305
(937) 848-3322
http://www.wake-up.org

Copyright © 2016
Wake Up America Seminars, Inc.
and its licensors.

All rights reserved.

Larry W. Wilson

The Lamb's Book of Life

Table of Contents

Chapter 1 -	A Short Overview	5
Chapter 2 -	Jesus Found Worthy	21
Chapter 3 -	The Humiliation of Jesus	27
Chapter 4 -	The Origin of Sin	45
Chapter 5 -	When Was Jesus Found Worthy?	55
Chapter 6 -	The Lamb Receives the Book	79
Chapter 7 -	Seven Revelations About Jesus	87
Chapter 8 -	Four Judgments/Four Living Creatures	91
Chapter 9 -	The Four Royal Horsemen	103
Chapter 10 -	First Seal - Salvation Through Faith Alone . . .	117
Chapter 11 -	Second Seal - Bible Translated / Distributed . .	131
Chapter 12 -	Third Seal - Judgment of the Dead	139
Chapter 13 -	Fourth Seal - Judgment of the Living	153
Chapter 14 -	Fifth Seal - Believers Martyred	165
Chapter 15 -	Sixth Seal - Second Coming	179
Chapter 16 -	Seventh Seal - Book of Life Opened	187
Appendix A -	Monotheism Versus Tritheism	197
Appendix B -	The Physical Appearing of Lucifer	221

Chapter One
A Short Overview

"When I was woven together in the depths of the Earth, your eyes saw my unformed body. All the days ordained for me were written in your book before one of them came to be. How precious to me are your thoughts, O God! How vast is the sum of them!" (Psalms 139:15-17, italics mine)

(To keep this overview as simple and short as possible, Bible texts and supporting arguments are kept to a minimum in this chapter. They will be provided in the rest of this book.)

The book of Revelation contains several exciting stories and one story reveals that the Father wrote a book before angels and human beings were created. Because the Father knows everything (omniscient), He wrote a complete history of sin's drama (this includes everyone's thoughts, words, and actions). God wrote this history to resolve problems He knew would come later. After He completed the book containing future history, He sealed it by affixing seven seals on it. Then, He put the book in a safe place.

Millions of people have heard about the seven seals of Revelation, but very few of them know about the book that God sealed with seven seals! Obviously, the contents of this book are much more important than the seals which keep the book closed. Of course, the seven seals are very important and breaking each seal goes hand-in-hand with the book, but we first should focus on the nature and content of the book.

A History of Life Before Creation

The Father has infinite wisdom and the Bible reveals that He is deliberate and purposeful in everything He does. I have found four reasons why He wrote a complete history of life before life was created.

First, the Father foreknew that sin would arrive first in Heaven and then on Earth. He foreknew that after angels and human beings were created, His biggest problem would be to prevent a *third* outbreak of sin and to justify why His "sudden death" law exists. (After sin's drama is over, the Father will enforce an eternal law that says "a sinner will die the very day he sins.") He had to develop a system that would prevent sin from occurring again in a universe with beings exercising free will.

Second, the Father foreknew He would be at the center of a great controversy among the angels in Heaven and the people on Earth. He knew a third of the holy angels would become suspicious and hate Him, ultimately choosing someone else to be their lord and master. The Father foresaw the suffering, pain, death, and agony which would accompany the curse of sin on Earth. Since He is the omnipotent Ruler of the Universe, He knew that He would be blamed for the rise of sin. When the Father sealed the book before creation, He set a date when the entire universe will see the contents of the book. At the end of a 1,000 year millennium, after the seventh seal is broken, the book's contents will astonish everyone. Ultimately, the information within the book will exonerate the Father and vindicate His actions.

Third, the Father wrote this book and sealed it because He cannot afford to reveal what He knew until the right time. If anyone reads the book before that appointed time, the Father could never prove that He is a God of love and allows His children to exercise free will. Moreover, He could never exonerate Himself from Lucifer's sophisticated accusations and lies. Do not underestimate Lucifer's crafty intelligence. The devil concocted many clever lies to malign the Father before He forced Lucifer from Heaven and the slander was so effective that even one third of the holy angels believed it! These angels had sinless natures. They were not inherently rebellious toward God before their disaffection. They had been joyful and happy in Heaven until Lucifer caused them to doubt God's integrity. Because the Father foreknew that He could only defend Himself after sin had fully matured, he did not answer the questions the devil's lies produced. Instead, because He foreknew the events that would occur in Heaven and on Earth, He wrote down everything that would happen. He sealed the book with seven seals, knowing that the sensitive information contained in the book would eventually exonerate Him.

Finally, the Father chose to write a "prerecorded history book" because He foresaw a peculiar problem. As Almighty God, His infinite ways are unlike the finite ways of His children. He has infinite wisdom, foreknowledge, and unlimited power. Therefore, He knows today what His children will understand ten thousand years later. God's infinite powers make Him incomprehensible and His subjects will never understand at a particular time what He is doing. *Living in the presence*

Chapter 1 – A Short Overview

of an eternal and infinite God, a God who cannot be understood, is only possible through love and faith. God's children have to trust and obey Him even when they do not understand Him. They have to believe that He is always righteous, fair, and loving without regard for the circumstances. This is what faith in God means.

Suppose the Father sets up a really wonderful experience for His children that will take 10,000 years to unfold. Let us assume that 10,000 years later, His children finally reach a point where they understand His original purpose. The only way His subjects can adore and worship Him during 10,000 years of mystery is through faith and love. This is why He wants us to study Him and His ways, because the more we know about Him the greater our faith and confidence in Him will be. Faith in God, when viewed in reverse, always makes sense. Our infinite Father (a being who lives in unapproachable light, whose finite subjects can never completely understand Him) chose to write a book so that one day, He could explain Himself so completely that finite beings would never question his motives or great love again.

The Father is omnipotent (all powerful) and omniscient (all knowing), but He would take His own life before using any of these powers to manipulate or control His subjects. With the evidence from His book, He will prove that He can be trusted to be a God of love. He gives His subjects freedom to exercise free will. Of course, free will does not mean that God has no laws. On the contrary, His subjects can choose to obey or disobey His laws which are the product of infinite wisdom. At the appointed time, the seventh seal on the book will be broken. A changeless and eternal God will demonstrate for all eternity that He can be trusted to keep an infinite distance between His foreknowledge and His omnipotence. This infinite distance means that He will not use either power for personal advantage. Instead, He will only use these powers to ensure that righteousness and truth are forever exalted. This concept may seem simple, but there is far more to this matter than meets the eye. It is one of the most profound stories in the Bible.

A Book Sealed with Seven Seals

The angels who live in God's presence and human beings who walk by faith with Him study the Father's actions closely, so He does nothing without careful forethought. He is constantly dropping clues so that those wanting to know Him can know more about Him. Those who do not care to know much about Him are not offended by His clues. The

Father is the king of courtesy and respect. He respects our choices. If someone does not want to know or love Him, God will not endlessly pester that person. The Father can be present or absent within any heart. The owner of the heart has a choice.

One clue which the Father has given to us is the number seven. It is no accident there are seven churches, seven seals, seven trumpets, seven thunders, seven heads which are seven mountains and seven kings, seven angels, and seven bowls in the book of Revelation. There are also seven days in a week, as well as a cycle of seven years and a week of seven years in the Jubilee Calendar. Jesus spoke seven times on the cross, there are seven colors in the rainbow, and there are seven continents. It appears that the number seven indicates full-fill-ment, as in perfect completion. If we add the years in genealogical Bible records, beginning with Adam and Eve, continuing through the reigns of the kings in Bible history, and including the eighteen prophetic time periods announced in Daniel and Revelation, the Bible describes *seven* millenniums for the duration of sin's drama on Earth!

If we apply the idea of "full-fill-ment" to the seven seals, two ideas quickly emerge. First, the Father perfectly sealed His book to ensure the contents are revealed when the *day* for which the book was written arrives. Second, the Father deliberately put seven seals on His book because the breaking of each seal is part of a seven-step process that will be completed on the *day* of His exoneration. I believe the breaking of each seal is associated with a stunning process called "the revelation of Jesus Christ."

The Book Contains Sensitive Information

Every government and many corporations on Earth create "top secret" information. Every adult knows that prematurely releasing sensitive information can have unintended or negative consequences. Because the Father is all knowing, He foreknew that Lucifer and his followers would rebel and they would be expelled from Heaven. He also foreknew the details surrounding the fall of Adam and Eve that Cain would kill Abel, and that Jesus would suffer and die on the cross. He even foreknew the names and actions of the religious leaders and soldiers who participated in Jesus' death. Of course, all of these things are included in His book, as well as the motives, thoughts, words, and actions of each person involved. There is information in the book that requires the utmost security and this explains why He physically sealed the book with seven seals. Looking at the end of sin's drama, the Father foreknew who would be saved from the penalty for sin and who would not. He foreknew the creation of angels and human beings, along with their eternal destinies before they were created. The Father wrote each being's outcome in His book. Because His history book will endure as a testimony for all eternity to come, the Father blotted out the names of those who will be destroyed by fire at the end of the 1,000 years.

Given the sensitive nature of such information, if the book was exposed prematurely or fell into the hands of His adversaries, the Father could never escape taunts of predestination, ridicule, and condemnation. Throughout eternity the charge would be repeated, "God is not a God of love." His own children would claim He predestined certain angels and human beings to be saved and others to be destroyed. They would say He even wrote down the results before life was created! His adversaries would claim He is condemned by His own words maintaining He is a God that owns and manipulates His subjects according to *His* free will and His subjects do not have free will or any say about their destiny.

The Father has implemented a plan to end these allegations and exonerate Himself from any hint of manipulation. First, He wrote a book, sealed it seven times, and put it away. Then, when the angels were first created, He assigned certain angels to serve as recording angels with special "camcorders" to record life in real time. Each recording angel records a life from beginning to end including our motives, thoughts, words, and actions. They miss nothing. The Father, with complete integrity, predetermined that the records of the recording angels would be used to judge the eternal destiny of human beings. *The book sealed with seven seals is not opened or used to judge human beings.*

The Great White Throne Judgment

The Bible teaches that Jesus has been appointed to judge sinners. **"The Father judges no one, but has entrusted all judgment to the Son."** (John 5:22) **"For we must all appear before the judgment seat of Christ, that each one may receive what is due him for the things done while in the body, whether good or bad."** (2 Corinthians 5:10) When each person's case comes before Jesus, He will see and review everything the recording angels recorded: **"For God will bring every deed into judgment, including every hidden thing, whether it is good or evil."** (Ecclesiastes 14:12)

Chapter 1 – A Short Overview

At the end of the 1,000 years, the Holy City will come down from Heaven and settle on Earth. The saints (who were taken to Heaven at the Second Coming) will descend with the Holy City as it comes down from Heaven and the wicked will be resurrected so that everyone who has ever lived on Earth will be present. The wicked will stand outside and the saints will be inside the Holy City. Billions of people and all of the angels (including Lucifer and his followers) will be in attendance. Jesus will sit on a high and glorious white throne that shines brighter than the Sun.

After everyone has been gathered, Jesus will stand and a hush will fall over this innumerable host. Solemnity and sobriety will be in the atmosphere as a glorious Jesus is about to take action.

Jesus will call for the recordings made by the recording angels (the books of records). These books will be opened and suddenly, everyone (angels and human beings) will see a vivid panorama. Each being will see a movie of his own life and observe his motives, thoughts, words, and actions as they happened. Each being will also see his responses to the voice of God in his heart. Was there habitual submission or rebellion? As the movie continues, each being will see the plan of salvation. The wicked angels will see God's patience and grace He extended to them before they reached the point of no return in their rebellion. Every human will see what the Father did to save repentant sinners. Everyone will see Jesus' birth, ministry, suffering, and death when He came to Earth. Everyone will be overwhelmed with God's love for sinners. Finally, Jesus will inform each angel and human being about his eternal destiny. Each person will actually see the moment that Jesus examined his life prior to the second coming and determined his destiny. They will either see the joy that followed for those that were declared righteous or the sorrow that overtook Jesus and Heaven's host for those who could not be saved. At the end of this panoramic presentation, everyone (angels and humans alike) will fall to the ground before Jesus:

> **"'By myself I have sworn, my mouth has uttered in all integrity a word that will not be revoked: Before me every knee will bow; by me every tongue will swear. They will say of me, 'In the Lord alone are righteousness and strength.' ' All who have raged against Him will come to Him and be put**

> to shame. But in the Lord all the descendants of Israel will be found righteous and will exult." (Isaiah 45:23-25)

The righteous will fall on their faces before Jesus, completely amazed that He saved them. They realize they do not deserve the gift of eternal life or even the lowest place in the kingdom. They are overwhelmed by Jesus' selfless sacrifice and the gift of His righteousness. Each person exclaims, "Worthy, worthy, worthy is the Lamb of God who took away my sin. My salvation belongs to you, the Lamb who was slain for me."

The wicked will also fall on their faces before Jesus, recognizing His judgment is righteous and true. The evidence is impeccable, the record is true; it cannot be twisted or distorted. Jesus has treated them with generosity, offered them life and every opportunity. They realize their rebellion against the Holy Spirit was their own doing and they accept Jesus' judgment. They are sorry for who they are, but realize they cannot change the person they have become and they own the penalty for their sins.

Jesus Breaks the Seventh Seal

After the "This is Your Life" movie has ended, Jesus will tell the innumerable host to stand. He has something everyone must see. Jesus turns to a table and lifts "The Book of Life." The book has one remaining seal on it. After Jesus tells everyone about the origin and nature of the book, He opens the seventh and final seal. Another movie begins and it will last about 30 minutes. Everyone silently gazes at the sky and sees the contents of the book! It is identical in every way to the books of the records made by the recording angels. Even more amazing, everyone sees the names of angels and human beings which were blotted out of the book, even before angels and human beings were created!

Each wicked angel and human being will find his life perfectly recorded in the Book of Life. However, each wicked being will find his name missing and each righteous being will find his sins covered by the righteous life of Jesus! What a stunning revelation! Amazingly, the Father foreknew who would end up inside the Holy City and outside the Holy City before angels and human beings were created.

Here are three facts that can be distilled from this once-in-an-eternity moment:

First, the Father can prove that He foreknew everything about everybody before any life was created. Identical histories, one written before history began and the other written in real time, prove this fact.

Second, because identical histories exist in writing, the Father is exonerated from the accusation that He uses omniscience and omnipotence to manipulate the eternal destiny of His subjects. He foreknew the rise of sin as well as each individual's motives, thoughts, words, and actions, but He has given everyone free will and freedom to exercise this free will. He even paid the price for sin so that every repentant sinner would have eternal life! Therefore, each person's choice has made him a participant in one of two groups standing before the throne, saved or doomed. After seeing the movie of their lives, everybody confesses that their position inside or outside the Holy City was a result of personal choice. Each person has already admitted to Jesus that he was carefully and thoughtfully judged in righteousness and in truth. Everyone has confessed that Jesus took into account everything possible and he has been more than fair. The wicked stand outside the Holy City because they responded to the Holy Spirit's voice with rebellion and the righteous stand inside the Holy City because they responded to the Holy Spirit's voice with submission.

Third, it is important to understand that the Father does not judge anyone, that is, He does not determine the eternal destiny of anyone. The Father has appointed Jesus to be the judge of mankind because first, Jesus has walked in our shoes. He knows what life as a human being is like on Earth and the Father has ordained that human beings are to be judged by a peer. This is both righteous and fair. Second, the Father has not permitted Jesus to know what is written in "The Book of Life." As our judge, Jesus has to examine each person's record on its own merit. The Father ordained that Jesus had to judge the record of each person's life before millions of watching angels (intelligent, reasoning witnesses). The Father did this because He wants the holy angels to see just how deliberate, careful, and generous Jesus is in judging every case. Remember, these angels will live with the Father and Jesus throughout eternity. Therefore, if trust, faith, and love for God is to endure forever, the Father and Jesus must act in open and transparent ways. Not even the slightest hint of inappropriate behavior can be found in God's ways or the knowledge will fester into a third rebellion.

In closing, think about this: If Jesus had foreknowledge and knew what the Father had written in "The Book of Life" about each being's

Chapter 1 – A Short Overview 13

eternal destiny and the outcome of His judgment perfectly aligned with the book sealed with seven seals, intelligent angels and human beings would quickly see through the ruse. Heaven would be a conspiracy if this happened. The Father and Son would be seen as co-conspirators, one merely defending the other. If the Father and Jesus judged angels and human beings according to foreknowledge, then the claim that God's subjects have free will is a cruel joke. The Father would be condemned by His own words and Jesus would be found to be a co-conspirator, merely keeping the Father on the throne. If that were true, the devil and his followers would have been right to rebel against Jesus and the Father.

God, the Father, put this amazing story in the book of Revelation so that all who are preparing to spend eternity with the Godhead can appreciate what they have done to redeem human beings. God is about to act and those who know the reasons for His actions will be prepared when the remaining seals are opened.

The Father established four eternal laws and wrote a book before any life was created.	Why?
God's government is based on the rule of law. Later, He will use the book to solve a mystery.	What are the four laws?

The laws are: (1) Each being must love God with all of his heart, mind and soul, (2) Each being must love his neighbor as he loves himself, (3) Each being must worship the Creator and (4) If a being sins, he will be put to death.

The first two laws are well known and worshiping the Creator makes sense, but the fourth law seems out of character for a God of love.

God told Adam that if anyone ate from the forbidden tree, the sinner would die on the day that he sinned. (Genesis 2:17)This penalty was based on the fourth law.

So the basis for sudden death in Eden is found in the fourth law which God established before any life was created?

Yes. When the Father established the four laws He knew that rebellion would occur. He also knew that He would be blamed for it.	If God gives His children the power of choice, how can He be blamed if they choose to rebel?
Consider this: After living in Heaven for a long time, the highest created being, Lucifer, started a rebellion by accusing God of being unfair.	Unfair about what?

Lucifer was a covering cherub and he wanted to be honored and worshiped like Jesus. The Father would not permit it.

Lucifer became unhappy because he wanted more than the Father permitted him to have.

So, Lucifer accused the Father of being unfair. Lucifer's anger and jealousy caused him to lead a third of God's angels into open rebellion. This is how sin began in Heaven and Lucifer has been blaming God for being unfair ever since.

Lucifer's attack on the Father went something like this: "God says He is a God of love, that His children have the power of choice, but look at His laws. He says we have to love and obey Him, but the day we exercise our power of choice, He will kill us. This is not divine love, this is divine tyranny!"

Even though they sinned, God "stayed" the execution of Lucifer and his followers until the universe could understand the nature of sin

Earlier, you mentioned a book. What mystery does the Father's book resolve?

The Father wrote a book detailing the life of every being. He sealed it with seven seals.

At the end of the 1,000 years in Revelation 20, Jesus will open the book and reveal its contents.

The Father will then prove that He knew everything about everyone, including Lucifer. The Father will show that He foreknew the painful consequences and price that would come with the curse of sin.

And most of all, the Father will confirm that everyone was allowed to exercise the power of choice.

When everyone sees that the Father's book is identical to the daily records special angels recorded in real time, the truth about God's ways and character will become self-evident. The Father is not righteous because He says so, His is worthy of honor and worship because the evidence proves He is a God of love.

This is amazing! The Father's book will be identical to the daily records recorded by special angels.

The Father wants everyone to know that He will not use His foreknowledge to manipulate His children.

Why was the Father's book sealed with seven seals?

The Father knew from the beginning which angels and human beings would have to be destroyed. Therefore, if the contents of His book were prematurely exposed, intelligent beings would wonder forever if He predestined some subjects for eternal death and others for eternal life. So He sealed His book with seven seals.

Incidently, after the Lamb was found worthy to receive the book, John called it, "The Lamb's Book of Life."

Because the seventh seal is broken at the end of the 1,000 years, does this mean the Book of Life has nothing to do with a person's salvation?

That's right. The Bible says the Book of Life is only opened at the end of the 1,000 years. (Revelation 20:12)

Are human beings judged from other records kept in Heaven?

When a person is born, a recording angel makes a flawless record of that life in real time, just as it unfolds. Each recording includes our words, thoughts, motives, and actions.

As Judge, Jesus carefully examines each recording before reaching a decision for eternal life or death. Jesus does not know what is in the Father's book until the final seal is broken.

Now I get it. The Father will not use His foreknowledge to manipulate us. His children have free will; the freedom to choose. Even if He had to give up His own Son to save sinners, the Father always gives His subjects the power of choice! Truly, He is a God of love!

Chapter 2
Jesus Found Worthy

> "Then I saw in the right hand of Him who sat on the throne a scroll with writing on both sides and sealed with seven seals. And I saw a mighty angel proclaiming in a loud voice, 'Who is worthy to break the seals and open the scroll?' But no one in Heaven or on Earth or under the Earth could open the scroll or even look inside it." (Revelation 5:1-3)

Because many Christians do not understand the events described in Revelation 5, they do not appreciate the importance of the events described. Let us consider the background for these events. About A.D. 95, while John was serving a prison sentence on the Isle of Patmos, he had a vision of an event in Heaven that would occur seventeen centuries later. John saw a glorious being sitting on a throne with millions of angels and 24 human beings assembled around Him. A solemn convocation was underway and during this meeting the Father produced a book sealed with seven seals. He offered the book to anyone who was qualified to break the seals and reveal the contents of the book. Even though John does not explicitly say what the qualifications were, by further study we can determine them. The assembled host conducted a thorough search, but they could find no one in the whole universe (dead or alive) worthy to receive the book. Then, Jesus offered Himself as a candidate to receive the book. The assembly closely scrutinized Jesus and after thoroughly vetting Him, they found that he was worthy and the Father agreed. The Father gave Jesus the book and He began breaking the seals. The events described in this scene were profoundly important and we will examine some themes about this convocation and the worthiness of Jesus.

Jesus Represented as a Lamb

John describes Jesus in Revelation 5:6 with language that is essential to understanding this story: **"Then I saw a Lamb, looking as if it had been slain, standing in the center of the throne, encircled by the four living creatures and the elders. He had seven horns and**

seven eyes, which are the seven spirits of God [the seven angels who stand before God – Revelation 8:2] **sent out into all the Earth."**

Jesus is represented in this scene "as a Lamb looking as if it had been slain" because this representation of Jesus reveals the qualifications for opening the book. Jesus appears as if He had been slain, demonstrating the qualification that mattered most to the Father was "proof of fidelity to His will." Long before any life was created, the Father conceived a plan to redeem sinners. When Adam and Eve sinned, the Father was willing to implement His plan because their sin was not open defiance. According to the plan, Jesus volunteered to give His life for Adam and Eve. Jesus came to Earth and died on the cross to do the Father's will. Therefore, when John saw Jesus looking like a lamb that had been slain, this representation demonstrates "proof of fidelity to the Father's will." Jesus carried out the Father's will, even giving up His eternal life so that sinners might inherit it!

In his vision, John viewed a scene in Heaven that would occur in the eighteenth century, seventeen centuries after his vision. The first step in the final phase of God's plan to resolve the sin problem was to find someone worthy to break the seals and open the book. The Father was looking for someone who would perfectly execute the plan which He created before any life was created.

The Father has perfect foreknowledge and omnipotence (all power), so if He opened the book that He had written, He could only prove He had foreknowledge. The Father does not need to prove that He has perfect foreknowledge. The Father has a larger problem! He needs to prove that He will not use His perfect foreknowledge and His omnipotence to manipulate or control His subjects. He needs to prove that He is a God of love and this task is far more difficult. He wants to prove to everyone that He has given His subjects the freedom to exercise free will. He will not interfere with the exercise of free will under *any* circumstance. In God's universe, everyone is free to exercise power of choice and of course, experience the consequences that come with this freedom.

At the appointed time, the Father will prove that there is an infinite distance between His omnipotence and His foreknowledge and He can be trusted to keep a wall of separation between them. The Father wants the universe to see there is absolutely no selfishness within Him. He is not a divine bully or an eternal dictator that rules the universe merely because He has the power to do so. He is not an omnipotent lawmaker

Chapter 2 – Jesus Found Worthy 23

that creates self-serving laws when needed. Instead, He is a God of love. He wants the universe to see that He will only use His omnipotence and foreknowledge to benefit His subjects. He is not a God of love because He says so. He is a God of love because His actions speak for themselves. As long as God is the Ruler of the universe, He will deeply love, provide for, and delight those who put their faith in Him. If a subject chooses to rebel against His government of righteousness and truth, that subject may freely rebel against Him and receive the consequences. The great obstacle for His finite subjects is for them to understand God's law, which is based on His infinite wisdom, requiring a sinner's death on the day he sins. Reasoning beings, before they had knowledge of good and evil, would not understand this law is righteous and necessary. For example, if the Father had annihilated Lucifer the day he sinned, Lucifer's closest friends may have thought that Lucifer's claim that God was not a God of love was correct.

Requirements to Open the Book

The Father needed someone who did not have foreknowledge and did not know what was inside His book to open it. Additionally, the Father needed the individual to achieve specific prerequisites before opening the book

First, the recipient of the book must be able to carry out His plan to redeem without the slightest deviation. This qualification was necessary so no one throughout eternity could charge that the Father's plan to resolve the sin problem was unfair, defective, or inadequate. Second, the recipient of the book must be able to correctly and appropriately reveal everything about Jesus which the Father ordained. Finally, the recipient of the book must be willing to impose incredible suffering on the inhabitants of Earth (during seals four and five). When these three qualifications were presented, I am sure everyone in the convocation was stunned and dumbfounded. I believe John heard and understood the qualifications. John also understood the seriousness of what was at stake and when no one was found worthy to exonerate the Father, he cried.

Before Jesus was found worthy to receive the book, everyone at the convocation knew that the Father intended to recuse Himself from the process of concluding sin's drama. Because the Father was on trial, the challenge was to find someone who could do everything required and eternally exonerate the Father. Whoever was found worthy would receive sovereign authority over everything in Heaven and on Earth. When the angels concluded that no created being could do the job, Jesus offered Himself as a candidate. The angels and the elders quickly realized Jesus was the *only* solution. Jesus had shown perfect fidelity to the Father's will in circumstances that went far beyond the experience of any other person. Jesus had overcome every temptation and perfectly carried out the Father's plan of redemption, even to the point of giving up His own life. This made Him "the Lamb of God." **"He was oppressed and afflicted, yet he did not open his mouth; He was led like a lamb to the slaughter, and as a sheep before her shearers is silent, so He did not open His mouth."** (Isaiah 53:7)

In Revelation 5:6, John describes "the Lamb" as having seven horns and seven eyes, which are seven spirits, or seven angels, (Hebrews 1:14; Zechariah 1:8-10; 6:1-5) sent out into all the Earth. After the angelic host and the 24 elders considered the qualifications necessary to receive the book and approved Jesus, only then did the Father approve Jesus. Jesus was not His choice, He was their choice. The angels and the elders saw that the task of opening the book determined the necessary qualifications. In other words, the Father had not written the required qualifications that would eliminate everyone but Jesus.

Jesus Received Sovereign Power

After the Father approved their unanimous choice, He gave Jesus sovereign power over the universe. (Daniel 7:13,14; Ephesians 1:9,10) This omnipotent power is represented by the seven horns in Revelation 5:6. In John's day, a horn was a symbol of power or authority. (2 Samuel 22:3; Psalms 18:2; Luke 1:69) Therefore, seven horns mean a perfect, complete fulfillment of power or sovereign power. Also, the seven angels who stood before the Father (Revelation 8:2) were also given over to Jesus. These magnificent and capable beings are the same seven angels of the seven churches, the seven trumpets, and the seven bowls. These seven angels will serve important roles during the seven trumpets and seven bowls.

In Revelation 5:6, John saw the four living creatures surround Jesus. In Revelation 4:6, the four living creatures surrounded the Father's throne, but in Revelation 5:6, the four living creatures surrounded Jesus. This change of position indicates that Jesus has authority over the Holy Spirit because Jesus now reigns as Almighty God. My understanding is the four living creatures are a representation of the third

Chapter 2 – Jesus Found Worthy

member of the Godhead, the Holy Spirit. The Holy Spirit is a deity, a separate, distinct God just like the Father and Jesus. Four identical living creatures represent one deity because the Holy Spirit is omnipresent. He lives everywhere, in the north, east, west, and south at the same time. The four living creatures are covered with eyes, representing the power of the Holy Spirit. He sees everything occurring in the universe in real time. When the four creatures surround Jesus, it means the Holy Spirit now connects all creation with Jesus who reigns on the throne as Almighty God. Jesus predicted this: **"He will bring glory to me by taking from what is mine and making it known to you."** (John 16:14)

After Jesus was found worthy to receive the book with seven seals, Heaven responded with joyful singing! Notice how the seven attributes of sovereign power are enumerated in this song: "In a loud voice they sang: **'Worthy is the Lamb, who was slain, to receive power and wealth and wisdom and strength and honor and glory and praise!' Then I heard every creature in Heaven and on Earth and under the Earth and on the sea** [Psalms 145:21, a phrase indicating universal praise – obviously people on Earth or under the Earth knew nothing about this event], **and all that is in them, singing: 'To Him who sits on the throne and to the Lamb be praise and honor and glory and power, for ever and ever!' The four living creatures said, 'Amen** [so be it]**,' and the elders fell down and worshiped."** (Revelation 5:12-14, insertions mine)

The apostle Paul knew a day was coming when Jesus would have authority over everything in Heaven and on Earth. He wrote: **"And He** [the Father] **made known to us the mystery of His will according to His good pleasure, which He purposed in Christ, to be put into effect when the times will have reached their fulfillment – to bring all things in Heaven and on Earth together under one head, even Christ."** (Ephesians 1:9,10, insertion mine) The prophet Daniel also saw Jesus given sovereign power in the same convocation: **"In my vision at night I looked, and there before me was one like a son of man, coming with the clouds of Heaven. He approached the Ancient of Days and was led into his presence. He was given authority, glory and sovereign power; all peoples, nations and men of every language worshiped him. His dominion is an everlasting dominion that will not pass away, and his kingdom is one that will never be destroyed."** (Daniel 7:13,14)

Chapter 3
The Humiliation of Jesus

"And being found in appearance as a man, He humbled Himself and became obedient to death – even death on a cross! Therefore God exalted Him to the highest place and gave Him the name that is above every name, that at the name of Jesus every knee should bow, in Heaven and on Earth and under the Earth, and every tongue confess that Jesus Christ is Lord, to the glory of God the Father." (Philippians 2:8-11)

Before we can completely understand Revelation 5, we must appreciate the level of degradation to which Jesus humbled himself. This is what makes the breaking of the seven seals so important. Each broken seal unleashes a new revelation about Jesus! However, the story of the seals begins before Earth was created. Please be patient and take your time to consider my understanding of this momentous story.

Long before Jesus was born, the Father decided the time and place of his birth, as well as the names of his parents. The Father also ordained that Jesus, the Creator of mankind, would live among human beings as one of them. The Father also decided Jesus' physical appearance would be very plain, in fact, the lowest of mankind. He would not have a majestic, beautiful, or attractive appearance. (Isaiah 53:2) The Father deliberately chose this humble appearance because the Father is the king of humility and ordained that all created beings would be given a physical appearance greater than that of the Creator.

The Bible indicates that Jesus lived among the angels as Michael, the archangel, before He lived on Earth. His physical appearance as an angel was not majestic, beautiful, or attractive in any way, but Lucifer, the first angel created, *the other covering cherub*, was the most glorious being ever created! (Ezekiel 28:12-14) The physical contrast between Michael and Lucifer could not have been starker.

The Book of Life

Remember, the Father wrote a book and sealed it with seven seals prior to the creation of angels or human beings. (Revelation 17:8; Psalms 139:15,16) After Jesus was found worthy to receive the book sealed with seven seals, John refers to it as "The Lamb's Book of Life." (Revelation 13:18; 21:27) Since this is the *only* book the Lamb receives in Revelation's story, the book sealed with seven seals must be "The Book of Life." Interestingly, "The Book of Life" is a book about life.

The Father foreknew every detail involved in the drama with sin, so He designed a process that would expose the humble Creator to the universe as a separate, coeternal God who is His equal in every way. The Father determined that as each of the seals was broken, more information would be revealed about Jesus.

One day the universe will see that Jesus, a God equal to Himself and a perfect mirror of Himself, was willing to forfeit His own life for sinners because of His love for them. When Jesus is fully revealed, everyone will see that a very humble Jesus is actually a mirror of a very humble Father. They are equals in humility, power, glory, and divine prerogatives. (Philippians 2:9,10)

Jesus the Son of God

Jesus is not the Father, the Father is not the Holy Spirit, and the Holy Spirit is not Jesus. The Bible teaches there are three Gods and each of them is a separate, distinct, coeternal member of the Godhead. (Please see Appendix A for an in depth study on this topic.) Before the Godhead formed the Trinity, Jesus had the same prerogatives, powers, authority, and glory as the Father. The Father has ordained that Jesus will be revealed because He wants all living beings to see a perfect mirror of Himself. The Father, Jesus, and the Holy Spirit were equals in every way until the Holy Spirit and Jesus subjugated themselves to the Father. Jesus is not a created being and He has never been a lesser God than the Father. In fact, the Father Himself calls Jesus, "God" (See Psalms 45:7 and Hebrews 1:9.) and Jesus refers to Himself as God Almighty! (Exodus 6:3; compare Isaiah 44:6 with Revelation 1:17)

Many Christians do not understand the *title*, "Son of God." Some people mistakenly infer that Jesus is an offspring of the Father, created a little lower than the Father. Jesus is a member of the deity just like the Father and the title "Son of God" refers to a state of submission

Chapter 3 – The Humiliation of Jesus 29

(humiliation). Jesus willingly entered this state to save mankind on the day that Adam and Eve sinned.

Before creating human beings or angels, the three distinct members of the Godhead made several decisions that would endure for all eternity. The strongest influence in all the universe, divine love, was behind the decisions. The three Gods, decided that one God, the God we now call the Father, would become invisible and live in a glorious light that was so bright that no one could ever see Him or approach Him. (1 Timothy 1:17; 6:16; John 6:46) The Father's glory serves an important purpose, it displays the awesome power and majesty which all three members of Deity actually have.

The Godhead also decided that one God, the one we call the Holy Spirit, would become an omnipresent conduit between the Father and all created beings. The Father and Jesus are not omnipresent, but this is not a limitation because the Holy Spirit is everywhere in real time. He sees and hears everything going on in the universe and communicates instantaneously with the Father and Jesus. Even though the Holy Spirit sees everything, no one can see Him. Even though He can hear everything and has a mind of His own, He does not speak on His own. (John 16:13) His role involves connecting a two-way channel between the Godhead and each member of creation. The Holy Spirit attempts to convey the Father's love, joy, peace, kindness, goodness, gentleness, and faithfulness – the fruits of the Spirit (Galatians 5:22) – to every being in the universe. Because the Holy Spirit is the *only* conduit that exists between the throne of God and all created beings, blaspheming the Holy Spirit is an unpardonable sin. (Matthew 12:31,32) This means that if the Holy Spirit ever gives up on a being who defies and rebels, there is no further contact between God and that person. Lucifer, a third of the angels, and King Saul provide illustrations of blasphemy against the Holy Spirit. (1 Samuel 28:6)

Finally, the three members of the Godhead decided that one God, the God we call Jesus, would be their only visible representative. Jesus' character is a perfect mirror of the Father and the Holy Spirit. (John 14:9; Colossians 2:9) Before Jesus created Earth, He lived among the angels as Michael the archangel. (Exodus 3; Judges 2; Jude 1:9; Revelation 12:7) Then, about four thousand years after Adam and Eve sinned, Jesus humbled Himself, came to Earth, and lived as a man. (Man was created lower than the angels. Hebrews 2:7) The Father wants everyone to see what He would do and how He would live if He walked "in our shoes." What a beautiful example of the Father's humility!

The Godhead also chose that Jesus would serve as the spokesperson for the Father. Of course, on special occasions the Father speaks directly to the angels, but Jesus provides instruction and edification. There are a few instances in the Bible where the Father actually spoke so that human beings could hear Him and when He did, He always exalted Jesus! (Luke 3:22; Matthew 17:5; John 12:28) Because Jesus is the Father's spokesperson, when Jesus came to Earth, He did not come here to do His own will or to speak His own words! The Father spoke from Heaven and *His words* came out of Jesus' mouth. The Holy Spirit (the conduit) made this possible. Jesus said, **"These words you hear are not my own; they belong to the Father who sent me."** (John 14:24) In a prayer Jesus said to the Father, **"For I gave them the words you gave me and they accepted them."** (John 17:8) When Jesus speaks, He speaks for the Father and this explains this illustrious title, "The Word." John says of Jesus, **"In the beginning was the Word, and the Word was with God, and the Word was God. He was with God in the beginning** [before anything was created]. **Through Him** [the Word] **all things were made; without Him nothing was made that has been made. . . . The Word became flesh and made His dwelling among us. We have seen his glory, the glory of the One and Only, who came from the Father, full of grace and truth."** (John 1:1-3,14, insertions mine)

Jesus and the Holy Spirit gave their ability of omniscience (foreknowledge) over to the Father, so the Father is the only member of the Godhead that exercises foreknowledge. Jesus and the Father gave their omnipresence (ability to be everywhere at once) to the Holy Spirit, so the Holy Spirit is the only member of the Godhead that can be everywhere at once. The Holy Spirit and Jesus gave up their prerogative of omnipotence (unlimited power), so the Father is the all-powerful ruler of the universe. The Godhead (Trinity) sacrificed these powers between themselves to benefit a universe full of children. We see in the Trinity a dynamic display of divine love, each God yielding to the other two out of divine love each day. This is how and why they function as One God ($1/3 + 1/3 + 1/3 = 1$).

The Father foreknew the circumstances surrounding the fall of Lucifer and the angels and He foresaw the fall of Adam and Eve. Because they

Chapter 3 – The Humiliation of Jesus

gave their foreknowledge to the Father, Jesus and the Holy Spirit did not know these events in advance. Because of His foreknowledge, the Father could write a history book and also create an intricate plan to save mankind before history began. The Father's plan required Jesus to die, but He did not know the price for salvation until He approached the Father to see what could be done to save Adam and Eve from death. Peter said of Jesus, **"He** [Jesus] **was chosen** [by the Father as the only one who could die for man] **before the creation of the world, but** [He] **was revealed in these last times for your sake."** (1 Peter 1:20, insertions mine)

Jesus Is the Creator

Many Christians do not know that Jesus is the creator; therefore, a few words about this topic are necessary. The Bible begins with the words, **"In the beginning God created the Heavens and the Earth."** (Genesis 1:1) The Hebrew word translated God is *'elohiym*. *'Elohiym* is plural and it literally means "Gods," but most translators have chosen to avoid argument over this point (even though in Genesis 1:26 the translators clearly indicate the plurality of the Godhead saying "Then God said, **'Let *us* make man in *our* image, in *our* likeness.'** " Genesis 1:26, italics mine) Because the Father, Son, and Holy Spirit are three separate Gods who live in perfect harmony with each other, we can be sure that all three were present at Earth's creation! Even the angels shouted for joy! (Job 38:7) Jesus was the Creator, the Father observed, and the Holy Spirit hovered over the surface of Earth, ready to connect the hearts and minds of a new creation with the Godhead.

The very first verse in the Bible indicates that Earth is the result of intelligent design. This verse also points to Jesus who is the Creator of everything that exists. (John 1:10,14; Isaiah 45:18) Jesus is described in the Bible with many titles including Almighty God, Jehovah, Lord God, The Word, Son of God, Master, and Savior. Whatever the Father wants, Jesus creates and whatever Jesus creates belongs to the Father. Notice what Paul says about Jesus, **"In the past God** [the Father] **spoke to our forefathers through the prophets at many times and in various ways, but in these last days He has spoken to us by His Son, whom He appointed heir of all things, and through whom He made the universe."** (Hebrews 1:1,2)

A few verses will clarify the role of Jesus as the Creator. The apostle Paul wrote that Jesus is the Creator of everything that is in Heaven and on Earth: "**For by Him** [Christ] **all things were created: things in Heaven and on Earth, visible and invisible, whether thrones or powers or rulers or authorities; all things were created by Him and for Him. He is before all things, and in Him all things hold together.**" (Colossians 1:16,17, insertion mine)

At Mt. Sinai, the Creator of Earth spoke to Israel saying, **"I am the Lord your God, who brought you out of Egypt, out of the land of slavery. . . . Remember the Sabbath day by keeping it holy. Six days you shall labor and do all your work, but the seventh day is a Sabbath to the Lord your God. For in six days the Lord made the Heavens and the Earth, the sea, and all that is in them, but He rested on the seventh day. Therefore the Lord blessed the Sabbath day and made it holy."** (Exodus 20:2,8-11) Fourteen centuries after saying this, Jesus was on Earth walking with His disciples. The Pharisees accused Him of breaking the Sabbath after He and His disciples picked and ate some grain while walking through a grain field on a Sabbath. Knowing that He is the Creator of the Sabbath, carefully consider the meaning of His words: **"Then He** [Jesus] **said to them** [His critics]**, 'The Sabbath was made for man, not man for the Sabbath.** [Men should not worship the Sabbath, men should worship the Creator of the Sabbath.] **So the Son of Man** [standing before you, the Creator of Heaven and Earth] **is Lord even of the Sabbath** [and as its Creator, I will show you how it should be observed].'** "** (Mark 2:27,28, insertions mine) There are many more texts in the Bible indicating that Jesus is the Creator, but one more should resolve the issue for now. John wrote, **"The Word became flesh and made His dwelling among us."** (John 1:14) **"He was in the world, and though the world was made through Him, the world did not recognize Him."** (John 1:10)

When Adam and Eve Sinned

After Jesus created Adam, the Lord gave Adam this command: **"And the Lord God commanded the man, saying, Of every tree of the garden thou mayest freely eat: But of the tree of the knowledge of good and evil, thou shalt not eat of it: for in the day that thou eatest thereof thou shalt surely die.'"** (Genesis 2:16,17, KJV) The underlying basis for this command is an eternal law which declares, "a sinner must die the day he sins."

Chapter 3 – The Humiliation of Jesus

After Jesus created Adam and Eve, Lucifer deceived Eve. Out of love for Eve, Adam deliberately sinned to share the consequences of Eve's guilt. One would think that since Adam was living in a sinless state, he would have sought the Creator's help to resolve Eve's disobedience. However, Adam loved Eve more than He trusted God and this weakness, even within a sinless being resulted in a fateful choice. Before fulfilling His promise to kill the guilty pair "the very day" they sinned, Jesus hurried to the Father to see if anything could be done to save Adam, Eve, and their future offspring from eternal death. I believe Jesus learned certain elements about the plan of salvation that day for the first time. The Father had ordained a plan for salvation before any life was created. The Father's plan was a closely guarded secret because its features and functions were designed to be understood and applied only after the plan became necessary.

I understand that prior to Earth's creation, a rebellion broke out in Heaven. Lucifer and his followers were not offered a plan of redemption because the Father did everything possible to correct His wayward children over a long span of time. I am speculating that it took considerable time, perhaps 7,000 years, for Lucifer's arguments to penetrate and infect a third of the holy angels. Nevertheless, a third of the holy angels reached a point in their rebellion where they blasphemed the Holy Spirit. When the Holy Spirit told the Father there was no hope of saving these angels, the Father postponed His sudden death law (a sinner dies the day he sins) and cast them out of Heaven. The Father temporarily stayed the execution of Lucifer and his followers for the larger benefit of the universe. Because the Father has infinite wisdom and foreknowledge, He wants the universe to see the malignity of sin's curse and its consequences so that after sin is finally eliminated from the universe, the curse of sin will never spread again. God offers no atonement for defiance. Only the Holy Spirit (who intimately reads each heart and mind) determines when the point of no return is reached. He is the member of the Godhead who determines when persistent defiance becomes "unpardonable." (Matthew 12:31)

The Meeting between Jesus and the Father

In a perfect universe, sin is never justifiable and there is no excuse for violating any of God's laws. The Father sends wisdom and strength to anyone who asks and has a thousand solutions for every temptation.

After Adam and Eve sinned, I believe they were also spared from immediate execution under the sudden death law. My understanding is that before Jesus executed them as he had promised, He went to see the Father. I can imagine a meeting between Jesus and the Father went something like this: The Father told Jesus He had a plan to save sinners who had not blasphemed the Holy Spirit. Then, the Father explained to Jesus that no sin can be forgiven because the curse of sin immediately begins to function within a sinner the moment he sins. *The curse of sin is the withdrawal of God's sustaining power to live.* God can implement the curse suddenly (God kills the sinner outright – as in the case of 185,000 soldiers (Isaiah 37:36)) or the curse can be lingering, when God withdraws life gradually (as in the case of growing old, getting weak and dying from disease). During the curse of sin, God continues to give life to sinners (up to a maximum of 969 years for Methuselah). When God finally removes the curse of sin from the universe, the result of sin will be instant death (a sinner will die the day he sins). Because sinless beings can choose to sin and/or be enticed into sin, God will not again permit the curse of sin to spread. Two instances of sin are enough.

God is the only source and sustainer of all life. All created beings (such as animals, birds, and fish) live from one breath to the next because God sustains life. Because of sin, disorder and chaos begins in the sinner's body, even at the cellular level, and the sinner eventually dies.

Jesus knew from Lucifer's rebellion that when a sinless being sins, the sinner immediately loses a propensity for righteousness. When the curse of sin takes over, a loving and selfless being suddenly becomes selfish and rebellious. Jesus created the angels and mankind in the image of God so they had humble attitudes, loved righteousness, and exalted truth. However, the curse of sin changes the image of God into the image of Lucifer. Every sinner has a propensity for arrogance, selfishness, and rebellion toward God. Sinners also have a propensity for predatory behavior and will take advantage of others if/when possible. The divergence between a noble, sinless being and a sinner defaced by sin's curse is enormous; this is why sinners are called "fallen beings."

The Price for Salvation

Until Adam and Eve sinned, Jesus could not know the actual price for salvation. I believe the Father told Jesus that "the sudden death law" hanging over Adam and Eve could be postponed for a while so that

Chapter 3 – The Humiliation of Jesus

they and their offspring could have access to redemption *if* Jesus, the Creator was:

1. Willing to become a man and live within the physical limitations of mankind.
2. Willing to live as a despised Jew. He would be sent to Earth at a time when the Romans ruled the world and the Jewish nation's apostasy would be at its peak.
3. Willing to speak every word which the Father commanded Him to say.
4. Willing to face and overcome every temptation known to mankind.
5. Willing to face and overcome extreme temptations to exercise divine power which would remain intact.
6. Willing at all times to display the patience, love, kindness, and humility of the Father.
7. After living a sinless life, willing to endure extreme suffering from the hands of men before dying on a cross.

The Father explained that if Jesus successfully executed these steps, the Father would have:

1. A legitimate way of restoring the righteousness that Adam and Eve had lost (Jesus would produce this righteousness by overcoming every temptation and through His blood, the Father could transfer Christ's righteousness to sinners).
2. A legitimate way for carrying out the penalty for sin on sinners while sparing repentant sinners from death (the law requiring the death of sinners cannot be changed or cancelled, but a sinner's guilt could be transferred to Lucifer, the father of sin).
3. A legitimate way for bestowing eternal life on repentant sinners (the Father would transfer to repentant sinners the eternal life which formerly belonged to the Creator).

If Jesus accomplished all that the plan of redemption entailed, God would resurrect Jesus from the dead and would give Him a special kingdom containing everyone that was redeemed. This kingdom would be exalted above the angels. The redeemed would serve as kings and priests, and manage the universe. They would testify throughout the universe that the only way to be saved is the way of genuine love and the curse of sin would never again infect the universe. If a billion years later, a person chooses to exercise free will and is tempted to sin, millions of ex-sinners, all having experience with the curse of sin and the knowledge of good and evil, will help him understand that sin is not the answer and sinning comes with a dreaded curse. If that person does not listen to these witnesses and stubbornly proceeds to blaspheme the Holy Spirit, God will destroy him on the day that he sins as the law demands. Everyone in the universe will sadly, but gratefully understand the immediate execution of that sinner. When the drama with sin is finally over, there will never be further atonement for sin. Jesus will never need to die again because there will be no further atonement for sin. So, Jesus and His kingdom of kings and priests will never end.

This was the Father's offer and solution for preventing a third instance of sin's curse. When Jesus learned of the Father's profound solution, Jesus did not hesitate. Incredibly, Jesus immediately humbled Himself right there to carry out the Father's plan.

The Incredible Nature of Jesus' Love

Jesus accepted the Father's plan, only because of Jesus' love. Jesus loved the Father and He quickly understood the wisdom behind the Father's larger plan to prevent a third instance of sin's curse. Jesus also loved Adam and Eve and He understood that either He had to carry out the demand of the law (killing the guilty pair) or He could offer them redemption by carrying out the Father's plan. Knowing there was a risk of failure, Jesus nevertheless humbled Himself to implement the Father's plan. This is the greatest act of humiliation ever recorded.

"And [God] being found in appearance as a man, He humbled Himself and became obedient to death – even death on a cross!" (Philippians 2:8, insertion mine) **"During the days of Jesus' life on Earth, He offered up prayers and petitions with loud cries and tears to the One who could save Him from death, and He was heard because of His reverent submission."** (Hebrews 5:7)

If the holy angels had any doubts about the Father's love for His subjects or the Creator's love for those He had made, such thoughts vanished that day. They clearly saw the Father and a very humble Jesus were One in purpose, plan, and action. The Father's and the Creator's love for their subjects overwhelmed the angels! Lucifer and his followers were shocked when Jesus did not kill Adam and Eve. Even in their

Chapter 3 – The Humiliation of Jesus

blind rebellion and hatred for God, the fallen angels were amazed to learn there was a plan to save sinners. This made Lucifer and his followers very angry toward God because God had a plan to save mankind but no plans to save one third of the angels!

The Bible summarizes the outcome of the meeting between the Father and Jesus saying: "I [Jesus] **will proclaim the decree of the Lord** [the Father]**: He said to me, 'You are my Son** [subject]**; today I have become your Father** [Master]. [If you are successful] **Ask of me, and I will make the nations your inheritance, the ends of the Earth your possession. You will rule them with an iron scepter** [you will have a kingdom whose rule cannot be broken]**; you will dash them** [your enemies] **to pieces like pottery. Therefore, you kings, be wise; be warned, you rulers of the Earth. Serve the Lord with fear and rejoice with trembling. Kiss** [submit to the authority of] **the Son, lest He be angry and you be destroyed in your way, for His wrath can flare up in a moment. Blessed are all who take refuge in Him.'** " (Psalms 2:7-12, insertions mine)

The phrase, "You are my Son" needs a little explanation. The Hebrew word translated "son" is *ben* and it means "a subject" or someone under authority. When Jesus subjected Himself to the Father to carry out the Father's plan and in all things to do the Father's will, the Father gave Jesus the title, "The Subject of God." (Psalms 2) In other texts, Jesus is called "The Lamb of God." (John 1:29) Both verses reveal that Jesus became willing to carry out the Father's will. Unfortunately, the title, "Son of God" has created many goofy ideas over the centuries which have nothing to do with the realities involved.

Two Sons Set Apart for Service

Please consider these two verses: **"But the angel said to him: 'Do not be afraid, Zechariah; your prayer has been heard. Your wife Elizabeth will bear you a son, and you are to give him the name John.'** " (Luke 1:13) **"But after he** [Joseph] **had considered this** [divorcing Mary]**, an angel of the Lord appeared to him in a dream and said, 'Joseph son of David, do not be afraid to take Mary home as your wife, because what is conceived in her is from the Holy Spirit. She will give birth to a son, and you are to give Him the name Jesus, because He will save His people from their sins.'** " (Matthew 1:20-21, insertions mine)

First, the angel told Zechariah that he was to name his son, "John." Next, the angel told Joseph that he was to name his son, "Jesus." These two families were not permitted to name their sons because both sons were set apart for God's service, not limited to the dominion of their parents. Like the prophet Jeremiah, God set them apart before birth. (Luke 1:15,35; Jeremiah 1:5)

Prior to his birth, God selected John (the Baptist) to proclaim the Messiah's arrival. No prophet had ever been given a greater honor. One day, Jesus told some Pharisees who had gone to the Jordan River to question John if he might be the Messiah: **"Then what did you go out to see? A prophet? Yes, I tell you, and more than a prophet. This is the one about whom it is written: 'I will send my messenger ahead of you, who will prepare your way before you.' I tell you the truth: Among those born of women there has not risen anyone greater than John the Baptist; yet he who is least in the kingdom of Heaven is greater than he."** (Matthew 11:9-11)

No Sacred Name

Some Christians *insist* that the name Jesus should not be used, maintaining that Jesus must be called a Hebrew name such as "Yah," "Yashua," "Yehoshua," or "Yahweh." This claim has no merit because first, the Father Himself avoided Hebrew names when He named John and Jesus. Second, man should not usurp the Father's authority. The Bible says, **"It is by the name of Jesus Christ of Nazareth, whom you crucified but whom God raised from the dead, that this man** [has been healed and you can see that he] **stands before you healed. He is 'the stone you builders rejected, which has become the capstone.' Salvation is found in no one else, for *there is no other name under Heaven* given to men by which we must be saved."** (Acts 4:10-12, insertion and italics mine) Third, the name "Jesus" is mentioned more than a thousand times in the New Testament because that's the name the Holy Spirit inspired Bible writers to use. The idea of using a sacred name is fiction.

From secular and Bible history, we know that the names "John" and "Jesus" were very common Jewish names used at the time of Christ's birth. (Acts 13:6; Colossians 4:11; Mark 5:37; Acts 15:37) The Father imposed this humility on both men and their lives were a demonstration of it. Matthew described John saying, **"John's clothes were made of camel's hair, and he had a leather belt around his waist.**

Chapter 3 – The Humiliation of Jesus

[John looked like a homeless mountain man.] **His food was locusts** [a bland fruit that grew in the region] **and wild honey."** (Matthew 3:4, insertions mine)

Isaiah reports Jesus' humility: **"He grew up before Him** [the Father] **like a tender shoot, and like a root out of dry ground. He had no beauty or majesty to attract us to Him, nothing in His appearance that we should desire Him. He was despised and rejected by men, a man of sorrows, and familiar with suffering. Like one from whom men hide their faces He was despised, and we esteemed Him not."** (Isaiah 53:2,3, insertion mine)

The only element that makes a name or title holy is divinity. Regardless of the many names or titles that identify Jesus in the Bible, we should not carelessly use any of His names or titles. (Exodus 20:7). For example, one of the highest and most exalted titles given in the Bible for God is "Father" and Jesus tells us to address the Ruler of the Universe with this endearing title, "Our Father." (Matthew 6:9) Because **"Father" is an exalted title for the Father, He forbids anyone from calling a clergyman, "Father."** (Matthew 23:9)

Michael is Jesus

Because Jesus' humility is a new subject for many people, another aspect of His humility needs investigation. Jesus lived in Heaven before He created the world and He lived among the angels in the form of a very humble angel. The angels called Him Michael. The name Michael is like the name Jesus in that both names indicate how closely Jesus identifies with those He creates. To the angels, Jesus is Michael *the* archangel (the prefix *arch* means "over" or "above" all angels). To mankind, Michael is Jesus, the Savior of the world, King of kings, and Lord of lords, the "archman," if you will. Many people are offended when they hear someone say that Jesus is also Michael because they do not understand this topic properly. Four books in the Bible offer information about Heaven's highest angel (who is also Heaven's most humble angel).

1. **"But even the archangel Michael, when he was disputing with the devil about the body of Moses, did not dare to bring a slanderous accusation against him, but said, 'The Lord rebuke you!' "** (Jude 1:9) Michael is identified as *the* archangel in this text. Sometimes, Bible students use this verse to infer that

Michael is not Jesus because Michael refers to the Lord as a third person saying, **"The Lord rebuke you."** This objection is superficial. Notice Zechariah 3:2: **"The Lord said to Satan, 'The Lord rebuke you, Satan! The Lord who has chosen Jerusalem, rebuke you!'"**

The third person reference in Zechariah 3:2 is identical to Jude 1:9. In both cases, Michael is speaking and Michael speaks with divine authority to terminate a discussion between Himself and the devil. Lucifer has no recourse. When the devil tempted Jesus in the wilderness, Jesus did not slander the devil nor rail against him. Speaking to Lucifer with divine authority, Jesus said, **"Do not put the Lord your God** [me] **to the test."** (Matthew 4:7, insertion mine) Both Jesus and the devil knew who He was and the devil retreated.

2. **"For the Lord Himself will come down from Heaven, with a loud command, with the voice of the archangel and with the trumpet call of God, and the dead in Christ will rise first."** (1 Thessalonians 4:16) Before we examine the details of this verse, we need to consider three statements that Jesus made. Notice what Jesus says about His voice: **"I tell you the truth, a time is coming and has now come when the dead will hear the voice of the Son of God and those who hear will live."** (John 5:25) Jesus said the dead will hear His voice. Jesus said, **"For my Father's will is that everyone who looks to the Son and believes in Him shall have eternal life, and I will raise him up at the last day."** (John 6:40) Jesus has the keys to death and said, **"I am the Living One; I was dead, and behold I am alive for ever and ever! And I hold the keys of death and Hades** [Greek: the grave]**."** (Revelation 1:18, insertion mine)

These four texts will harmonize only if the archangel is Jesus. The Lord Himself will come down from Heaven and having the keys of death and the grave, He *will speak with the authority of the archangel* and call the dead to life at the last day. When Jesus appears in glory at the Second Coming, all of the angels will be with Him. (Matthew 25:31) Because He is the archangel, He will be their commander. The dead will hear His voice at the last day. Some people try to avoid the weight of evidence by saying the archangel joins with the Lord in raising the dead. Obviously, Almighty God does not need an angel to help Him raise the dead.

Chapter 3 – The Humiliation of Jesus

Paul merges two perspectives about Jesus in 1 Thessalonians 4:16. From man's point of view, Jesus is the Redeemer who resurrects the dead. From the angel's point of view, Michael, the archangel, is the Commander-In-Chief who leads the heavenly host. Jesus has great authority rising from two identities. He is the Redeemer of mankind and the Commander-in-Chief of angels.

3. **"At that time Michael, the great prince who protects your people, will arise. There will be a time of distress such as has not happened from the beginning of nations until then. But at that time your people – everyone whose name is found written in the book – will be delivered. Multitudes who sleep in the dust of the earth will awake: some to everlasting life, others to shame and everlasting contempt."** (Daniel 12:1,2)

I understand the seven bowls in Revelation 16 will begin when Michael *stands up*. This suggests that prior to this time, Michael is seated and we know this is true because Paul says, **"We do have such a high priest, who sat down at the right hand of the throne of the Majesty in Heaven, and who serves in the sanctuary, the true tabernacle set up by the Lord, not by man."** (Hebrews 8:1,2)

When Michael stands up, His work as man's Savior is terminated and a time of greatest distress will begin on Earth. Michael is identified as the *great prince* who protects God's people. It is true that a prince becomes a king when the kingdom is handed over to him. Currently, Jesus is "a prince in waiting" and waiting for Earth to become His footstool. (Psalms 110:1; Hebrews 1:13; Revelation 11:17) The Bible says Jesus will take possession of Earth during the Great Tribulation, at the time of the seventh trumpet. (Revelation 11:15-19) His first action as King of kings and Lord of lords will be to pour out seven bowls of vengeance on His enemies, all who have the mark of the beast. (Revelation 15 and 16)

One text in the book of Daniel is sometimes used to support the idea that Michael is not Jesus. **"But the prince of the Persian kingdom resisted me twenty-one days. Then Michael, one of the chief princes, came to help me, because I was detained there with the king of Persia."** (Daniel 10:13) This text describes an event when Gabriel needed Michael's help to overcome the devil's influence over the king of Persia.

At first, it may seem strange that Michael is called *"one* of the chief princes," especially if He is *the* archangel. This particular language can be easily harmonized if you can accept two concepts. First, Jesus lived among the angels as "one" of them, just like He lived among mankind as "one" of us. In this sense, Michael looked like the other chief princes of Heaven. Second, in Heaven's order, the highest rank is that of a servant leader. Jesus said, **"The greatest among you will be your servant."** (Matthew 23:11) When Jesus lived on Earth, He did not awe the multitudes with His power and glory. He did not lord His divine authority over mortals or rule from an exalted throne. He did not surround Himself with an entourage of 10,000 servants. Even though Jesus is a God in His own right, He humbled Himself and became a subject (son) to the Father and even death itself. He lived as a humble servant of man and Michael lived the same way in Heaven. Servant leadership is the order in God's kingdom and Gabriel refers to Michael as one of the chief princes because He functioned as that. Keep this parallel in mind: Jesus *appeared* to be one of us and from the perspective of the angels, Michael *appears* to be one of them.

4. **"And there was war in Heaven. Michael and his angels fought against the dragon, and the dragon and his angels fought back. But he was not strong enough, and they lost their place in Heaven."** (Revelation 12:7,8) In this text, Michael and Satan are described as commanders, each with an army of angels. Lucifer is the Prince of Darkness and Michael is the Prince of Peace. Jesus ascended to Heaven shortly after His resurrection on Sunday morning to claim the Father's promise that Earth would be His possession if He successfully met the terms and conditions set forth in the Plan of Redemption. Lucifer realized that if He could no longer present himself in Heaven's councils as the Prince of this world (Job 1) and lost this exalted position, he and his followers would eventually be destroyed. Fallen angels waged this war to save themselves from certain death. It is ironic to note that Michael and Lucifer were very close friends at one time. It is also interesting to note that each time the name Michael (the archangel) is used in the Bible, it is directly or indirectly associated with conflict between Jesus and Lucifer.

Now that we have examined the four texts that mention Michael by name, there is good reason to believe that Michael is Jesus, but the Bible has more evidence proving this fact.

Chapter 3 – The Humiliation of Jesus

Michael is Jehovah

In the Old Testament, Jesus is often identified as "the angel of the Lord." Three excellent examples are in the following texts. Pay careful attention to which entity is speaking in each text. When Abraham was about to slay Isaac as a sacrifice, the Bible says, "But the angel of the Lord called out to him from Heaven, 'Abraham! **Abraham! . . . Do not lay a hand on the boy,' He said. The angel of the Lord called to Abraham from Heaven a second time and said . . . 'I swear by myself, declares the Lord** [Jehovah]**, that because you have done this and have not withheld your son, your only son, I will surely bless you and make your descendants as numerous as the stars in the sky and as the sand on the seashore. Your descendants will take possession of the cities of their enemies, and through your offspring all nations on Earth will be blessed, because you have obeyed me.'"** (Selections from Genesis 22:11-18, insertion mine). Did you notice in these verses that "the angel of the Lord" is actually God, the Lord Jehovah (Jehovah means "eternal God")?

The second example is even more illuminating. One day when Moses was tending his sheep, he noticed a bush blazing with flames of fire. The Bible says, **"There the angel of the Lord appeared to him in flames of fire from within the bush. Moses saw that though the bush was on fire it did not burn up. So Moses thought, `I will go over and see this strange sight – why the bush does not burn up.' When the Lord saw that he had gone over to look, God called to him from within the bush, 'Moses! Moses!' And Moses said `Here I am.' `Do not come any closer,' God said. 'Take off your sandals, for the place where you are standing is holy ground.' Then he said, 'I am the God of your father, the God of Abraham, the God of Isaac and the God of Jacob.'"** (Exodus 3:2-6) Did you notice again that "the angel of the Lord" is God?

The third text should remove all doubt. **"The angel of the Lord went up from Gilgal to Bokim and said, 'I brought you up out of Egypt and led you into the land that I swore to give to your forefathers. I said, 'I will never break my covenant with you, and you shall not make a covenant with the people of this land, but you shall break down their altars.' Yet you have disobeyed me. Why have you done this? Now therefore I tell you that I will not drive them out before you; they will be thorns in your sides and their gods** will be a snare to you." When the angel of the Lord had spoken these things to all the Israelites, the people wept aloud, and they called that place Bokim. There they offered sacrifices to the Lord [Jehovah]." (Joshua 2:1-5, insertion mine)

There is only one angel (the angel of the Lord) who can be God, has the authority of God, and speaks for God. His name is Michael, the archangel. He is "the Word." He was with the Israelites day and night and He provided for all their needs, including their food and water. Notice what Paul wrote, **"They all ate the same spiritual food and drank the same spiritual drink; for they drank from the spiritual rock that accompanied them, and that rock was Christ."** (1 Corinthians 10:4) After reviewing these verses, we can easily solve the mystery. The angel of the Lord is God. There is only One angel who can be called God. He is the Archangel and His name means "One who is like God."

Chapter 4
The Origin of Sin

"Son of man, take up a lament concerning [Lucifer] **the** [real] king of [the evil city of] **Tyre and say to him:** 'This is what the Sovereign Lord says: 'You were the model of perfection, full of wisdom and perfect in beauty. You were in Eden, the garden of God; every precious stone adorned you: ruby, topaz and emerald, chrysolite, onyx and jasper, sapphire, turquoise and beryl. Your settings and mountings were made of gold; on the day you were created they were prepared. You were anointed as a guardian cherub, for so I ordained you. You were on the holy mount of God; you walked among the fiery stones. You were blameless in your ways from the day you were created till wickedness was found in you. Through your widespread trade you were filled with violence, and you sinned. So I drove you in disgrace from the mount of God, and I expelled you, O guardian cherub, from among the fiery stones. Your heart became proud on account of your beauty, and you corrupted your wisdom because of your splendor. So I threw you to the Earth; I made a spectacle of you before kings. By your many sins and dishonest trade you have desecrated your sanctuaries. So I made a fire come out from you, and it consumed you, and I reduced you to ashes on the ground in the sight of all who were watching. All the nations who knew you are appalled at you; you have come to a horrible end and will be no more.' " (Ezekiel 28:12-19, insertions mine)

Note: This chapter on the origin of sin represents my "best guess." Because God is changeless, I have merged Bible facts and parallels from Christ's life to assemble this story. Even though some aspects of this story are not included in the Bible, I believe there is enough detail in the Bible to assemble the scenario presented here. The primary purpose of this story is to contrast the humility of Jesus with the arrogance, ignorance, and self-importance of Lucifer. Lucifer's beauty, high position, and desire for worship led him to despise Jesus and the *eternal* gospel. As you consider this story, do not forget that Lucifer's campaign against the Father was very clever. Lucifer executed this deception so well that a third of the holy, intelligent angels, were deceived by his arguments and lies. The development of sin in Heaven and on Earth affirms that God will not, under any circumstances, prohibit His children from exercising their power of choice.

Before we can understand how the sin problem will be resolved to never appear again, we must start with the origin of sin. Someday, people may question God's ways and ask the very same questions that Lucifer once asked.

The Rise of Sin

There was a time in Heaven when the angels poorly understood Jesus. The angels called (and they still call) Jesus by the name, Michael, the archangel, long before mankind called Him Jesus. The angels were delighted to worship Michael whenever and wherever they saw Him. Physically speaking, there was nothing special about His appearance. Michael looked like an ordinary angel and mingled among the angels in Heaven with the same humility that He later displayed among men on Earth. In both cases, His physical appearance did not reveal that He was in fact, the Creator of the universe.

Even though the name Michael means "One who is like God," the angels never questioned the origin of Michael or the order of life in Heaven. They were very happy and felt safe. All of the angels were fully engaged with learning and doing new things every day. God's universe is endless and full of ceaseless wonders. To make matters even better, Michael occasionally conducted classes in different parts of the universe and sitting at His feet was a very special treat. Michael was their favorite teacher and Lucifer served as a substitute teacher. Lucifer also served as leader of the angels when Michael was elsewhere, but Lucifer was not the archangel. For a long time, Lucifer was very close to Michael. Michael and Lucifer spent much time together and Lucifer had many leadership responsibilities. In all appearances, Lucifer was an extraordinary angel.

Chapter 4 – The Origin of Sin 47

Lucifer held the highest position given to any created being. He stood on the left side of God's brilliant throne and Michael stood at God's right hand whenever convocations with the Father were held. The angels worshiped the Father on a regular basis and they also worshiped Michael whenever they saw Him. The angels always looked forward to worshiping the Father who lives in unapproachable light. The angels were always delighted to hear what the Father had to say and listen to reports of the wonderful things that He did.

The angels knew the Father was the Supreme Ruler, the Most High God of the universe. His gifts to the angels constantly renewed their love and adoration for Him. The angels also worshiped Michael whenever they saw Him because they understood *by faith* that He was their Creator. They also understood that Jesus was the source of life within each angel. In Him, the angels moved and had their being. Even though the angels believed these things about Michael, they had no idea how His creative powers worked.

At creation, Adam and Eve did not see Michael create the Earth because they were created last, on the sixth day of the week. In fact, Adam did not see Jesus create Eve because Jesus put Adam into a deep sleep! Similarly, the angels did not watch Jesus create the universe. Jesus created the angels *after* He created the universe. This fact is important to this story because the angels did not witness Michael exercising His awesome creative powers *before* Lucifer fell. The angels knew that Michael had created them, but they embraced this truth and worshiped Jesus on the basis of *faith alone*. The angels did not see Michael's creative power in much the same way that all of Creation Week was hidden from human view.

Over time, Lucifer became jealous of Michael. His jealousy began when he coveted 'the worship' that was directed at *the other covering cherub*. The angels worshiped Michael, but they did not worship Lucifer. Michael could also enter the unapproachable light surrounding the Father, but Lucifer could not. Finally, Michael looked like an ordinary angel and Lucifer did not. Lucifer was created as a model of perfection; he was more beautiful than any other angel. Lucifer eventually became jealous of Michael because he allowed his passion for self-adoration to overrule self-control. Lucifer's jealousy began with vanity and his desire for entitlement. He began to think more of himself than he did of Michael and he coveted the way Michael was worshiped. Lucifer nursed his envy for a long time before he made a fatal choice.

Lucifer's Vanity

Lucifer found a clever way to exalt himself above Michael without raising the suspicions of the other angels. Lucifer began by using his perfect beauty and exalted position as a covering cherub as a way to elevate himself *into equality with* Jesus among the angels that were his closest friends. Over time, Lucifer argued to be fair, the angels really should worship *both* covering cherubs. Lucifer's angel friends did not suspect that Lucifer had an evil intent. They had sinless natures (no knowledge of good and evil), loved Lucifer, and deeply respected his caring leadership. As a result, some angels did not see anything inherently wrong with worshiping 'the other covering cherub.' However, there was something about this that did not seem right to most of the angels. As time went by, Lucifer gained followers because he promoted those who worshiped him to higher positions and with this, the concept of politics began in Heaven. Suddenly, two parties existed in Heaven; angels loyal to Lucifer and angels loyal to Jesus. Happiness and innocence began to evaporate. Tensions displaced happiness. Attitudes and allegiances began to go in different directions and this became very unsettling.

Lucifer avoided direct conflict with Michael and he presented his arguments in secret meetings with the angels, using the excuse that his endeavor was all about fairness. One of his favorite arguments went like this: "How can it be fair of God to permit the angels to worship one covering cherub and not the other?" Many angels sided with Lucifer and concluded that Lucifer was right – God was unfair. Angels loyal to Lucifer said he was just as important as Michael because he was the *other* chief prince! As disaffection for the Father and Michael grew, the devil twisted everything that Michael said. He made right appear wrong. He made Michael's actions appear self-serving and ultimately harmful to the angel's welfare, although nothing harmful ever happened. Lucifer raised many questions and doubts about God's government which God had not addressed. Lucifer also presented clever arguments which ultimately caused one-third of the angels to doubt that the Father was fair and Michael was actually the Creator of the universe. Remember, no angel had seen Michael create anything at that time, so Lucifer's arguments gained some traction with sympathizers.

Chapter 4 – The Origin of Sin

Lucifer's campaign against the Father went on for a long time. The campaign undermined the joy of Heaven and Lucifer's disdain for Michael became widely known. Of course, the Father knew everything that was going on all along. Time after time, the Father and Michael kindly addressed Lucifer's undertow, but Lucifer and his followers would not relent. God warned them repeatedly that their disaffection would bring about their destruction, but they mistook God's patience as indecisiveness and His threat of destruction as evidence of tyranny.

Lucifer told his followers, "The Father cannot tolerate a challenge and Michael cannot tolerate the possibility of competition. The Father is not a God of love and I can prove it! You have heard Him say that it is His way or sudden death." Remember, there is a divine law that requires immediate death for anyone who sins. God's law was *also* imposed on Adam and Eve in the Garden of Eden, but this law will not be implemented until the knowledge of good and evil has matured. After the drama of sin is completed, if someone defies the testimony of ex-sinners and the urging of the Holy Spirit, God will destroy that sinner the day he sins. This is to prevent the spread of sin's curse and everyone will understand that God is both righteous and fair. Before He created Earth, only God had the knowledge of Good and Evil. In the future, if someone chooses to sin defiantly, God's children will not question the sudden destruction of that sinner because everyone will understand what sin does. The Father will not permit a third instance of sin. Sin and its curse will not permeate God's universe again.

God's Demand

Lucifer's controversy with the Father came to a head at a special convocation which the Father organized. As usual, Lucifer called the meeting to order. The angels gathered around God's throne and typically, before the Father's glorious presence filled the temple with brilliant light, Michael arrived and took His position on the right side of the throne. When Michael took His position on that day, one-third of Heaven's angels refused to bow down before Him. This had never happened before. Suddenly, the Father's glorious presence filled the temple. His presence was unusually brilliant and of course, the service stopped.

The Father spoke and commanded everyone to stand up and carefully consider His words. He began by describing Lucifer's self-promotion and jealousy of Michael and his subsequent campaign to gain the adoration and worship of the angels. The Father's words were specific and highly embarrassing. He revealed incidents and conversations that were not common knowledge. He also exposed many lies about Jesus which Lucifer had made up. In short, the Father exposed the controversy that Lucifer had with Jesus and Himself. Then, the Father said, "Let everyone hear and understand this eternal truth: Fear Michael who, like myself, is Almighty God. Give Michael the honor and glory that God is due. Worship Michael your Creator as you worship me, because He made you and the Heavens and all that is in them. In Him, you move and have your being. The hour of your judgment has come. Bow down and worship Him or you will be removed from Heaven!"

Every angel was caught by surprise. The angels were forced to make a decision that would affect their eternal destiny. There was a rustle of movement in the temple as the loyal angels quickly bowed before Michael, but Lucifer, sensing this would be his last day in Heaven, broke the awkward silence with his commanding voice. He spoke defiantly, "I will not worship Michael." Then, Lucifer pointed to his followers who were still standing and said, "We do not think the Father is fair. You claim to be a God of love, but you give us no choice! You say, 'obey and live, disobey and die!' How loving is this? Is it fair that the Father requires us to worship and honor Michael while ignoring the exalted position of *the other covering cherub*? You say that Michael is the Creator, but we have not seen any evidence of His creative powers! Many of us think that your government is based on arbitrary whim and it is secured through your mighty powers. You and your tattletale, Michael, have conspired to keep us as your slaves and if we rebel, you threaten to kill us. This is not right, this is not fair, this is not love and we will not bow down and worship Michael."

Lucifer's defiant response to the Father was shocking. The silence that followed was unbearable. Heaven had never experienced anything like this! Lucifer and his followers remained standing before the Father. One-third of the angels had disobeyed a direct order! They had been warned of the consequences of rebellion and still, they openly defied the clearest evidences of the Father's will. They refused to bow down before Michael, who we now know is an Almighty God, who lives in the form of an angel. Suddenly there was a frightening sound like the sizzle and searing crackle of nearby lightning. A tremendous burst of light blinded the angel's eyes and immediately, a deafening crash of thunder

Chapter 4 – The Origin of Sin

followed. The ground trembled and a great crevice opened up. Lucifer and his angels were thrown into the crevice and instantly, the crevice was closed. Lucifer and his angels were cast out of Heaven at the speed of lightning. The drama was so overwhelming and it happened so fast that the remaining angels remained prostrate on their faces until the Father spoke again. He said kindly, "My children, today *your faith in Christ* has saved you. Stand up and behold your Creator!"

This dramatic event defined Michael in a new way that the angels had not considered. Prior to Lucifer's expulsion, they were innocent and naive. They lived in a sinless universe and had sinless natures. The angels naturally loved each other and were delighted to serve the Father, the Archangel, and Lucifer. The angels had not seen sin or rebellion, so they could not understand the malignant effects that sin produces. The knowledge of good *and evil* began to unfold for the angels on that day.

The Angels See Creation

After Lucifer and his followers were expelled from Heaven, the angels witnessed for the first time, Michael's awesome creative power. They watched in awe as He created the Earth and all that is in it. **"For He spoke, and it came to be; he commanded, and it stood firm."** After watching the creation of Earth and millions of life forms in six twenty-four-hour days, the angels shouted for joy (Job 38:7) and worshiped Michael as though He was a new Deity in Heaven! It was so exciting. Suddenly, the Michael they had known was so much more than the archangel. He was so humble in appearance, yet His creative powers were awesome and divine! Later, when the heavenly angels saw Jesus die on the cross, they gained a perspective on the depth of God's love that words cannot convey. On that day, the angels knew that Jesus was not an angel and He was not a man. He is the Alpha and The Omega; He is Almighty God, just like the Father. Jesus lived as an angel so that He could show the angels how the Father would live if He were an angel. Jesus also lived as an angel so that He could tell the Father about the perspectives of the angels. What amazing love!

One last point. The angels did not see Jesus create Earth until their faith in Him as their Creator had been tested. In other words, *after* Lucifer and his angels were cast out of Heaven, the angels saw Michael create something for the first time. Similarly, the saints will not see Jesus create until their faith in Him has been tested. At the end of the 1,000 years, Jesus will destroy Lucifer and all the wicked. Then, the saints will observe Jesus exercise His creative power. He will create a new Heaven and a new Earth! Whether in Heaven or on Earth, Jesus' creative powers and other facts about Him are hidden for a time, because *faith in Christ* is always and forever the key to eternal life.

God Allowed Lucifer to Live

I hope you can see that there was a time when the angels did not understand who Michael/Jesus was. This knowledge was not revealed until their faith in Him was tested. The angels could not know what sin was all about until sin occurred, but a bittersweet thing has happened because of sin. The Father permitted Lucifer and his angels to live for a while so that the nature, scope, and the universe could clearly understand the consequences of sin. The Father's decision to allow sin to mature has produced an enormous amount of suffering and death, but this enormous suffering has been offset by two wonderful developments.

First, God wants everyone on Earth to understand that He has provided a plan of salvation from sin. He has given His subjects the power of choice. Human beings have free will. Sin exists in the universe today because Lucifer and his followers *chose* to sin and rebel. At the end of the 1,000 years, Jesus will destroy Lucifer and his followers – not because He dislikes them or they offended Him. In fact, Jesus loves the wicked angels, but He must destroy Lucifer and his followers because sin produces predators. Lucifer was moved by selfishness and jealousy to prey upon innocent angels. After Lucifer was banished from heaven, his hatred for Jesus caused him to prey on Eve. Cain was moved by jealousy to kill Abel. Throughout the ages, history has revealed that the wicked are predators and they always prey on the innocent and the righteous. The curse of sin always exploits the innocent. This is why God destroyed the world with a flood in Noah's day. This is why Sodom and Gomorrah were burned to the ground. Sin results in predatory behavior and this is why sin and those who love it must be destroyed. On the other hand, the Father and Jesus have made redemption possible. If a person wants to know God and live a better life, God will give him the power to do so. Surrender to God's will is the beginning of eternal life. Each born again believer gets to taste the joy and peace of eternal life which will occur in due time. Strength and grace from God enable sinners to overcome passion and the power of sin!

Chapter 4 – The Origin of Sin

Second, by allowing Lucifer to live and flourish for a time, God chose the curse of sin to reveal the depths of His love for His creation. Because of sin, the plan of salvation has revealed much about the Father and Jesus that would have remained obscure for billions of years! The Father wisely permitted sin to exist for a period of time so that once it is destroyed, everyone will know why sin is not permitted in the universe again. No one who has been freed from sin's curse will ever want to repeat the drama of sin.

The Father made lemonade out of a lemon! Entry of sin into the universe has disclosed our Creator, Jesus Christ! We know much more about Him than ever before. He is the Creator of Heaven and Earth, He is also Almighty God. He is the only antidote for sin. The Creator is the Savior of mankind and a mirror of the Father's character. It is ironic that God created Lucifer and his angels with sinless natures, yet they chose to rebel. On the other hand, the offspring of Adam and Eve were born with rebellious natures, but many sinners will be saved. Even though the saints were born in a naturally rebellious state, they chose to submit to the urging of the Holy Spirit. Christ's atonement will save these people and, one day, the redeemed of Earth will repopulate Heaven! The Father will restore Heaven to three-thirds and this time, it will be better than before, because one-third of God's house will include beings that have conquered rebellion! They lived in sin and overcame it through Christ's power.

Obedience or Faith

On the surface, the eternal gospel appears to boil down to Lucifer's argument, "Obey and live, disobey and die." This choice appears to produce salvation through obedience rather than faith. Here is the way faith in Christ and the eternal gospel mixes together.

Before Lucifer was expelled from Heaven, He became a liar. He was a master at misrepresenting the Father and Jesus. He skillfully made them appear to be evil and one-third of Heaven's holy angels, very intelligent beings, believed his lies! Lucifer's cunning and sophistry are beyond measure. If the demands of the eternal gospel were placed before the people of Earth *at any other time* than during the Great Tribulation, one could argue that the eternal gospel boils down to "obey and live, disobey and die!" However, to be a testing truth based on faith, the eternal gospel *requires a special setting,* a context where God Himself clearly presents His will and each person understands the consequences of his decision. This is the way it happened in Heaven and this is the way it must happen on Earth! Notice the requirements:

Because sin has physically separated human beings from God's presence, the eternal gospel must include unimpeachable evidence to prove that worshiping Jesus is the Father's will. This requires shattering the religious paradigms of the world so that Muslims, Jews, Hindus, Catholics, Atheists, Protestants, and all others can make an informed decision. Jesus will speak through the lips of the 144,000 and they will perform signs and wonders as often as needed. Jesus is anxious to save the honest in heart within all religious systems. Jesus is no respecter of persons and He is the Creator of *all* mankind. Therefore, to be fair and impartial to all religious backgrounds, the eternal gospel has to be presented with the clearest evidence that the eternal gospel is the Father's will. This is why God will empower His Two Witnesses for 1,260 days.

The eternal gospel must be presented by *inspired* people having *inspired* words. Human argument will not be sufficient. Spiritual things are spiritually understood. Consider the current religious gridlock on Earth. One religious man cannot prove the superiority of his religious beliefs to another religious man. More people have been killed on Earth because of religion than for any other reason. Therefore, the Holy Spirit will give the 144,000 a testimony that will penetrate through the confusion with great power. Jesus will speak through the mouths of the 144,000. The honest in heart will be troubled at first by the demand of the eternal gospel, but they will be moved by the testimony of Jesus to obey His commands.

Worshiping the Creator will come with consequences, but defiance will also come with consequences. Everyone will be forced by circumstances to take a side in the conflict. Jesus will ensure that His gospel will reach the entire world. The Holy Spirit will convict the world of sin, righteousness, and judgment. The eternal gospel will convict the honest in heart that defiance is sin. They will worship Jesus as the Creator because it is the righteous thing to do (God's will). Finally, everyone will be judged according to their decision. If a person rejects the eternal gospel, he will defy the Holy Spirit and defying the Holy Spirit leads to the unpardonable sin.

Chapter 5
When Was Jesus Found Worthy?

> "In my vision at night I looked, and there before me was one like a son of man, coming with the clouds of heaven. He approached the Ancient of Days and was led into his presence. He was given authority, glory and sovereign power; all peoples, nations and men of every language worshiped him. His dominion is an everlasting dominion that will not pass away, and his kingdom is one that will never be destroyed." (Daniel 7:13,14)

Revelation 5 does not indicate when Jesus was found worthy to receive the book sealed with seven seals. For 18 centuries, Bible scholars used some of Paul's writing and assumed that Jesus was found worthy shortly after His ascension since John did not reveal specific timing for the seals. This assumption has caused confusion because scholars have not been able to produce a consistent explanation for the nature and purpose of the book or the seven seals. During the 19th century, some Christians accepted the idea of a pre-tribulation rapture and today, many scholars now believe that Revelation 5 will occur after Christians are raptured from Earth. It is interesting that both assumptions result in the idea that no one needs to understand the seven seals because they were fulfilled centuries ago or they will be broken after Christians are in Heaven. Both explanations are harmful.

I believe the Bible indicates the scene in Revelation 5 occurred in 1798. My conclusion is based on the understanding that God has linked certain events in Heaven with certain events on Earth. God knows that we cannot see events occurring in Heaven, so He has aligned prophetic events in Heaven with events on Earth. This linkage enables us to determine the dates for specific events occurring in Heaven by observing when linked events occur on Earth. I like to call this linkage, the *Heaven Earth Linkage Law*. When diagrammed, the law looks like the chart on the following page.

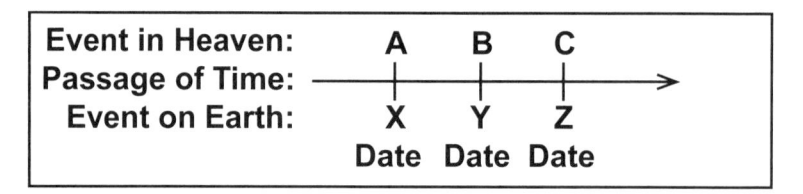

```
Event in Heaven:    A    B    C
Passage of Time: ───┼────┼────┼───▶
Event on Earth:     X    Y    Z
                  Date Date Date
```

The Importance of Prophetic Chronology

God placed the key to dating the scene in Revelation 5 in the book of Daniel. The books of Daniel and Revelation flow together as one book, written by two men separated from each other by six centuries. These two books tell one story and they are inseparably linked by seven different events. They use the same rules of interpretation because they contain the same type of prophecy.

The book of Daniel contains five prophecies and the book of Revelation contains twelve prophecies. Many Bible students overlook the importance of Daniel's prophecies because they do not understand the intimate relationship between Daniel and Revelation. The prophecies in Daniel are fascinating for three reasons:

First, Daniel's prophecies reveal a series of events which God foresaw. Think of these events as historical milestones which occur in chronological order. God described the same event in different prophecies to ensure that human beings can reach the conclusion that God intended. This repetition and enlargement are very beneficial because events in Daniel's prophecies can be aligned with each other. When the elements in each prophecy are aligned chronologically, they create a historical matrix that looks something like this:

Example of a Matrix

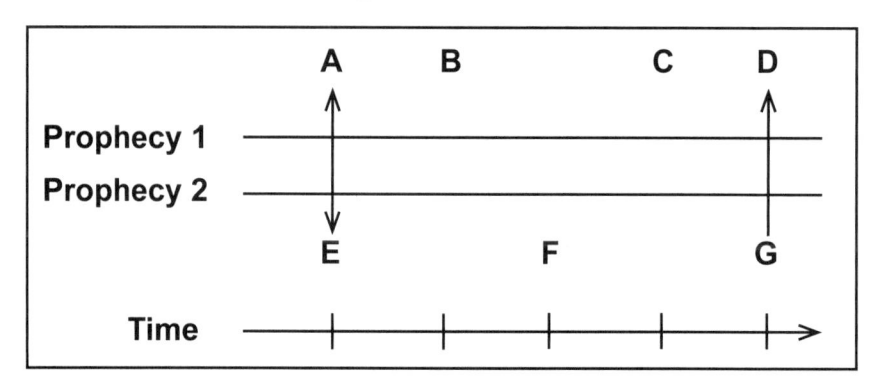

```
                  A      B           C      D
                  ↑                         ↑
Prophecy 1   ─────┼──────┼───────────┼──────┼─────
Prophecy 2   ─────┼──────┼───────────┼──────┼─────
                  ↓
                  E      F                  G

Time         ────┼──────┼──────┼──────┼──────┼──▶
```

Chapter 5 – When Was Jesus Found Worthy?

Consider the matrix on the previous page and notice that Prophecy 1 has four events and Prophecy 2 has three events. Suppose that event "A" and event "E" are two descriptions of the same event therefore, Prophecy 1 and Prophecy 2 have the same starting date. The starting date of each prophecy is important because the elements within a prophecy are given in chronological order. Let us suppose the date for event "D" in Prophecy 1 cannot be determined from the information in Prophecy 1, but the date for event "G" in Prophecy 2 can be determined with the information in Prophecy 2. If event "G" and event "D" are the *same* event, then we can know the date for event "D." This is the beauty of the matrix when the multiple events in the prophecies of the books of Daniel and Revelation are aligned. The matrix reveals answers to questions that could not be otherwise resolved.

The seventeen prophecies in Daniel and Revelation create a large and intricate matrix. This matrix includes every prophetic event mentioned in these two books. Because each prophecy in Daniel and Revelation flows in chronological order, identified events within the prophecies align perfectly. When all seventeen prophecies are viewed together, they produce one amazing story! No single prophecy stands alone; each prophecy contributes information that no other prophecy offers. The matrix allows us to identify which prophecies have been fulfilled and the prophecies that remain to be fulfilled. We can discover how and when events in Heaven and on Earth align through the *Heaven Earth Linkage Law*! You may need to consider this matrix for a few minutes because it produces answers to questions that are otherwise impossible to find, including when the scene in Revelation 5 occurs.

The second fascinating element in Daniel's prophecies is that Daniel links several events in Heaven with events on Earth. For example, Daniel describes a scene in Heaven where Jesus is inaugurated (Daniel 7:13,14) and he links it with the termination of the little horn's power. Daniel mentions the cleansing of Heaven's temple (Daniel 8:14) and he links it with the decree to restore and rebuild Jerusalem. Daniel reveals the date of Christ's death on the cross and this is linked to John's description of the war in Heaven. (Daniel 9:24-27; Revelation 12:7-9) Daniel mentions a day will come when Michael will arise from His throne in Heaven and God will pour His wrath on the wicked on Earth (Daniel 12:1) and John links this day with the beginning of the seven bowls. (Revelation 16) Because Heavenly events are associated with Earthly events, the "Heaven Earth Linkage Law" and the prophetic matrix are very important tools for the Bible student. Centuries ago, God hid these tools in plain sight. God designed that when the right time arrives, Bible students would completely understand apocalyptic prophecy.

Finally, the stories and prophecies in the book of Daniel are fascinating because a complete understanding provides enormous encouragement and inspiration. For example, these prophecies tell us that from the beginning, God has a master plan and He has been faithfully following this plan for millennia! God's plan is on time even though He has been executing His master plan for thousands of years. *In fact, there is no haste or delay with God because with God, timing is everything.* God sealed the keys of a wonderful trove of information to make the book of Daniel really valuable when the appointed time of the end arrives! (Daniel 12:4,9; 8:19) The Father did this because He has something to say to the final generation that He has not revealed to previous generations.

God's message to the final generation is huge. The Father wants everyone on Earth to know who Jesus really is and what He is all about. Approximately 75% of the world does not know Jesus or recognize Jesus as Deity, so the revelation of Jesus Christ as Almighty God will come as a huge shock to billions of people. Interestingly, most Christians will be surprised as well! Approximately two-thirds (or more) of the Christian world worships an icon they call Jesus. However, most Christians do not really know who Jesus is or what Jesus is about. When Christ's supreme authority over Earth is revealed, the Deity of Jesus Christ will also come as a huge shock to them!

The Father foreknew that after 6,000 years of sin's curse, the people of Earth would degenerate into a condition like Noah's day. (Matthew 24:37-39) The Father has a gospel of present truth for the final generation, because He wants to save as many people as possible. He wants the last generation to understand His actions, His purposes, and His love. During the Great Tribulation He will speak to the world through the lips of His servants, the 144,000, and our response to His gospel will determine our eternal destiny.

We can use this foundational information to learn when Jesus received the book sealed with seven seals in Revelation 5.

Chapter 5 – When Was Jesus Found Worthy?

Dating Revelation 5

Now that you are acquainted with the Heaven Earth Linkage Law and the concept of the matrix which the books of Daniel and Revelation produce, you need to know that dating the scene in Revelation 5 involves three steps. They are:

1. Timing the elements in Daniel 2
2. Timing the elements in Daniel 7
3. Aligning Daniel 7 with Revelation 5

Step 1 - Timing the Elements in Daniel 2

The first step in this process is to position the prophetic elements in Daniel 2. This prophecy is simple and straightforward. (Note: If you wish to investigate the prophecies of Daniel more thoroughly, please see my books, *Daniel: Unlocked for the Final Generation* and *Jesus' Final Victory*. These books can be freely downloaded from our website or inexpensive copies can be ordered.)

Jesus gave the vision recorded in Daniel 2 to King Nebuchadnezzar around 600 B.C. While in vision the king of Babylon saw the image of a metal man made of different metals. While the king was studying the metal man, a large rock came out of the sky and destroyed it leaving no trace of the image. Later, Daniel interpreted the vision for the king and told him that the metal man represented six kingdoms that would occur in chronological order. Then, God of Heaven (the Rock) would come down from the sky, utterly destroy the kingdoms of men, and establish a seventh kingdom that would never end.

This vision has been unfolding for 26 centuries! Today, we are living in the time period of the feet which represents the kingdom of Europe. Notice the chronological order and the duration of the kingdoms below:

Metal Man	Metal	Kingdom	Date
1. Head	Gold	Babylon	605-538 B.C.
2. Chest	Silver	Medes & Persians	538-331 B.C.
3. Thighs	Bronze	Grecia	331-168 B.C.
4. Legs	Iron	Rome	168-476 A.D.
5. Feet	Iron and Clay	Europe	476 - Present Time
6. Toes	Iron and Clay	10 kings	Future
7. Rock	Jesus	New Earth	Eternity

Chapter 5 – When Was Jesus Found Worthy?

Many Christians do not realize that the vision of the metal man has another dimension besides time. Now that we have observed the chronological progression of this vision, consider the *geographical expansion* of this vision over the past 26 centuries. Notice that this vision does not include the whole world until the kingdom of the toes arrives! (Daniel 2:42)

As you examine the list below, think of an archery target. King Nebuchadnezzar's vision starts with one kingdom in the center of the target. The "bull's eye" is the first kingdom, the tiny empire of Babylon:

1. The kingdom of Babylon – which was about the size of California
2. The kingdom of the Medes and Persians – about the size of Nigeria, two times the size of California
3. The kingdom of Grecia – about the size of Alaska, four times the size of California
4. The kingdom of Rome – about the size of Siberia, 12 times the size of California
5. The kingdom of Europe – about 24 times the size of California
6. The kingdom of the Toes – the whole world

For the past 1,540 years through the date of this book, this vision has centered on the feet. The feet represent the continent of Europe which consists of some strong nations (represented by iron) and some weak nations (represented by clay). By divine decree, the strong nations have never been able to eliminate the weak nations! The kingdom of the feet will continue to exist until the time arrives for the kingdom of the toes (which are also made up of iron and clay). During the forthcoming kingdom of the toes, God will give ten kings authority over the whole world. (Compare Daniel 2:42 with Revelation 17:12.)

Consider the chart below and notice how the centuries unfold. The first four kingdoms span 1,081 years (from the rise of Babylon to the fall of Rome) and the kingdom of the feet spans 1,540 years thus far. When the time comes for the kingdom of the toes, I believe they will rule over the world for about nine months.

Chapter 5 – When Was Jesus Found Worthy?

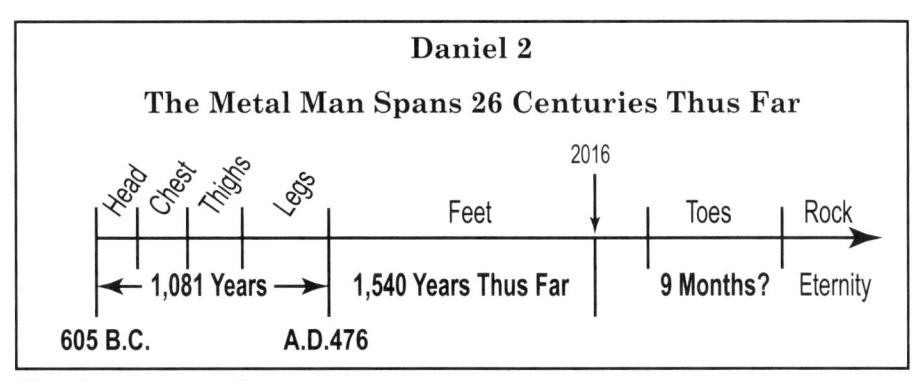

```
┌─────────────────────────────────────────────────────────────┐
│                         Daniel 2                            │
│           The Metal Man Spans 26 Centuries Thus Far         │
│                                    2016                     │
│    Head Chest Thighs Legs                                   │
│     |    |    |    |     Feet     ↓    | Toes  | Rock       │
│     |────1,081 Years────|1,540 Years Thus Far| 9 Months? Eternity │
│   605 B.C.          A.D.476                                 │
└─────────────────────────────────────────────────────────────┘
```

Not drawn to scale

Now that we have aligned the timing of the metal man vision with generally accepted historical data, we have a simple but powerful chronological framework. We have also noticed an expanding geographical framework. Soon, there will be a global upheaval on Earth and during the time ten kings rule over the world the Bible says, **"In the time of those kings, the God of Heaven will set up a kingdom that will never be destroyed, nor will it be left to another people. It will crush all those kingdoms and bring them to an end, but it will itself endure forever."** (Daniel 2:44)

Step 2 - Timing the Elements in Daniel 7

We will now proceed with the timing of the elements we can identify in Daniel 7. (For further study, please see my books, *Daniel: Unlocked for the Final Generation* and *Jesus' Final Victory*.) As you study the diagram below consider two features: First, God often uses repetition and enlargement. Traditionally, students of Bible prophecy have understood the first four kingdoms in Daniel 7 (represented by the lion, bear, leopard and monster beast) are *the same kingdoms* as the first four kingdoms represented by the metal man (represented by the head, chest, thighs and legs). God used repetition and enlargement to eliminate confusion in two areas. First, He wants us to date the kingdoms in Daniel 2 and Daniel 7 in history because dating these kingdoms moves us forward chronologically toward the establishment of His eternal kingdom. Second, repetition and enlargement locks down the identity of the four involved empires. This lock down is important because there were many empires on Earth during this time. However, the book of Daniel is not concerned with empires in places like India,

62　　　　　Chapter 5 – When Was Jesus Found Worthy?

Asia, Africa or the Western Hemisphere. Repetition and enlargement helps us understand that the legs of iron in Daniel 2 and the monster beast in Daniel 7 cover the same time period and they are the same kingdom (Rome).

Because we want to date the scene in Revelation 5, study the diagram below and notice that God inserted a period of 1,260 years (Daniel 7) into the time period for the feet (Daniel 2). The prophecies in Daniel and Revelation tell one story in chronological order and because all of the prophecies link together, they form a timely matrix. Notice in the diagram below that the Little Horn power in Daniel 7 ruled over Europe for 1,260 years and how this time period easily fits into the larger time period for the feet. This insertion is important because the time Jesus was found worthy *in Heaven* is directly associated with the termination of the little horn's power *on Earth* in 1798. When we examine some details in Daniel 7, we will see that the Heaven Earth Linkage Law clearly ties these two events together. This linkage enables us to date Revelation 5!

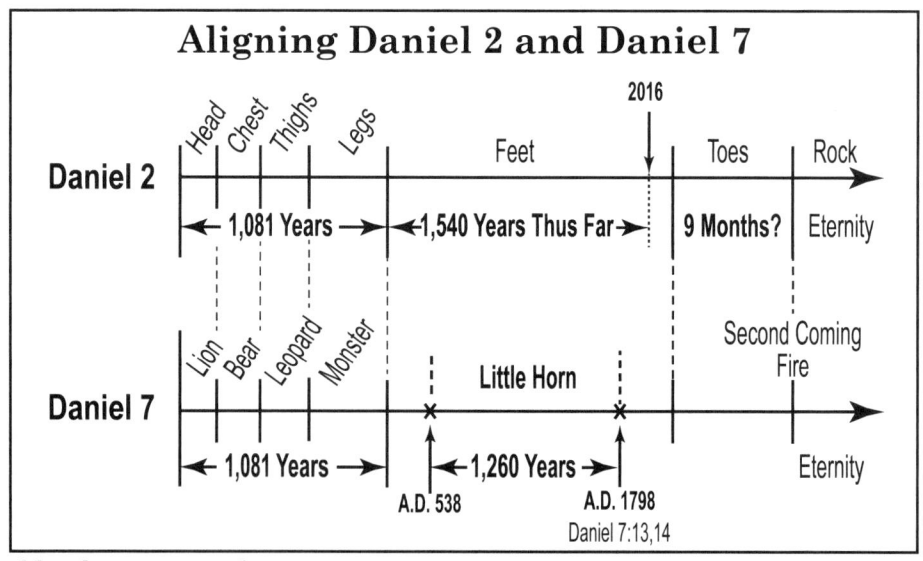

Aligning Daniel 2 and Daniel 7

Daniel 2: Head | Chest | Thighs | Legs | Feet (1,081 Years → 1,540 Years Thus Far →) | 2016 | Toes (9 Months?) | Rock | Eternity

Daniel 7: Lion | Bear | Leopard | Monster (1,081 Years →) | Little Horn (1,260 Years →) A.D. 538 – A.D. 1798 (Daniel 7:13,14) | Second Coming Fire | Eternity

Not drawn to scale

The Monster Beast Represents Rome

Because many Christians do not understand the vision described in Daniel 7, we must further consider some background information so we can appreciate the importance of 1798. (For an in depth discussion on these prophecies, please see Chapters 1 and 3 in my book, *Daniel:*

Chapter 5 – When Was Jesus Found Worthy? 63

Unlocked for the Final Generation and Chapters 9 and 10 in my book, *Jesus, The Alpha and The Omega*.)

Daniel wrote, "**In my vision at night I looked, and there before me was a fourth beast– terrifying and frightening and very powerful. It had large iron teeth; it crushed and devoured its victims and trampled underfoot whatever was left. It was different from all the former beasts, and it had ten horns. While I was thinking about the horns, there before me was another horn, a little one, which came up among them; and three of the first horns were uprooted before it. This horn had eyes like the eyes of a man and a mouth that spoke boastfully. . . Then I would know the truth of the fourth beast, which was diverse from all the others, exceeding dreadful, whose teeth were of iron, and his nails of brass; which devoured, brake in pieces, and stamped the residue with his feet; And of the ten horns that were in his head, and of the other which came up, and before whom three fell; even of that horn that had eyes, and a mouth that spake very great things, whose look was more stout than his fellows.**" (Daniel 7:7,8,19,20)

Daniel was frightened by this monster beast and wanted to know *the truth* about the fourth beast, the ten horns, and the little horn. If we are going to determine the identity of the fourth beast and the little horn that arose out of the monster beast, we have to consider *a dozen* specifications of the beast. With these specifications, we can identify a world power from past centuries that was very bold, powerful, blasphemous, and deadly that transitions to a power adored and respected by millions of people today. This transition is important to understand because God is not impressed with changing tides of public opinion. He sees the world in a very different light than human beings.

The truth that unfolds from this prophecy is not popular nor politically correct today, but a few centuries ago, the Protestants had no question about the identity of the fourth beast and the little horn power. Because the Protestant reformation died a century ago, many Protestant pastors and scholars now refuse to accept the *truth* about the identity of the fourth beast, its ten horns, and its little horn because the truth has become offensive. Nevertheless, sincere Bible students know that since God is the author of prophecy, those who love truth must follow it wherever it leads. Jesus said truth seekers are the kind of people whom God loves. (John 4:23)

Chapter 5 – When Was Jesus Found Worthy?

God identifies the fourth beast and the little horn that grew out of it with a dozen specifications:

1. The monster beast is the fourth empire in this vision.
2. The monster beast has unusual strength and it stomps its enemies.
3. The monster beast is different from the other beasts; it has crushing teeth of iron.
4. Out of the monster beast, ten horns (representing kings/kingdoms) will arise.
5. After the ten horns appear, a little horn will rise. As it rises to power, it will uproot three of the original horns – leaving a total of eight.
6. As the little horn grows and becomes powerful, it exhibits the same fierce qualities of its parent, the monster beast.
7. Eventually, the little horn dominates the other seven horns.
8. The little horn has a mouth; it blasphemes God by usurping His authority.
9. The little horn has eyes; it seeks out the saints of the Most High and wars against them for 1,260 years.
10. The little horn "thinks" it has authority to change God's times and laws.
11. The little horn will endure until the end of the world; in fact, it will speak boastfully during the Great Tribulation.
12. The monster beast and the little horn will be destroyed by fire at the Second Coming.

If we look at the specifications for the first three beasts in Daniel 7 and consider the twelve specifications concerning the fourth beast, history allows no leeway regarding the identity of this monster. Starting with the empire of Babylon, the fourth empire is Rome. Rome came to power after the fall of Grecia in 168 B.C. Roman soldiers nailed Jesus to the cross and destroyed Jerusalem in A.D. 70. Rome fell as an empire in 476 A.D. The ten horns that caused the fall of the empire represent ten ethnic nations that divided Rome. They were the Ostrogoths, Heruli, Franks, Vandals, Lombards, Visigoths, Suevi, Burgundians, Alamanni and the Anglo-Saxons.

The little horn that grew out of the ashes of Rome was the *Roman Catholic Church*. As the church grew in power, it was instrumental in "uprooting" three of the original ten horns, the Ostrogoths, Heruli, and Vandals. By A.D. 538, the little horn in Daniel 7 began ruling over the remaining seven horns of Europe. This reign lasted 1,260 years.

Chapter 5 – When Was Jesus Found Worthy?

The Little Horn Persecutes the Saints for 1,260 Years

One of the specifications of the little horn involves a 1,260 year period of time. Given the enormous length of this slice of world history, the specifications and identity of the fourth beast, the records of European history, and the geographical location of Christianity (Europe), no religious entity other than the Roman Catholic Church meets the specifications for the little horn. The angel said to Daniel, **"And he** [the little horn] **shall speak great words against the most High, and shall wear out the saints of the most High, and think to change times and laws: and they** [the saints] **shall be given into his hand until a time and times and the dividing of time."** (Daniel 7:25, KJV, insertions mine) We will limit our focus to two phrases in this text to assist us in dating the scene in Revelation 5. **"He shall speak great words against the most High"** and **"they** [the saints] **shall be given into his hand until a time, and times and the dividing of time."**

European history has documented the course of the Catholic Church through the centuries and Protestants should be concerned. The history of the Catholic Church runs parallel to that of ancient Israel and Protestantism has fared no better. All three religious systems are guilty of the same sin. They displaced God's Word with man-made traditions and ended up in apostasy. There are many honest and sincere individuals within Judaism, Catholicism, and Protestantism (and for that matter, all world religions). These individuals love God (as they know Him) and they faithfully uphold and adhere to their beliefs, but Daniel 7 is not about individuals. This prophecy is about *a religious system*. Many Jews, Catholics, and Protestants have not had any reason to question their religious system and God certainly understands this. However, in days to come, many honest individuals will be shocked and overwhelmed to learn that their religious system is blasphemous in God's sight. Unfortunately, many of the doctrines and ideas taught by their religious system have no basis or authority whatsoever.

Basis for Roman Catholic Doctrine

Currently, the Roman Catholic Church seems more popular than ever. Wherever the pope travels, large crowds greet him expressing appreciation, worship, and joy. This popularity makes the church appear benevolent, generous, loving, and charitable (this may be attributed to the affable personalities of Pope John Paul II and the present Pope Francis), but do not be fooled. As a religious system, the church has an iron backbone and history indicates that when the Church is not in a position to dictate, it "will go along to get along."

We need to step back in time and consider the absence of religious freedom when popes ruled over the kings of Europe during the Dark Ages. During that time period, Catholicism acted differently when it had absolute power. European history indicates the Catholic Church during the Dark Ages acted similarly to the Taliban when it ruled over Afghanistan. The following statements reflect some interesting thoughts about Catholic doctrine and belief.

Statement #1 (The Church Determines the Teachings of the Bible): "That a person with no other equipment than a knowledge of the English language and a seventeenth century English translation of the Bible in his hands is qualified to decide all matters of eternal consequence for himself and the rest of mankind, is the ridiculous conclusion to which the principle of private judgment can finally be brought. In such a process, the countless generations of devout people who have lived and died according to other beliefs simply count for nothing. The centuries of thought and prayer that have gone into the interpretation of the Bible for all these generations likewise count for nothing." [*Some Bible Beliefs Have to Be Wrong!*, Booklet #68, page 5, (1963), Imprimatur: Most Reverend John F. Whealon, Archbishop of Hartford, Knights of Columbus.]

Statement #2 (The Bible Needs an Interpreter): "Since the Catholic Church holds that the Bible is not sufficient in itself, it naturally teaches that the Bible needs an interpreter. The reason the Catholic Church so teaches is twofold: first, because Christ established a living church to teach with His authority. He did not simply give His disciples a Bible, whole and entire, and tell them to go out and make copies of it for mass distribution and allow people to come to whatever interpretation they may. Second, the Bible itself states that it needs an interpreter. . . . The Holy Spirit was given to the Church by Jesus Christ, and it is exactly this same Spirit who protects the Church's visible head, the Pope, and the teaching authority of the Church by never permitting him or it to lapse into error." [*Scripture Alone? 21 Reasons to Reject Sola Scriptura*, pages 21, 26, (1999), Joel Peters, Tan Books and Publishers, Inc., Rockford, Il.]

Chapter 5 – When Was Jesus Found Worthy?   67

Statement #3 (The Pope is Infallible When Speaking *Ex Cathedra*): "We teach and define it to be a dogma divinely revealed that the Roman Pontiff, when he speaks *ex cathedra*, that is, when acting in his office as pastor and teacher of all Christians, by his supreme Apostolic authority, he defines a doctrine concerning faith or morals to be held by the whole Church through the divine assistance promised him in Blessed Peter, he enjoys that infallibility with which the divine Redeemer willed His Church to be endowed in defining doctrine concerning faith and morals; and therefore such definitions of the said Roman Pontiff are irreformable of themselves, and not from the consent of the Church." [*The Papacy, Expression of God's Love*, page 29, (undated), Imprimatur: Most Reverend John J. Carberry, Archbishop of St. Louis, Knights of Columbus.]

Although you may not have heard these three concepts discussed, they are the bedrock of Catholic doctrine. In fact, these nonnegotiable themes spurred a Bible-based revolt during the 16th and 17th centuries and later, the "protesters" became known as Protestants.

Before we leave this section, one last concept must be considered. Many Catholics have not had any reason to objectively consider the Protestant experience or consider the teachings of Daniel 7. When presented with information that puts the Catholic Church in an unfavorable light, denial is the usual human response. Sincere Catholics cannot imagine or believe that their church system, the church they love, could be the little horn in Daniel 7! Even the recent exposure that many Catholic priests had been sexually abusing children for decades and their superiors covered these atrocities is interpreted by laymen as a problem with bad priests, not a bad church system.

Because truth can be inconvenient at times and truth is not always on our side, truth separates people. Attorney Richard J. Humpal once said, "When a man who is honestly mistaken hears the truth, he will either quit being mistaken or cease being honest." This segment in our study is not focused on bashing the Roman Catholic Church. This segment is focused on identifying the little horn in Daniel 7 because God linked the fall of the Roman Catholic Church with a very important event, the date Jesus was found worthy and inaugurated! Because God's Word is truth, it is important to understand and cherish truth no matter where it may lead.

The last resort of false religion is force. False religion will violate its own tenants to maintain its power over the people. The Jews did this to crucify Jesus, the Catholics did this to Protestants during the Reformation, and the Taliban have done this to Afghans. Religious conflict emanates hatred and hatred makes people cruel. On the other hand, freedom in Christ (2 Corinthians 3:17) is all about respect and sincerity, love for God and one another. God never approves when we violate His commandments. He has a thousand ways of solving problems that we know nothing about. True religion always embodies compassion and kindness. The beauty of Christianity is found in the joy of discovering our Creator and walking closely with Him from faith to faith, day by day.

Daniel 7:25 says the little horn would wear out God's saints, **"they** [the saints] **shall be given into his hand** [for example, the hand of the little horn] **for a time, times and half a time!"** (insertions mine) This verse should cause everyone who believes in a pre-tribulation rapture to rethink this position because this verse indicates that God Himself gave His saints over to the little horn to be persecuted for more than a thousand years! If a God of love subjected His saints to persecution for 1,260 years, the final generation should not expect to escape the coming persecution that will last 42 lunar months. (Revelation 13:5) Instead of delivering the saints *from* persecution, God handed His people over to the little horn for 1,260 years! Here are two reasons why a loving and all-wise God of love might do this:

First, persecution keeps God's people on their knees and their focus in His Word because this is where faith, strength, and peace are found. When life is easy, faith evaporates. Prayer becomes shallow and Bible study doesn't get very deep. Moses warned Israel: **"Be careful that you do not forget the Lord your God, failing to observe his commands, his laws and his decrees that I am giving you this day. Otherwise, when you eat and are satisfied, when you build fine houses and settle down, and when your herds and flocks grow large and your silver and gold increase and all you have is multiplied, then your heart will become proud and you will forget the Lord your God, who brought you out of Egypt, out of the land of slavery."** (Deuteronomy 8:11-14)

During the Dark Ages, the saints laboriously copied many Bibles, or portions thereof, by hand so that people could have the Word of God to study. The saints loved and honored the Word of God and in millions

Chapter 5 – When Was Jesus Found Worthy? 69

of cases, the Church sent them to the stake because the saints held God's Word in higher esteem than life itself. God gave His saints to the little horn so that His Word would endure. Otherwise, God's Word would have disappeared just as surely as the ancient parchments on which its earliest manuscripts were written.

Persecution also develops or eliminates faith. Give up faith and lose the persecution or live by faith and overcome the persecution. Persecution makes God's Word extremely precious. Ironically, God handed His saints over to the little horn to keep faith alive. The circumstances that cause faith to grow are the very circumstances that human nature hates the most! The selfish desires of the carnal nature include the pursuit or possession of pleasure, prosperity, power, unchallenged authority, limitless amounts of money, fame, and respect. On the other hand, our spiritual nature flourishes when faith becomes the air we breathe. Truth is precious to the spiritual nature and it has greater value than life itself. Abiding in the Lord and obeying the Lord is the essence of life with Christ. The Church in Rome wrongly used its power for political instead of spiritual reasons. Faith became a religious paradigm instead of a religious experience. Even today, people typically ask, "What faith are you?" Wouldn't it be better to ask, "What is your faith experience?" In summary, God wisely gave the saints over to persecution to preserve the Bible and to keep the faith of Jesus alive for 1,260 years!

What Is a Time, Times, and Half a Time?

Daniel 7:25 says the saints would be given over to the little horn for a time, times, and half a time. The phrase "a time (360 years), times (720 years) and half a time (180 years)" amounts to 1,260 years in length. This span of time began in A.D. 538 and ended in February 1798. (One system of tracking time is called the Jubilee Calendar. I believe this calendar was in effect between 1437 B.C. and A.D. 1994. During this time frame, a day in Bible prophecy is equivalent to a year of actual time. For an in depth discussion on the operation of the Jubilee Calendar, please see Chapter 6 in my book, *Daniel: Unlocked for the Final Generation* and Appendix A, "The Importance of 1994" in my book, *Jesus' Final Victory*.)

Until the sixteenth century A.D., men believed the Earth stood still and the Sun orbited our planet. Israel used 360 degrees of arc to represent a completed *circle* or *cycle* of the Sun. The Jews did not count a year as 365 days because there was either 354 or 384 days in their religious year. God gave Israel a solar/lunar calendar at the time of the Exodus (Exodus 12:1) to measure time and the cycles of the Sun and Moon determine the number of days in a year. Since the Sun appears to move about one degree of arc per day between equinoxes, using 360 degrees of arc (the number of degrees in a circle) to represent the length of a year was a practical method for measuring "a time." This type of averaging was also done for the length of a month. Even though a month is actually 29.53 days, the ancients counted a month (or a moon) as 30 days for purposes of calculation.

The Aramaic word, 'hiddan, is translated "a time" in Daniel 7:25 (and it is used elsewhere in Daniel). This word refers to "a set time" or "a turning." The word, 'hiddan can mean a set time like New Year's Day or it can be used to indicate "the turn" of the Sun when a new year begins. At the spring and fall equinoxes, the Sun appears to reverse its daily direction, hence the idea of turning is found in the word 'hiddan.

Revelation 12:14 also contains the phrase "a time, times and a half a time," and according to Revelation 12:6, this phrase represents 1,260 days. Some people question if the word "times" could mean more than two times. Actually, the word "times" can only be two times. Follow this logic: First, if we compare Revelation 12:6 with 12:14, we find that 1,260 days are "a time, times and half a time." Second, if "times" indicates more than two times, the span of time cannot be determined because no one knows how many "times" are indicated. Finally, historical evidence confirms that God had 1,260 years in mind when He defined this time period. The number of days in "a time, times and half a time" is determined by the following formula:

1. One **time** of the Sun equals one circle of 360 degrees of arc.
2. Two **times** of the Sun equals two circles of 360 degrees of arc or 720 degrees.
3. Half a **time** equals half a circle or 180 degrees of arc.
4. Total: 1,260 degrees of arc

Scholars accept that God gave the Jews a calendar in which a day of the week represented a year; a week of seven days equaled seven years. (See Leviticus 25; Numbers 14:34; Ezekiel 4:5,6.) Many Bible students understand the 70 weeks mentioned in Daniel to represent 490 years (that is, 70 weeks times seven days equals 490 days, and if each day represents a year, 70 weeks represent 490 years). If God used

Chapter 5 – When Was Jesus Found Worthy?   71

the Jubilee calendar to measure the 70 weeks in Daniel 9, it would be consistent to define the 1,260 days in Daniel 7 as 1,260 years because both time periods fall within the time frame of the Jubilee Calendar.

Even though Protestants in past centuries did not properly understand how the Jubilee Calendar worked, they did conclude the Church's power would end after 1,260 years. They believed that history and prophecy were in perfect harmony and several Protestants predicted the "wounding" of papal power before the event actually occurred in 1798. Amazingly, twenty-two centuries earlier, God revealed the little horn power to the prophet Daniel and told him it would persecute God's saints for 1,260 years. The power of the Catholic Church over Europe (the feet of the metal man) was broken in February 1798 when, during the French Revolution, General Berthier took the pope captive and put him in exile.

Step 3 - Aligning Daniel 7 with Revelation 5

History leaves no latitude about the identity of the fourth beast or the little horn. The fourth beast is Rome and the little horn is the Roman Catholic Church, the only religious entity that meets the specifications given in Daniel 7. Daniel 7:25 does not explicitly say when the 1,260 years of persecution would begin or end. However, by evaluating history and prophecy, we can determine these dates. The Bible says the little horn would prevail against the saints *until* the Ancient of Days took His seat in Heaven's courtroom and pronounced judgment in favor of the saints! (Daniel 7:21,22)

Historians say the French Revolution ended the power of the Catholic Church over Europe in 1798. However, there is more to the story. A Heavenly process was involved in this story that historians do not see. Daniel 7 does not give a starting or ending date for the 1,260 years because God wants us to understand that man did not determine the end of the 1,260 years. God removed the Roman Catholic Church from power so that it could not persecute the saints any longer. When the Ancient of Days took His seat in Heaven's courtroom and pronounced judgment in favor of the saints, He placed a restraining order on the authority and power of the Catholic Church in 1798. Daniel 7:20 aligns these events for us: **"The same horn made war with the saints, and prevailed against them;** *until* **the Ancient of days came** [to the court room and took His seat]." Using the Heaven Earth Linkage Law, we find the 1,260 years ended because the Ancient of Days took

His seat in Heaven (Daniel 7:9) and issued the restraining order. The pope was arrested in February 1798.

Counting backwards 1,260 years from 1798, we arrive at year A.D. 538 which is a date that can be justified as the date papal dominion began. In A.D. 533, Justinian issued a very important decree. This decree gave the pope authority to determine who was an orthodox Christian and who was not. The emperor Justinian issued this decree because he wanted to revive the broken empire of Rome and he dictated that everyone must be or become a Christian to be a member of the Holy Roman Empire. Justinian decreed that the pope was the proper person to determine who was orthodox. When Justinian issued the decree in 533, the pope was unable to function as the detector of orthodox Christians. He was involved in a different war of his own which included an argument over whether Jesus was a created being or an eternal being. Five years after Justinian issued the decree, Justinian's general, Belisarious, overcame the Italians in A.D. 538 and this enabled the pope to begin functioning according to Justinian's decree. By A.D. 538, three of the original tribal nations, the Ostrogoths, Heruli and Vandals, had been uprooted. The timing of these events is not coincidence. Clearly, God measures the time, a times and half a time recorded in Daniel 7 as 1,260 days. Using the Jubilee Calendar in which a day represents a year, the Catholic Church's authority over Europe began in A.D. 538 and ended in 1798. God emphasized this same time-period again in Revelation 12:6 and 12:14! In the final days of Earth's history, the final generation will need to understand this huge slice of time. This specification for the little horn will help billions of people to see and understand that a revived and modern papacy is not what they think it is.

Jesus Was Found Worthy and Inaugurated in 1798

The apostle Paul saw in a vision that a day was coming when the Father would give Jesus sovereign authority over everything in Heaven and on Earth. (2 Corinthians 12:2-7) Paul also knew that the Father would recuse Himself from the throne after giving Jesus sovereign authority so that Jesus could resolve the sin problem according to the Father's plan. (1 Corinthians 15:24-28) Even though Paul does not mention the book sealed with seven seals, we do know that about 25 years after Jesus ascended, Paul wrote about a future day when Jesus would take over the throne and exercise authority over everything in Heaven and on Earth. He wrote: **"And He** [the Father] **made known to us the**

Chapter 5 – When Was Jesus Found Worthy?

mystery of His will according to His good pleasure, which He purposed in Christ, to be put into effect when the times will have reached their fulfillment – to bring all things in Heaven and on Earth together under one head, even Christ." (Ephesians 1:9,10, insertion mine)

Paul also knew that Jesus would return the authority which the Father gave Him. Notice Paul's words: **"Then the end** [of sin's drama] **will come, when He** [Jesus] **hands over the kingdom** [returns everything given to Him] **to God the Father after He** [Jesus] **has destroyed all dominion, authority and power** [the kingdoms of men on Earth – remember the rock in the metal man vision?]. **For He** [Jesus] **must reign until He has put all His enemies under His feet. The last enemy to be destroyed is death** [the curse of sin]. **For He** [the Father] **'has put everything under his feet.' Now when it says that "everything" has been put under Him** [Jesus], **it is clear that this does not include God** [the Father] **Himself, who put everything under Christ. When He** [Jesus] **has done this** [resolved the sin problem], **then the Son himself will be made subject to Him** [the Father] **who put everything under Him, so that God** [the Father] **may be** [above] **all** [and] **in all."** (1 Corinthians 15:24-28, insertions mine)

Six hundred years before Paul was born, Daniel also saw the event when Jesus was coronated. Notice his words: **"In my vision at night I looked, and there before me was one like a son of man, coming with the clouds of Heaven. He approached the Ancient of Days and was led into his presence. He was given authority, glory and sovereign power; all peoples, nations and men of every language worshiped him. His dominion is an everlasting dominion that will not pass away, and his kingdom is one that will never be destroyed."** (Daniel 7:13,14)

I understand that the Father gave Jesus sovereign power in 1798 because the context in Daniel 7:9,10 points to 1798. After the Father convened a great meeting in Heaven, one of the first things He did was to issue a restraining order against the little horn (the papacy). This restraining order ended 1,260 years of persecution. Because the Heaven Earth Linkage Law aligns the fall of the papacy with Jesus going before the Father, we have a date for the scenes which Daniel, Paul, and John saw in vision.

Chapter 5 – When Was Jesus Found Worthy?

An apparent conflict exists because Jesus seems to have been given sovereign power and a kingdom in 1798. (An apparent conflict occurs when two Bible verses *appear* to say contradictory things.) Notice Jesus' words just before He returned to Heaven: **"Then Jesus came to them** [His disciples] **and said, 'All authority in Heaven and on Earth has been given to me. Therefore go and make disciples of all nations, baptizing them in the name of the Father and of the Son and of the Holy Spirit."** (Matthew 28:19,20, insertions mine)

The conflict arises because Jesus said that "all authority has been given to me" in A.D. 30 (at the time of His ascension), but according to prophetic timing Jesus received sovereign authority in 1798. The resolution to this conflict is that when it became clear that Israel would not accept Jesus as the Messiah and Jesus would not be able to establish the kingdom of God on Earth, the Father implemented "Plan B." According to this new plan, Jesus would not remain on Earth as "Plan A" required. Before Jesus returned to Heaven, the Father gave Jesus "all authority" to establish and manage a religious body (His church) on Earth. This transition between "Plan A" and "Plan B" is highlighted by two texts:

At the beginning of His ministry, Jesus said, **" 'The time has come,'** He [Jesus] **said. 'The kingdom of God is near. Repent and believe the good news!' "** (Mark 1:15) If Israel had cooperated with God and received Jesus as the Messiah, God would have established His kingdom on Earth as predicted in Daniel 9. **"Seventy 'sevens'** [weeks] **are decreed for your people. . . . to bring in everlasting righteousness . . . and to anoint the Most Holy** [One of Israel – Isaiah 1:4]**."** (Daniel 9:24) Under "Plan A," if Israel had received Jesus as the Messiah, Jesus would not have returned to Heaven. Instead, He would have stayed on Earth and after His death, He would have ruled on Earth from David's throne. (1 Kings 9:5) (For a discussion on the properties of "Plan A," please see Appendix B in my book, *Jesus' Final Victory*.)

When it became clear that "Plan A" could not be implemented, God put "Plan B" in motion. Jesus said to Peter: **"And I tell you that you are Peter** [a tiny pebble]**, and** [but] **on this rock** [pointing to Himself, the Rock of the ages - Psalms 18:2; 78:35] **I will build my church, and the gates of Hades will not overcome it."** (Matthew 16:18) God replaced His kingdom (Plan A) with His church (Plan B). Therefore,

Chapter 5 – When Was Jesus Found Worthy?

when Jesus ascended He did have "all authority" over His church, but He did not have sovereign authority over Heaven and Earth. This is proven by the fact that Daniel saw Jesus receive sovereign authority in 1798 and some twenty-five years after Jesus ascended, Paul pointed forward to a day when Jesus would be given authority over everything in Heaven and on Earth!

The Father waited to give Jesus sovereign authority because from the beginning, the Father foreknew everything about the rise of sin. To resolve the sin problem, the Father set a date (even before sin began) when He would give up His authority and throne. Because the Father foreknew that He would become the target of many accusations and lies, He chose to recuse Himself from the process of exonerating Himself. This is why He wrote the book and sealed it with seven seals. It is also why a careful and thorough investigation was conducted throughout the universe to find someone worthy to receive the book and break the seals. The Father's character and government are at stake. God's use of foreknowledge and omnipotence must be revealed and He must rescue and destroy sinners in a way that no one can levy a charge of unfairness or injustice against Him. All these steps had to be carried out with precision according to the plan which God created before sin began. Someone had to be found who was trustworthy and the only person who was found qualified to do the job was Jesus.

Jesus was found worthy because He had demonstrated the Father's love for sinners by coming to Earth and offering up His life as a sacrifice for sinners, Jesus had resisted and overcome all of Lucifer's clever temptations while He was on Earth, and Jesus had lived in perfect compliance with the Father's will while on Earth. Therefore, when the qualifications for receiving the book were enumerated, no one in the universe could measure up until Jesus was considered a candidate. The angels in Heaven rejoiced when they realized that Jesus was the most trusted person in the universe qualified to carry out the Father's will.

In 1798, when the Father gave Jesus the book sealed with seven seals, He also gave Jesus total control of everything in Heaven and on Earth. The Father also appointed Jesus as the judge of mankind because He had lived as humans live. The Father recused Himself from judging mankind because His plan must demonstrate that all of God's children have free will and the Father will not use His foreknowledge to determine the eternal destiny of any child.

After Jesus received the book sealed with seven seals from the Father, Heaven sang a new song about Jesus: **"And they sang a new song: 'You are worthy to take the scroll and to open its seals, because you were slain, and with your blood you purchased men [redeemed] for God from every tribe and language and people and nation.'"** (Revelation 5:9)

Daniel and John Compare Favorably

Before we conclude our investigation on the timing of Revelation 5, please review the following parallels between Daniel and John (insertions in [ ] mine):

Daniel 7:9: **"As I looked, thrones** [notice the plural] **were set in place."**

Revelation 4:2,4: **"before me was a throne . . . Surrounding the throne were twenty-four other thrones and seated on them were twenty-four elders."**

Daniel 7:10: **"Thousands upon thousands attended him; ten thousand times ten thousand stood before him."**

Revelation 5:11: **"Then I looked and heard the voice of many angels, numbering thousands upon thousands, and ten thousand times ten thousand."**

Daniel 7:9: **"The Ancient of Days took His seat. His clothing was as white as snow; the hair of His head was white like wool."**

Revelation 4:3,4: **"The One who sat there had the appearance of a jasper** [having a translucent brilliance, golden quartz color] **and carnelian** [having the multilayered brilliance of a ruby]. **The elders were dressed in white and had crowns of gold on their heads."**

Daniel 7:9,10: **"His throne was flaming with fire and its wheels were all ablaze."**

Revelation 4:5: **"From the throne came flashes of lightning, rumblings and peals of thunder. Before the throne seven lamps were blazing."**

Chapter 5 – When Was Jesus Found Worthy? 77

Daniel 7:13: "I saw one like a son of man. He approached the Ancient of Days."

Revelation 5:7: "The Lamb approached the Father sitting on the throne and took the scroll from His right hand."

Daniel 7:14: "He [the Son of Man] **was given authority, glory and sovereign power.**"

Revelation 5:9,12: "**They sang a new song, 'You are worthy to take the scroll and open its seals. Worthy is the Lamb, who was slain, to receive power and wealth and wisdom and strength and honor and glory and praise!'** "

Critics will maintain these parallels are not identical. While there are some variances between the parallels, we must consider that these parallels are not in conflict. If no other information was available, the parallels between Daniel 7 and Revelation 5 are not close enough to maintain absolutely that they are describing the same scene. However, when we add Ephesians 1:9,10 to these parallels, the differences between Daniel and John are more helpful than harmful because they give us two different perspectives. Daniel 2 and Daniel 7 do not seem to be parallels at first. The metal man and the four beasts are very different visions, but Bible students agree they offer two different perspectives on Babylon, Medo-Persia, Grecia, and Rome.

Summary

This chapter has been somewhat intricate because God hid the timing of Revelation 5 very well. Now that the book of Daniel has been unsealed and a matrix has formed, we can identify the timing of Revelation 5 with a high degree of certainty. In review, we have investigated the following points:

1. We have examined the operation of the Heaven Earth Linkage Law. God has linked certain events in Heaven with events on Earth so that we can determine the chronological timing within His plan.

2. We have examined the properties and benefits of a prophetic matrix as well as how alignment of chronological events of different prophecies resolve questions that are otherwise impossible to resolve.

3. We have aligned events in Daniel 2 (the metal man) with events in Daniel 7 (the four beasts) with the rise and fall of empires.

4. We have aligned events in Daniel 7 (the termination of the little horn's power and Jesus is given sovereign power) with events in Revelation 5 (Jesus found worthy to take the book and given sovereign power to break its seals).

5. We have identified the fourth beast in Daniel 7: Rome.

6. We have identified the little horn in Daniel 7: The Roman Catholic Church.

7. We have identified the 1,260 years allotted to the little horn: 538-1798.

8. We have linked the fall of the papacy in 1798 on Earth with Jesus receiving sovereign power in Heaven.

9. We have aligned Daniel's inauguration of Jesus in Daniel 7:13,14 with Paul's prediction that a time was coming when everything in Heaven and on Earth would be put under Jesus' authority. (Ephesians 1:9:10) We have also learned that John saw Jesus receive the seven attributes of sovereign power in Revelation 5:12. We now understand Paul's words that at the end of sin's drama (at the end of the 1,000 years), Jesus will return sovereign authority to the Father.

10. We have also considered that God gave authority to Jesus to manage His church just before His ascension and compared that to the sovereign authority given to Jesus in 1798 to resolve the sin problem.

When we synthesize these points, the year 1798 is the only date possible that Jesus could have been found worthy and inaugurated in Revelation 5. If this date is accurate, we also can identify that Jesus began breaking the seven seals in 1798.

Chapter 6
The Lamb Receives the Book

> "He who overcomes will, like them, be dressed in white. I will never blot out his name from the Book of Life, but will acknowledge his name before my Father and His angels." (Revelation 3:5)

Before sin began, the Father knew that sin would rise in Heaven and on Earth. Because the Father is a God of love, He created a sophisticated plan to resolve the sin problem, once for all eternity, so that the curse of sin could not contaminate His house again. His plan included writing a complete history of life in a book. Then, He sealed the book with seven seals to keep prying eyes from seeing His foreknowledge. Many people are surprised to learn that the book sealed with seven seals is actually called "the Book of Life." The following three steps will demonstrate that the book sealed up with seven seals is the Book of Life.

1. John mentioned the Book of Life six times in Revelation and he distinguished the Book of Life from other books that are in Heaven. (Revelation 3:5; 20:12) Daniel also made a distinction between "books" and "the Book [of Life]." (Daniel 7:9,10; 12:1) Daniel also mentioned "the Book of Truth" (Daniel 10:21) which, I believe, is another name for the Book of Life.

   Since the title, "Book of Truth" is only mentioned once in the Bible, my speculation is based on the following logic: Only the Father has foreknowledge. He wrote a perfect history of life before life was created and sealed it with seven seals. Therefore, when the Father sent Gabriel to tell Daniel about the future, Gabriel brought information from the Book of Life which the Father had revealed to Gabriel. Gabriel referred to the Book of Life as the Book of Truth because truth means, "nothing missing." Finally, Gabriel did not deliver the prophecies God gave to King Nebuchadnezzar (Daniel 2) and to Daniel (Daniel 2, 7 and 8). Instead, the Holy Spirit gave these prophecies through visions. Therefore, it appears that the Father (who alone has foreknowledge) revealed the future to the Holy Spirit as He did to Gabriel. This much is certain: After the Lamb was found worthy to receive the book having seven seals as described in Revelation 5, John referred to the book with a possessive noun, calling it, "the Lamb's Book of Life" (Revelation 21:27) or "the Book of Life belonging to the Lamb." (Revelation 13:8) The Lamb received only the book sealed with seven seals and since John referred to it as "the Lamb's Book of Life," we can conclude the Book of Life was sealed with seven seals.

2. The Book of Life is unlike the books of records that the angel's maintain. The Book of Life remains sealed until the end of the 1,000 years. (Revelation 20:12) The Book of Life is never opened or used when Jesus judges human beings. Since Jesus judges human beings according to their thoughts, motives, words, and actions, He uses the books of records which documents our choices in real time. (Ecclesiastes 12:14; 2 Corinthians 5:10; Daniel 7:9,10; Malachi 3:16; Revelation 20:12) When God created Adam and Eve, the angels recorded their thoughts, motives, words, and deeds in real time for as long as they lived. I understand the books of records were opened in 1844 and it is possible that Jesus examined Abel's record first since he was the first person to die. (Daniel 7:10; 8:14) The Book of Life was not opened in 1844. According to the Bible, the Book of Life is only opened once, at the end of the 1,000 years. (Revelation 20:12)

3. Third, we know that the book sealed with seven seals is the Book of Life because of the sensitive contents of the Book of Life. If everyone knew in advance who would be saved and who would be destroyed, the Father could never escape the charge of divine fraud. An all-knowing God who created children bound for annihilation could not be called a God of love. Even though no one but the Father knows the specifics in the book (Revelation 5:3), the Bible reveals the Father's purpose for the book as well as its contents.

Notice this Bible verse: **"If anyone's name was not found written in the Book of Life, he was thrown into the lake of fire."** (Revelation 20:15) Many Christians read this verse and assume the Book of Life contains only the names of the saved. They are partially correct when they interpret the title of the book to mean the "Book of Eternal Life." While the Book of Life does contain the names of people who will receive eternal life, it also includes the record of each person's life whom God gives the gift of life. The Father's book includes everyone and it describes the thoughts, motives, words, and deeds of all living beings.

Chapter 6 – The Lamb Receives the Book

God entered the name and record of each person who will receive the gift of life. God recorded each person's actions and choices in His book before anyone had the privilege of living. (See Psalms 139:16.) Even though the Father foreknew who would be saved and who would not, He did not blot out anyone's record of life. Instead, He simply blotted out the name of each wicked person.

Names Blotted Out

A little background information about the practice of "blotting out" names in record books may be helpful. In Bible times, God required the nation of Israel to keep very accurate records on family trees. Every Jew knew his tribal origin. We find many examples of this in the Bible. These accurate records allowed the lineage of Jesus to be traced to Abraham. In Luke 3, Jesus' lineage was traced to Adam. In the days of Jesus, it was the custom to enter the names of the offspring in the nation's official records because tribal lineage was important. When Rome destroyed Jerusalem in A.D. 70, Rome destroyed all of Israel's records. So, today there is no possible way to prove if a person is in fact, a biological Jew or which tribe he may belong.

God divided the land of Canaan according to the size and lineage of each tribe. (Numbers 26:53,54; Joshua 14:5) Interestingly, God designed polygamy as a method to keep a family name alive. **"If brothers are living together and one of them dies without a son, his widow must not marry outside the family. Her husband's brother shall take her and marry her and fulfill the duty of a brother-in-law to her. The first son she bears shall carry on the name of the dead brother so that his name will not be blotted out from Israel."** (Deuteronomy 25:5,6) Tribal lineage also determined temple responsibilities and duties among the priests. (Exodus 40; Numbers 4) Even more, those born through intermarriage were to be entered in tribal rolls. God said, **"No one born of a forbidden marriage nor any of his descendants may enter the assembly of the Lord, even down to the tenth generation."** (Deuteronomy 23:2)

Notice David's words regarding evil men; especially consider the nature and importance of being "cut off" or "blotted out" from God's people:

"O God, whom I praise, do not remain silent, for wicked and deceitful men have opened their mouths against me; they have spoken against me with lying tongues. With words of hatred they surround me; they attack me without cause. In return for

my friendship they accuse me, but I am a man of prayer. They repay me evil for good, and hatred for my friendship. Appoint an evil man to oppose him; let an accuser stand at his right hand. When he is tried, let him be found guilty, and may his prayers condemn him. May his days be few; may another take his place of leadership. May his children be fatherless and his wife a widow. May his children be wandering beggars; may they be driven from their ruined homes. May a creditor seize all he has; may strangers plunder the fruits of his labor. May no one extend kindness to him or take pity on his fatherless children.

May his descendants be cut off, their names blotted out from the next generation. May the iniquity of his fathers be remembered before the Lord; may the sin of his mother never be blotted out. May their sins always remain before the Lord, that He may cut off the memory of them from the Earth. For he never thought of doing a kindness, but hounded to death the poor and the needy and the brokenhearted. He loved to pronounce a curse – may it come on him; he found no pleasure in blessing-- may it be far from him." (Psalms 109:1-17)

If an Israelite committed an unpardonable offense, God commanded that certain offenders be "cut off" from His people. In some cases, they had to be put to death. When such a person was "cut off" from his family and nation, his name was blotted out of the tribal rolls. The scribes could not erase information on velum or parchment because they wrote these records of lineage, births, marriages, and deaths in ink. Moreover, a rebellious person might have had offspring and tribal lineage was a historical fact that could not be changed. However, the name could be blotted out with an ink blot so that the succeeding generations would not know the identity of the wicked person.

This crude but ancient practice helps to explain how God represented His actions to John. When the Father wrote out a complete history of life, He included everyone in His book that would receive life. If the Father had omitted the records of those who would be destroyed, His book would have been incomplete and worse, the books of records (the records made by angels in real time) would have information in them not included in the Book of Life. It is imperative that the Book of Life and the books of records are identical at the end of sin's drama. The Father must prove that everyone had free will and the freedom to act according to free will and that He foreknew what everyone would choose

Chapter 6 – The Lamb Receives the Book

to do. However, under no circumstances would the Father interfere with the exercise of anyone's free will. Therefore, after the drama with sin is completed, it is important that the Father's book is found to be identical with everything recorded (in real time) in the books of records for all eternity. Every life is a thread in the tapestry of history because all of us are Adam and Eve's created offspring and are related to each other. Therefore, the Father only blotted out the names of those who would refuse to submit to the Holy Spirit, but He left the record of every life intact for all eternity.

The sins of the saints will not be available forever to review after the Book of Life is opened and sin's problem has been resolved. God gives each person who follows the directives of the Holy Spirit and receives eternal life, the "righteousness of Christ" on judgment day. Christ created the record of His righteousness when He came to Earth. His life's record as a human being shows that He overcame every temptation and never sinned. Christ gives this perfect record of His righteousness to every repentant sinner when we are judged. Christ's righteousness will "cover" every sinner's record eternally and as far as I can tell, this is the only cover-up in recorded history that has the Father's approval. If there should be any future quibbling about this amazing gift, do not forget that billions of angels and 24 elders were eye witnesses when Jesus chose to bestow His righteousness on each sinner.

Remember, the Book of Life also has a record of the lives of angels. Because God foreknew who would choose eternal life and who would choose rebellion, He determined that no one should have access to His foreknowledge until sin's drama has been completed. This is why He perfectly sealed the Book of Life with seven seals and put it in Heaven's vault. The Book of Life will remain sealed until the 1,000 years are ended. The Book of Life has nothing to do with the judgment of mankind. Humanity is not judged or predestined to eternal life or death on the basis of God's foreknowledge. We are judged according to the angel's records of our words, thoughts, and deeds which are recorded as they transpire. (Revelation 22:12) Special angels chronicle our daily actions in the books of deeds. (See Daniel 7:9,10; Revelation 20:12; 2 Corinthians 5:10; Ecclesiastes 12:14 and Malachi 3:16.)

The Book (of Life)

Several Bible writers mention the Book of Life even though it is not always called by that name. Notice this conversation between the Lord and Moses: " 'But now, please forgive their sin [of Israel] but if not, then blot me out of the book you have written. The Lord replied to Moses, 'Whoever has sinned against me I will blot out of my book.' " (Exodus 32:32,33, insertion mine) Moses begged God to forgive Israel or blot his name out of the book that God had written! God responded by saying that whoever has sinned against Him would be blotted out. Some Christians have concluded that this text shows the Book [of Life] is a dynamic recording, that is, names are added and blotted out as needed. However, we know God wrote the Book of Life and sealed it with seven seals before He created the world. (Revelation 17:8) We also have learned that our eternal destiny has nothing to do with the Book of Life. Jesus determines the eternal destiny of dead people when he reviews the books of record which show motives, thoughts, words, and actions. (2 Corinthians 5:10; Ecclesiastes 12:14)

The Lord's response to Moses provides an assurance that the wicked were blotted out of the book even before God gave them life! Moses knew God had already completed the book! Notice the past-perfect tense: **"then blot me out of the book you have written."** Therefore, we need to understand God's response to Moses within a past-perfect context. In effect, the Lord's statement means, "When I wrote the Book of Life, I blotted out the names of those who would sin against me." This approach to Exodus 32:32 aligns with a statement in Revelation concerning the Antichrist's appearing during the Great Tribulation: **"The inhabitants of the Earth whose names have not been written in the Book of Life from the creation of the world will be astonished when they see the beast."** (Revelation 17:8)

This text shows the Book of Life was written from the creation of the world and shows the Father foreknew who will worship the beast and who will not. Even though God foreknows what we will do, the choice is ours to make! This is free will with the freedom God gives to everyone. Because God gives us the power of choice, we are responsible for our choices and actions. If we were mere robots, we would not have free will, any moral obligation, or responsibility.

King David knew about the Book of Life. He wrote, **"May they** [the wicked] **be blotted out of the Book of Life and not be listed with the righteous."** (Psalms 69:28, insertion mine) King David knew that God wrote his entire life record in the Book of Life long *before* he was born. David wrote, **"Your eyes saw my unformed body. All the days ordained for me were written in your book before one of**

Chapter 6 – The Lamb Receives the Book

them came to be." Psalms 139:16) Jesus alluded to the Book of Life when He said to His disciples, **"However, do not rejoice that the spirits submit to you, but rejoice that your names are written in Heaven."** (Luke 10:20) Paul mentions the Book of Life saying: **"Yes, and I ask you, loyal yokefellow, help these women who have contended at my side in the cause of the gospel, along with Clement and the rest of my fellow workers, whose names are in the Book of Life."** (Philippians 4:3)

Summary

While different Bible writers mention the Book of Life, God only showed John that it was sealed with seven seals. The Book of Life is an important topic because at God's appointed time, the seventh seal will be broken and God will reveal the contents of the book. The information inside the book will exonerate the Father eternally of all charges that He uses His foreknowledge and omnipotence to manipulate and control His subjects. Only the Father knows the specifics He wrote in the book, but we can determine that it contains a prerecorded history of life. When the Father wrote the book, He blotted out the names of those who will be lost. This highly sensitive information explains why the book had to be sealed seven times. After all Heaven found the Lamb worthy to receive this book from the Father in 1798, John referred to it as "the Lamb's Book of Life."

Chapter 7
Seven Revelations about Jesus

"I watched as the Lamb opened the first of the seven seals. Then I heard one of the four living creatures say in a voice like thunder, 'Come!' " (Revelation 6:1)

God prepared the book of life before life on Earth and in Heaven began and we now know why He sealed it with seven seals. These seven seals also have an important purpose. Long ago, the Father ordained that the seven seals on the Book of Life would be associated with seven revelations about Jesus. The Father has infinite love and wisdom and everything He does is always ultimately beneficial. The Father's ways never have unintended consequences. The Father foresaw the drama with sin was an opportunity to reveal many aspects of His universe. For instance, through the ministry and death of Jesus, we now can understand the ravages that come with the curse of sin, the depth of God's love for sinners, the properties of divine love, the character and nature of God's judicial system, the intricate balance between mercy and justice, the patience and longsuffering of a loving Father, and His thoughtfully designed plan to make lemonade out of the lemon of sin. Finally, at the end of the 1,000 years, all created beings will learn that the Father has not and will not use His foreknowledge or omnipotence to manipulate beings having free will. As a bonus, the Father has a wonderful surprise for everyone that will inherit eternal life. Because Jesus is an exact mirror of the Father, the revelation of Jesus Christ will be a perfect revelation of the Father!

Remember, before sin existed, the Father designed a process to resolve the sin problem that would take several thousand years to accomplish. When the time arrived to start the final chapter in this plan, the Father summoned the angelic host and the twenty-four elders. (Revelation 4-6; Daniel 7:9,10,13,14) At that time, the Father gave Jesus sovereign power to break the seven seals.

The twenty-four elders surrounding the throne are people who were resurrected when Jesus died on the cross (Matthew 27:52) and went to

Heaven when Jesus ascended. (Ephesians 4:8) God selected two witnesses from each of the twelve tribes and gave them "front row seats." They have occupied this exalted position because they are there as members of a special jury. The Father resurrected 24 human beings (think of them as first fruits of the dead) to observe the process He is using to resolve the sin problem. The Father is using these elders because the process involves the judgment of sinners (e.g., the redemption and the annihilation of human beings) and the 24 observers are there to maintain total transparency in the judgment process. These 24 elders are ex-sinners and the Father has given them substantial authority. If any elder witnesses a presentation or decision on another human being that appears to be incomplete, unfair, or improper, that elder has the authority to halt the judgment process until a satisfactory resolution is produced. The Father has placed 24 ex-sinners (peers of the people being judged) around the throne and given them the authority to halt the judgment process to show that He is love. He is more than fair!

When Jesus was considered as a candidate to receive the book sealed with seven seals, everyone agreed (including the 24 elders) that Jesus was the only being worthy of the task. Jesus' perfect compliance with the Father's will, a victorious life over every temptation, and His shed blood made him worthy to redeem man. (Revelation 5:9, John 6:38; Hebrews 5:7-10) No one but the Creator could meet the required specifications. We must not focus on Christ's accomplishments as amazing and surreal as they are. Instead, we need to focus on the task ahead of Jesus, His use of sovereign power to break the seven seals!

Before sin began, the Father planned that opening each seal on the Book of Life would initiate a new campaign on Earth. Also, when each seal is broken, we receive a new revelation about Jesus. This is why the book of Revelation is called, "The Revelation of Jesus Christ." The book of Revelation contains seven revelations that will sweep away a thousand mysteries about Jesus. Jesus is far more than an angel or a man. Jesus is a God just like the Father is a God!

My understanding is that Jesus received the Book of Life in 1798 and He broke the first seal at that time. If indeed, a new revelation about Jesus occurs in Heaven and on Earth when each seal is broken, we should be able to find distinctive evidence of this. As the revelation of Jesus grows in glory and intensity, all creation will see a full disclosure of our Creator at a point in time. This day will occur at the end of the thousand years because each being who received life will be there. After

Chapter 7 – Seven Revelations About Jesus

the Father has given Jesus all the power, glory, praise, and accolades that can be given, Jesus does not retain this power forever. Jesus will not eternally bask in glory and fame that will eclipse the Father. Instead, Jesus will choose, once again, to be subject to the Father so that the Father can be God Most High and Jesus can live among His created beings as one of them. What a stunning revelation about the love, humility, and meekness of the Godhead! And the eternal bonus that goes with this knowledge is this: "Like Father – like Son!"

The seven seals are associated with these seven revelations of Jesus:

      Seal 1: The salvation of Jesus
      Seal 2: The teachings of Jesus
      Seal 3: The judgment seat of Jesus
      Seal 4: The authority of Jesus
      Seal 5: The faith of Jesus
      Seal 6: The glory of Jesus
      Seal 7: The Deity of Jesus

Chapter 7 – Seven Revelations About Jesus

Chapter 8
Four Deadly Judgments
The Four Living Creatures

> "Each of the four living creatures had six wings and was covered with eyes all around, even under his wings. Day and night they never stop saying: 'Holy, holy, holy is the Lord God Almighty, who was, and is, and is to come.'" (Revelation 4:8)

Throughout the centuries, Christians have generally believed that Jesus began breaking the seals shortly after He ascended to Heaven. This idea has been perpetuated, but it is faulty because there is nothing within Revelation 4-6 indicating that Jesus was found worthy to receive the book sealed with seven seals shortly after He returned to Heaven. Revelation 5 does indicate that Jesus had been slain, (Revelation 5:6) but this is not particularly helpful because Revelation 13:8 describes Jesus as **"the Lamb that was slain from the creation of the world."** The timing of the convocation in Revelation 4-6 was not revealed in the book of Revelation and the book of Daniel (which indicates the timing) was sealed until the time of the end! Early Christians did not have access to the rules governing the interpretation of apocalyptic prophecy or Daniel's matrix, so they tried to understand Revelation 4-6 by *assuming* that Jesus was found worthy to receive the book shortly after He returned to Heaven.

This assumption, like the assumption that Earth stood still and the Sun orbited around Earth, has been harmless, but it has introduced more confusion than it resolved. In the sixteenth century, before Copernicus proved that Earth orbited the Sun, the orbits of heavenly bodies were very difficult to calculate. However, once astronomers understood that Earth traveled around a stationary Sun, they could determine the orbits of heavenly bodies much more easily. The timing of Revelation 4-6 works the same way. When a person understands the timing of Revelation 4-6, the purpose of the Father's book and the meaning of the seven seals will make sense just as the Bible reads. I do not believe that Jesus began breaking the seals shortly after He ascended to Heaven.

Apocalyptic prophecy is written in a way that it will only make sense when we use valid rules of interpretation. If we do not use valid rules, private interpretations will flourish. (A private interpretation is an interpretation which people cannot discover on their own. A private interpretation requires that an external authority serve as interpreter.) Even though we have not yet examined the meaning of the seven seals, a short discussion on the fourth seal will demonstrate how the seven seals have been distorted for many centuries.

Consider the fourth seal: **"When the Lamb opened the fourth seal, I heard the voice of the fourth living creature say, 'Come!' I looked, and there before me was a pale horse! Its rider was named Death, and Hades was following close behind him. They were given power over a fourth of the earth to kill by sword, famine and plague, and by the wild beasts of the Earth."** (Revelation 6:7,8)

A person does not have to be a Bible scholar to understand that when the fourth seal is broken, the Bible gives us a big hint that the result will be extremely deadly. The rider's name on the horse is "Death" and the grave (Greek: *Hades*), like an accompanying vulture, follows close behind to consume the dead. The Bible says Death will have power to kill 25% of Earth's population. How does Death kill 25% of the Earth? Even more, why would Jesus kill 25% of Earth's population? These are reasonable questions even though they border on fantasy because killing 25% of Earth's population (presently 7.3 billion people) is unimaginable!

You might be surprised to learn that the rider on the horse will use the *same* deadly judgments which God has used since Bible times. These judgments are sword, famine, plague, and wild beasts. (Compare Leviticus 26:12-39 with Ezekiel 14:12-21) Two selections from the Old Testament reveal that God previously described His four judgments and justified their use. The first passage is a selection of verses from "The Song of Moses." The Israelites were required to memorize and sing this song. (Incidentally, the redeemed will also sing this song in Heaven! See Revelation 15:3.) God gave the second declaration to Ezekiel just before King Nebuchadnezzar was sent to plunder and destroy Jerusalem in 586 B.C. Take a few moments to absorb these divine declarations because when the fourth seal is broken approximately two billion people will die.

Statement 1: The Song of Moses   1437 B.C.

"Jeshurun [a poetic name of endearment given to Israel. God used this name to indicate His affection for Israel, as though His people

Chapter 8 – The Four Living Creatures

were His pet.] **grew fat and kicked; filled with food, he became heavy and sleek. He abandoned the God who made him and rejected the Rock his Savior. They made him jealous with their foreign gods and angered him with their detestable idols. They sacrificed to demons, which are not God, gods they had not known, gods that recently appeared, gods your fathers did not fear. You deserted the Rock, who fathered you; you forgot the God who gave you birth. The Lord saw this and rejected them because he was angered by his sons and daughters. . . . I will heap calamities upon them and spend my arrows against them. I will send wasting *famine* against them, consuming pestilence and deadly *plague*; I will send against them the fangs of *wild beasts*, the venom of vipers that glide in the dust. In the street the *sword* will make them childless; in their homes terror will reign. Young men and young women will perish, infants and gray-haired men."** (Selections from Deuteronomy 32:15-25, insertion and italics mine)

Statement 2: Concerning the Destruction of Jerusalem 586 B.C.

"The word of the Lord came to me: 'Son of man, if a country sins against me by being unfaithful and I stretch out my hand against it to cut off its food supply and send *famine* upon it and kill its men and their animals, even if these three men Noah, Daniel and Job were in it, they could save only themselves by their righteousness,' declares the Sovereign Lord. 'Or if I send *wild beasts* through that country and they leave it childless and it becomes desolate so that no one can pass through it because of the beasts, as surely as I live,' declares the Sovereign Lord, 'even if these three men were in it, they could not save their own sons or daughters. They alone would be saved, but the land would be desolate.' Or if I bring a *sword* against that country and say, 'Let the sword pass throughout the land,' and I kill its men and their animals, as surely as I live, declares the Sovereign Lord, 'even if these three men were in it, they could not save their own sons or daughters. They alone would be saved.' 'Or if I send a *plague* into that land and pour out my wrath upon it through bloodshed, killing its men and their animals, as surely as I live,' declares the Sovereign Lord, 'even if Noah, Daniel and Job were in it, they could save neither son nor daughter. They would save only themselves by their righteousness.' For this is what the Sovereign Lord says: 'How much worse will it be when I send against Jerusalem my four dreadful judgments: *sword and famine and wild beasts and plague* to kill its men and their animals!'" (Selections from Ezekiel 14:12-21, italics mine)

God has used four deadly judgments on many occasions to punish people and to cauterize the growth of sin. Of course, a God of love is reluctant to implement these judgments, but He is moved by divine justice (Genesis 15:16; Leviticus 18:24) when extended mercy has no redeeming effect. (For a study of the "Full Cup Principle," please see Chapter 2 in my book *Warning! Revelation is about to be fulfilled*.) The Bible says that God destroyed the world in Noah's day because man's thoughts were constantly evil. Geneses 6:5) The Bible indicates that God destroyed Sodom, Gomorrah, and Jerusalem because of degenerate behavior. (Genesis 18,19; Ezekiel 5) God destroyed His own people in A.D. 70 because of arrogance and decadence. God's patience with sin and sinners has a limit. God even cast Lucifer and his followers out of Heaven when the limit of God's patience was reached. God destroys people, cities, and nations when extended mercy cannot produce repentance and reformation. (Genesis 19; Leviticus 18; Colossians 3:5,6; Revelation 18 and 20)

Unfortunately, Christians do not hear much about God's wrath and this silence has led many people to diminish the reality of God and our accountability to Him. Several texts in the Bible highlight God's four dreadful judgments and these judgments were *always* exercised within the context of corporate punishment. (Please review Leviticus 26, 1 Chronicles 21; Jeremiah 14; 27; 44; Ezekiel 6.) This means that sword, famine, plague, and wild beasts were "group punishments." With this background information, we return to the issue of Christians attempting to interpret and identify the correct timing of the fourth seal.

History Cannot Produce a Fulfillment of the Fourth Seal

For twenty centuries, Christian expositors have made various claims of fulfillment for the fourth seal, but no one has presented a convincing solution. The problem is the scope of destruction is so huge (25% of Earth's population) that it should be very easy to identify the evidence of God's wrath if indeed this seal has been broken! Additionally, the fourth seal has to occur between the breaking of the third seal and the fifth seal. The chronological timing of the fourth seal creates issues which negate the argument that the fourth seal has been broken pre-

Chapter 8 – The Four Living Creatures

viously. Bible students who believe the fourth seal has been fulfilled should be more concerned about the absence of a clear and convincing fulfillment, but alas, it is human nature to distort prophetic details that are not understood and/or to dismiss events in the book of Revelation as mysterious symbols.

If the fourth seal was broken previously, no student can identify the year it occurred or show when Jesus punished the *whole* world by killing only a quarter of it. A few Christians have argued the bubonic plague which swept through Europe in the sixth, fourteenth, and seventeenth centuries could be a fulfillment of the fourth seal. These epidemics were horrible, but they were limited to Europe. Even if the bubonic plague killed 25% of Europe's population, this event did not fulfill the specification of the fourth seal. The death that occurs during the fourth seal represents death for 25% of the whole world. There was nothing supernatural about the bubonic plague and obviously, it was not God's punitive judgment on the whole world. It was self-inflicted; a consequence of poor sanitation and standing filth.

Because the Protestant reformation grew out of persecution, many reformers in the seventeenth, eighteenth, and nineteenth centuries claimed the fourth seal covered a period of a thousand years when the Church of Rome persecuted all who refused to obey its laws. The total number of martyrs during the Dark Ages (around A.D. 500 to A.D. 1500) has been estimated to be as low as ten million and as high as fifty million. No student of Protestant history doubts the saints were persecuted horribly during the Dark Ages, but this interpretation cannot satisfy the specifications given in the fourth seal for two reasons. First, the Bible indicates that God's four judgments, sword, famine, plague, and wild beasts, are punitive and corporate. This means they are *always* directed at nations who have filled their cup of iniquity. Therefore, Bible students cannot apply the fourth seal to the saints who were burned at the stake or imprisoned for their faith during the Dark Ages. Second, the Bible says that when the fourth seal is broken, 25% of Earth's population dies. Even if the Catholic Church did put fifty million saints to death, this does not meet the specifications of the fourth seal. The scope of destruction involves the whole world and the breaking of the fourth seal will harm every nation.

A few Christians (grasping at straws) have suggested the fourth seal was broken about 1918, when at the height of its deadly grip, the world's worst outbreak of influenza killed twenty-five million people in a single year! Between 1914 and 1918, nine million people died from World War I. The influenza outbreak was horrible and it followed on the heels of a horrible war, but both events did not come close to killing 25% of the world's population.

History cannot produce a single fulfillment for the fourth seal because the scope of the fourth seal is so large that nothing in the past measures up. A fulfillment of apocalyptic prophecy occurs only when all of the specifications of the prophecy are met. There is no event in history that meets the specifications of the fourth seal because the fourth seal is in the future, not the past.

A Mighty Display of Divine Authority

Now that we understand the specifications for the fourth seal and are aware of no evidence supporting that this seal was previously fulfilled, please consider the following explanation. I believe Jesus will soon break the fourth seal and when He does, four judgments will kill 25% of Earth's population and the Great Tribulation will begin. God's wrath will break out and come as an overwhelming surprise for billions of people. Unfortunately, Jesus will reveal His sovereign authority and everyone on Earth will experience it. Jesus must do this because humanity is so arrogant, religiously diverse, and degenerate that a mighty display of divine authority is the only remaining solution. Earth's cup of iniquity is overflowing.

The Four Living Creatures

If you want to understand the first four seals, you have to understand the role of the Holy Spirit in the first four seals. It is not coincidence that Revelation 4 and 5 include information about the four living creatures. They are intimately involved in the story of the seven seals because the Holy Spirit rides each of the four horses sent from Heaven's temple. I believe the four living creatures represent the third member of the Godhead, the Holy Spirit. (Note: Many Christians have not considered the composition and nature of the Godhead. The Bible teaches that the Father is not the Son, and Jesus is not the Holy Spirit. The Godhead consists of three separate deities and the Holy Spirit is a separate, coeternal, Deity just like Jesus and the Father. For an in depth study on this topic, please see Appendix A.)

Chapter 8 – The Four Living Creatures

I know that many people may not understand the four living creatures represent the Holy Spirit, but we will see that this is the only solution that will fulfill all of the specifications given for the four living creatures. Consider this rule of interpretation: "Apocalyptic language can be literal, symbolic or analogous. To reach the intended meaning of apocalyptic prophecy, the student must consider: (a) the context, (b) the use of parallel language elsewhere in the Bible, and (c) relevant statements in the Bible which define the symbol if an element is thought to be symbolic."

If we follow and properly apply valid rules of interpretation, we will arrive at the intended meaning of apocalyptic prophecy. Therefore, to determine whom the living creatures represent, we have to consider all of the specifications which John provides:

1. John saw four living creatures surrounding God's throne.
2. Each creature had six wings.
3. Each creature was full of eyes.
4. Each creature had four faces: a lion, a calf, a man, and a flying eagle.
5. The four creatures never rest from giving praise and glory to God.

Before we reach for a conclusion with these specifications, we need to also consider the use of parallel language in the Bible. Consider what Ezekiel wrote in Ezekiel 1 and Ezekiel 10 because he, too, saw the four living creatures!

1. The four living creatures have the appearance of a man. (1:5)
2. Each living creature has four faces, four wings and four hands. (1:6,7)
3. Each living creature has the faces of a lion, ox, man, and eagle. (1:10)
4. The four living creatures appeared to be on fire. Lightning flashed from the four living creatures. (1:13)
5. The four living creatures traveled at the speed of light. (1:14)
6. Above the four living creatures was a great sparkling expanse that looked like a sheet of ice. (1:22)
7. A glorious throne rested above the four living creatures, in the middle of this sparkling expanse. (1:26)
8. The bodies of the four creatures were covered with eyes. (10:12)

9. Four whirling wheels of light were located beside each creature. (1:15,16;10:16)
10. The power within the four creatures came from the four wheels beside each creature. (1:20; 10:17)

Even though John and Ezekiel have slight variations in descriptions, there is no question that these two men saw the *same* four living creatures. God is able to expand our understanding of the topic by giving John and Ezekiel different descriptions of the living creatures. This is why there are four gospels! Matthew's perspective is not sufficient, so we need the other gospel writers' perspectives to better understand Jesus' ministry and teachings. Without Paul's additional perspective, Christianity would have been much different today.

When the idea is presented that the four living creatures represent the Holy Spirit, people wonder about the strange idea that the power within the four creatures was not within the creatures but inside the four wheels beside the creatures. Notice this passage:

"When the cherubim moved, the wheels beside them moved; and when the cherubim spread their wings to rise from the ground, the wheels did not leave their side. When the cherubim stood still, they also stood still; and when the cherubim rose, they rose with them, because the spirit of the living creatures was in them." (Ezekiel 10:16,17)

To help Ezekiel understand the ministry of the Holy Spirit, God represented the power within the four living creatures as separate from the four living creatures. This indicates that the Holy Spirit is not limited to any particular shape, being, person, or form. The Holy Spirit can assume any shape, at any time, at any place all at the same time. He can assume the shape of a dove (Matthew 3:16) or He can enable a donkey to speak (Numbers 22). The Holy Spirit can be deadly, too! Remember, He killed Ananias and Sapphira (Acts 5).

When the fifteen specifications John and Ezekiel provided are consolidated, we can make the following conclusions:

1. The four living creatures are identical or, in other words, four clones of the same entity. They stand closest to God and His throne. This representation suggests there is an omnipresent being who can take any form and remain alive! They are called "the four living creatures" because the power to give life is within them. The 24

Chapter 8 – The Four Living Creatures   99

elders are not called, "the 24 living elders" and the angels are not called "the living angels." The four living creatures are "living creatures" because the power of life is within them. Additionally, the four living creatures exist in the north, south, east, and west, the four points of a compass, all at the same time.

2. The four living creatures are covered with eyes. This indicates the Holy Spirit instantly sees everything occurring in the universe. The eyes, signifying the Holy Spirit's omnipresence, indicate Deity because the Holy Spirit serves as the eyes and ears of Jesus and the Father. The Holy Spirit sees everything in the universe instantly and reported in real time. The amount of data that flows from the Holy Spirit every millisecond is unimaginable.

3. Ezekiel and John saw the same four faces on each living creature. Each face describes certain challenges which the Holy Spirit "faces." For example, the Holy Spirit has intelligence. He knows God's ways and will as well as mankind's thoughts, motives, words, and deeds (this ability is represented by the face of a man – Ecclesiastes 8:1). The Holy Spirit has divine strength (represented by the face of an ox – Numbers 23:22). The Holy Spirit is deadly and can destroy anything that has been created (represented by the prowess of a lion – Numbers 23:24). The Holy Spirit travels at warp speed, much faster than light (represented by six wings). When necessary, the Holy Spirit can swoop down and catch any prey wherever or whatever it may be (represented by the face of an eagle – Deuteronomy 28:49).

4. The Holy Spirit is as selfless and humble as Jesus and the Father. The Holy Spirit extolls the Father's majesty, generosity, wisdom, love, goodness, and grace perpetually. The Holy Spirit's highest work is to bond God's children with the Father and Jesus in spirit and in truth. The Holy Spirit constantly brings glory to the Father and Jesus by exalting them. (John 16:14) The Holy Spirit also serves as a conduit between God and His children. He takes God's happiness, joy, and goodness and shares it with everyone willing to receive it producing "the fruit of the Spirit." (Galatians 5:22-24)

When we incorporate all the features that Ezekiel and John specify, the four living creatures point to one person, the Holy Spirit. The really cool thing about the Holy Spirit is if it wasn't for His ministry, no one would ever know God! The Holy Spirit's job is to reveal the other two Gods. He is perfect at this because He is just like them, a selfless member of Deity like the Father and Jesus.

The Unpardonable Sin

Because the Holy Spirit is a critical member of Deity, we need to understand that sinning against the Holy Spirit is the unpardonable sin. Jesus said: **"And so I tell you, every sin and blasphemy will be forgiven men, but the blasphemy against the Spirit will not be forgiven. Anyone who speaks a word against the Son of Man will be forgiven, but anyone who speaks against the Holy Spirit will not be forgiven, either in this age or in the age to come."** (Matthew 12:31,32)

Jesus' words resolve a very important issue. Many people believe and teach that the Holy Spirit is an *influence* that comes from the Father or Jesus. These people often deny that the Holy Spirit is a separate Deity, thinking this will avoid the issue of polytheism. However, the Bible does not teach polytheism. Instead, it teaches tritheism (three separate Gods bound together by love who are one in purpose, plan, and action).

If the Holy Spirit is just an influence, no one could sin against the Holy Spirit because a person cannot sin against an *influence*. For example, a person cannot sin against the influence of magnetism, a puff of cold air, or the tug of a river's current, because these are inanimate influences. On the other hand, the Holy Spirit is a living being who has authority, has eyes, can speak and hear, and can exert influence in the heart of anyone He wishes. (Luke 2:25-27; Ezra 1:1) The sinner, the Father, or Jesus does not determine or declare that a person has committed the unpardonable sin. The Holy Spirit Himself makes that determination. He alone can do this because He is Deity. When the Holy Spirit speaks to us, we can either submit to Him or reject Him because He is a God, a member of the Godhead.

If you would like to prove to yourself that the Father, Jesus, and the Holy Spirit are separate, distinct, coeternal members of the Godhead, try this simple experiment. In mathematics, we say that if a, b, and c have the same value, we can substitute one of these three variables for another at any time. Using a similar approach, if we say that the Father, Son, and Holy Spirit are the same God (expressing Himself in three different ways), we should be able to go through the Bible and substitute any mention of God with any title for God and we should

Chapter 8 – The Four Living Creatures

reach the same conclusion. Obviously, this approach does not make any sense.

Let us carry this concept to its logical conclusion (to avoid polytheism) and see what we find: "Jesus wrote a book and sealed it with seven seals before the world was created. At the appointed time, Jesus searched for someone to open His book, but He found that only Himself was worthy to receive the book from Himself. So, after passing the book from His right hand to His left hand, He proceeded to break the seals. Each time Jesus breaks open a seal, He reveals more of Himself to the universe. At the end of sin's drama, the Holy Spirit will open the book and prove that He foreknew everything that would happen and He never has done anything wrong. Then the Father will give back to Himself the sovereign authority which He gave to Himself in 1798 so that the Father might be all in all."

If this silly scenario was true, intelligent angels and the redeemed would have to conclude the Father has been deceitful. He wrote a book to exonerate Himself and after searching through the universe to find someone worthy to open it, it turns out that only He was worthy. Then, He concluded the sin problem according to His own wisdom and He exonerated Himself accordingly. After concluding the sin problem, He returned the authority which He had given to Himself so that He could be Almighty God again. Obviously, this is nonsense.

The book of Revelation will only make sense if a Bible student properly understands the separate and distinct roles of the Father, Son, and Holy Spirit. Many verses in the Bible support the conclusion that the four living creatures represent the Holy Spirit. When we examine the four horsemen in Revelation 6, you will see what I mean.

Chapter 9
The Four Royal Horsemen

"The angel answered me, 'These are the four spirits of Heaven, going out from standing in the presence of the Lord of the whole world.' " (Zechariah 6:5)

The First Four Seals

Please review the breaking of the first four seals and notice that four royal horsemen are sent out from God's throne.

Seal #1   White Horse

"And I saw when the Lamb opened one of the seals, and I heard, as it were the noise of thunder, one of the four beasts [the one that had the face of a lion] **saying, Come and see. And I saw, and behold a white horse: and he that sat on him had a bow; and a crown was given unto him: and he went forth conquering, and to conquer.**" (Revelation 6:1,2, KJV, insertion mine)

Seal #2   Red Horse

"**And when He had opened the second seal, I heard the second beast** [the one that had the face of an ox] **say, Come and see. And there went out another horse that was red: and power was given to him that sat thereon to take peace from the Earth, and that they should kill one another: and there was given unto him a great sword.**" (Revelation 6:3,4, KJV, insertion mine)

Seal #3   Black Horse

"**And when He had opened the third seal, I heard the third beast** [the one having the face of a man] **say, Come and see. And I beheld, and lo a black horse; and he that sat on him had a pair of balances in his hand. And I heard a voice in the midst of the four beasts say, A measure of wheat for a penny, and three measures of barley for a penny; and see thou hurt not the oil and the wine.**" (Revelation 6:5,6, KJV, insertion mine)

Seal #4   Pale or Dappled Horse

"**And when He had opened the fourth seal, I heard the voice of the fourth beast** [the one that had the face of an eagle] **say, Come** and see. And I looked, and behold a pale horse: and his name that sat on him was Death, and Hell followed with him. And power was given unto them over the fourth part of the Earth, to kill with sword, and with hunger, and with death, and with the beasts of the Earth." (Revelation 6:7,8, KJV, insertion mine)

These eight verses speak volumes with very few words. The first four seals describe four tasks assigned to the Holy Spirit. The Holy Spirit is represented as four horsemen. As Jesus breaks each of the first four seals, He gives a command to the Holy Spirit and the Holy Spirit invites John to "come and see" the action. While many people have heard of the four horsemen of the Apocalypse, preachers and artists who have painted scary and grotesque pictures of the four horsemen have badly distorted the meaning of the four horsemen. Few people have any idea why four horsemen are even part of this vision, even though the solution to this mystery is quite simple.

Royal Horses and Royal Horsemen

In ancient times, there were no telephones, faxes, satellites, high speed internet connections, televisions, or radios. In those days, kings dispatched couriers on fast horses throughout their kingdoms to deliver laws, edicts, bulletins, political directives, and other information that was pertinent to the administration of the kingdom. The person in charge of the couriers lived in or near the king's residence so the king could dispatch royal couriers at a moment's notice. The king's commands could have no delay. Royal couriers rode special horses that had been bred and trained for stamina because the king's subjects could be hundreds of miles away from the throne.

During the time of Queen Esther, King Artaxerxes naively issued a decree which allowed the Persians, at an appointed time, to kill all of the Jews and take their possessions. (Esther 3:9-11) However, Queen Esther learned of the plot and she cleverly exposed wicked Haman. Haman had masterminded the plan because he hated the Jews, especially her uncle, Mordecai. When King Artaxerxes discovered that he had been duped into granting a decree to kill all of his wife's people, he executed Haman on the gallows which Haman had prepared for Mordecai. The king then asked Mordecai to write an emergency edict which the king sent to all the Jews throughout his kingdom, notifying them that they could use arms to defend themselves. **"Mordecai wrote in**

Chapter 9 – The Four Royal Horsemen

the name of King Xerxes, sealed the dispatches with the king's signet ring, and sent them by mounted couriers, *who rode fast horses especially bred for the king.* The king's edict granted the Jews in every city the right to assemble and protect themselves; to destroy, kill and annihilate any armed force of any nationality or province that might attack them and their women and children; and to plunder the property of their enemies. . . . **The couriers, riding the royal horses, raced out, spurred on by the king's command.**" (Esther 8:10-14, italics mine)

The parallel between Esther 8 and Revelation 6 should be obvious. King Artaxerxes dispatched horsemen from the throne room in the same fashion that God dispatches four horsemen from His throne when Jesus breaks the first four seals. God used the imagery of horses and riders because that was how couriers were used in John's day. The four horsemen of the Apocalypse represent the Holy Spirit who is sent to Earth to accomplish four missions.

The use of parallel language is important to help us understand apocalyptic prophecy. Parallel language helps us to interpret the language God gave us in Revelation. As you read the following passage, notice how the number and color of the horses in Zechariah 6 paralleled the horses in Revelation 6. Also note the four horses are identified as "the four spirits of Heaven." The prophet Zechariah wrote, **"I looked up again – and there before me were four chariots coming out from between two mountains – mountains of bronze! The first chariot had red horses, the second black, the third white, and the fourth dappled – all of them powerful. I asked the angel who was speaking to me, 'What are these, my lord?' The angel answered me,** *'These are the four spirits of Heaven* [the four living creatures], *going out from standing in the presence of the Lord of the whole world.* **The one with the black horses is going toward the north country, the one with the white horses toward the west, and the one with the dappled horses toward the south.' When the powerful horses went out, they were straining** [having difficulty] **to go throughout the Earth. And he said, 'Go throughout the Earth!' So they went** [again] **throughout the Earth. Then he called to me, 'Look, those going toward the north country have given my spirit rest** [they have accomplished my objectives] **in the land of the north.' "** (Zechariah 6:1-8, insertions and italics mine)

God's wrath against Israel in 605 B.C. came from the north. (Jeremiah 25:9) After 70 years in Babylon, God delivered His people through a decree issued by King Cyrus, but Cyrus' decree was not enough to get the temple rebuilt and the homeland resettled. The Persian kings ultimately issued three more decrees and this is the lesson presented in Zechariah 6. When needed, the Lord can send the Holy Spirit to favorably incline the hearts of pagan kings to help His people. **"In the first year of Cyrus king of Persia, in order to fulfill the word of the Lord spoken by Jeremiah,** *the Lord moved the heart of Cyrus* **king of Persia to make a proclamation throughout his realm and to put it in writing."** (2 Chronicles 36:22, italics mine)

Even though Zechariah 6 does not mention riders on the horses (they are assumed to be in the chariots), the point remains that God represented the four living creatures who stood before the throne of God to Zechariah as the four spirits of Heaven. The horses have the same colors found in Revelation 6. However, the Holy Spirit is not actually four living creatures or four horses. God used these representations of the Holy Spirit so that human beings can understand the divine processes and powers that exist outside the realm of human comprehension and ability.

Four Horns and Four Craftsmen

One more sample of parallel language will help to clarify the connection between the four living creatures and the Holy Spirit. Notice these verses from a vision recorded in Zechariah 1: **"Then I looked up and there before me were four horns! I asked the angel who was speaking to me, 'What are these?' He answered me, 'These are the horns that scattered Judah, Israel and Jerusalem.'** Then the Lord showed me four craftsmen. I asked, 'What are these [four craftsmen] **coming to do?' He answered, 'These are the** [four] **horns that scattered Judah so that no one could raise his head, but the** [four] **craftsmen have come to terrify them** [the enemies of Jerusalem] **and throw down these horns of the nations who lifted up their horns against the land of Judah to scatter its people.'"** (Zechariah 1:18-21, insertions mine) This vision reveals an awesome truth. King Nebuchadnezzar was not the four horns that brought down Jerusalem even though historians would say that he did. The four horns (or four powers) that brought down Jerusalem were the four living creatures. The Holy Spirit aroused and empowered King Nebuchadnezzar to accomplish God's will and the Holy Spirit delivered

Jerusalem into the hands of a pagan king, King Nebuchadnezzar! (Daniel 5:18,19) God told Jeremiah, **"I will summon all the peoples of the north and *my servant* Nebuchadnezzar king of Babylon,' declares the Lord, and I will bring them against this land and its inhabitants and against all the surrounding nations. I will completely destroy them and make them an object of horror and scorn, and an everlasting ruin.'"** (Jeremiah 25:9, italics mine)

It is interesting that God calls Nebuchadnezzar "my servant" in Jeremiah 25:9 even though the king did not recognize the God of Israel as the Most High God until many years later. (Daniel 4:34-37) The Lord instructed the Holy Spirit (four horns) to arouse Nebuchadnezzar, and years later, the Holy Spirit (four craftsmen) was instructed to rebuild the city. God told the Holy Spirit to raise a destroyer for Jerusalem and He did. Then, God told the Holy Spirit to set His people free and He did. Cyrus issued the decree right on time! (2 Chronicles 36:22) Then, God told the Holy Spirit to raise a builder so that Jerusalem might be rebuilt and He did. **"So he said to me, This is the word of the Lord to Zerubbabel** [the rebuilder]: **Not by might nor by [human] power, but by my Spirit,'** [You will overcome the obstacles and rebuild the temple.] **says the Lord Almighty. What are you, O mighty mountain** [of obstacles]? **Before Zerubbabel you will become level ground** [and enable his success].'" (Zechariah 4:6,7, insertions mine)

Summary

When we compare parallel language from the books of Esther and Zechariah with Revelation 6, the mystery of the four living creatures is easily resolved. The four living creatures represent the Holy Spirit. He is the omnipresent "Enabler/Destroyer" through whom God's will is accomplished on Earth. Now we know who the four living creatures are, why the Holy Spirit is represented as four couriers on horseback, and that 1798 is the date when Jesus was found worthy to break the seven seals (see Chapter 5), we are now ready to examine the seven seals. You need to see how Jesus will resolve the sin problem and exonerate God's government!

The seven seals on the Book of Life can be compared to the wrapping paper on a gift. One purpose for the wrapping paper is to hide the gift until it is time to open it.

Does the Father have something to hide?

Yes. The information written in the Book of Life has to remain a secret until the drama with sin is completed.

In addition to this, the Father foreknew the incredible sacrifice which Jesus would make to save sinners. Therefore, He set up a process whereby Jesus would be fully revealed. A new revelation about Jesus occurs with the breaking of each seal.

So there is much more to Jesus than being the Son of God?

Yes! Jesus has many attributes.

For example. . . .

The Father wants everyone to know that:

– Jesus is a co-eternal, separate and distinct member of deity.
– Jesus is the Creator of everything that exists.
– Jesus is the judge of mankind
– Jesus is the Savior of the world.
– Jesus is called the "Word of God" because He speaks for the Father.

Finally, the Father wants the universe to know that Jesus is His equal in every way!

I see.

How does the breaking of each seal on the Book of Life reveal these attributes of Jesus?

Jesus was found worthy to receive the Book of Life in 1798. He promptly broke the first seal and Protestantism began to proclaim that salvation comes only through faith in Him.

But billions of people do not know Jesus or believe that He is the way to salvation.

Is there hope for those people?

Yes, from the beginning of sin, the Father has had a provision in the plan of salvation for saving people who do not know Jesus.

Near the end of the age, the Father's plan of salvation includes the revelation of Jesus to everyone on Earth! This process grows larger with the breaking of each seal.

Jesus broke the second seal in 1800. This seal pertains to the translation and global distribution of the Bible – which contains the teachings of Jesus.

This is fascinating. Because He foreknew that Jesus would be willing to die for sinners, the Father prepared a process before the world was created whereby Jesus would be exalted at the end of the age and revealed to the whole world as the Savior of sinners!

That's right! Jesus broke open the third seal in 1844 and He began judging the dead at that time.

How are dead people judged?

2 Corinthians 5:10 says that everyone must stand before the judgment seat of Jesus. Because He has lived as one of us, He will be compassionate.

John 5:22 says the Father has appointed Jesus as our judge. Keep in mind that the daily records made by special angels are a flawless testimony. Our words, actions thoughts, and motives show whether or not we love God above everything else and our neighbors as ourselves.

What happens when Jesus breaks the fourth seal?

The next seal to be broken is the fourth. When Jesus breaks this seal, the wrath of God begins. The whole world will be shaken, terrified and overwhelmed by Jesus who sits on the throne as Almighty God.

Sounds frightening. What will take place?

There will be a global earthquake, a third of Earth will be burned up by wildfires, two asteroid impacts will occur, and darkness caused by volcano eruptions will cause global famine. About two billion people will die.

This display of divine wrath will get the full attention of the world. Everyone will be frightened. Finally, the survivors will give due consideration to the gospel of Jesus which will be presented by 144,000 prophets.

Isn't there a less devastating way for Jesus to overcome the world's religious and political diversity?

If there was an easier and more productive way to judge the living and save sinners from the penalty for sin, you can be sure that the Father would have used such a plan. The story of Noah's flood teaches that it is very difficult for sinners to let go of rebellion against God.	I know the Bible talks about Noah's flood and the destruction of Sodom, Gomorrah, and Jerusalem. I believe that God will destroy the world with fire at the end of days, but I had not considered that Jesus would destroy the Earth prior to His return!
The wrath of God will cause everyone on Earth to be overwhelmed with shock and awe. People from every religious background will be willing to listen to a gospel that is contrary to what they have previously believed.

At the same time, the religious and political leaders of Earth will unite in a global effort to appease God so that His wrath will cease. | What will they do? |

World leaders will create many new laws. They will tell people that decadent behavior must end. Everyone must obey and worship God as they say or be punished. The problem is that man's laws will be contrary to the laws of God. Persecution will follow for those who obey Jesus. When Jesus breaks the fifth seal, many people will die as martyrs.

Clearly, the fifth seal indicates martyrdom. How does this seal reveal more about Jesus?

The slaughter of millions of innocent saints will reveal the faith that Jesus had in the Father when He was on Earth. The martyrs will be deliberate, calm, and eloquent in their testimony. They will present the gospel of Jesus without fear or hesitancy.

When Jesus breaks the sixth seal, He and the Father will come to Earth in clouds of glory. The kings, the generals, the rich, and the rest of the wicked will run for cover. They do not want to see their faces!

What happens to the wicked at the Second Coming?

The glory of Jesus will be revealed. He will destroy all of the wicked at the Second Coming. He will throw some into a lake of fire and the rest will die when He gives the command. The birds will eat their flesh.

I am beginning to see how the attributes of Jesus are revealed with the breaking of each seal.

What happens when the seventh seal is broken?

The seventh seal is broken at the end of the 1,000 years. Jesus will then open the Book of Life and the contents will exonerate the Father. Everyone will also understand the amazing role which Jesus played to save sinners.

Everyone will see that Jesus is an Almighty God just as the Father is an Almighty God. This revelation will have profound beauty throughout eternity because Jesus will live among His children as one of them!

What an amazing story! To think that an Almighty God would lay down His life for sinners is totally overwhelming. Now, I understand the words of Jesus: "If you have seen me, you have seen the Father." (John 14:9)

Chapter 10
First Seal – Salvation Through Faith Alone

"I watched as the Lamb opened the first of the seven seals. Then I heard one of the four living creatures say in a voice like thunder, 'Come [here, John]!' I looked, and there before me was a white horse! Its rider held a bow, and he was given a crown, and he rode out as a conqueror bent on conquest." (Revelation 6:1,2, insertion mine)

Seal #1   White Horse – 1798 – Salvation through Faith Alone Promoted

The English translation of Revelation 6:1,2 can be misleading. The Greek text indicates the first horseman in Revelation 6 rode out of Heaven's temple carrying a *toxon*. Depending on how the Greek word *toxon* is used, it can be an archer's bow or a winner's ribbon, an ornamental bow made of fabric (like a blue ribbon award – see Strong's Concordance G5115). It may be confusing that a Greek word can have two different meanings, but even in the English language, the word "bow" can have several meanings. For example, we can see a bow in the clouds (a rainbow), a person can bow as a courtesy, a person can wear an ornamental bow (a blue ribbon), and we can use an archer's bow. Because the rider on the white horse is also carrying a crown (the Greek word *stephanos* means a crown of victory), His bow is not for war. The rider's bow is for those who have overcome the world, persevere in faith, and win the crown. Therefore, the bow (*toxon*) should be considered a winner's ribbon rather than an archer's bow.

A *stephanos* is a crown of laurel, a crown of victory, like an athlete would wear at the Olympics. A *stephanos* is not to be confused with a *diadema*. A diadem is a crown that a king wears; it denotes authority and dominion. Paul indicates one day, Jesus will give each saint a crown [*stephanos*] of righteousness. Notice, **"Now there is in store for me the crown [*stephanos*] of righteousness, which the Lord, the righteous Judge, will award to me on that day – and not only to me, but also to all who have longed for His appearing."** (2 Timothy 4:8, insertion mine)

The Greek syntax in Revelation 6:1,2 also indicates the work of this horseman takes time and considerable effort. Literally, the Greek says, *the rider went out overcoming that he might overcome.* The Holy Spirit is attempting to overcome the two greatest enemies of truth, arrogance and ignorance. Arrogance and ignorance are great enemies in matters of religion. According to Revelation 4:7, the first living creature has the face of a lion. This living creature is associated with the first seal and He invites John to "come" and see His actions. The Holy Spirit "faces" an enormous challenge on Earth. He must overcome many false religious paradigms during the duration of the first seal. His mission is to reveal the truth about Jesus to the world. The Holy Spirit left Heaven's temple when Protestantism became free of persecution and a numberless group of saints "marching in" at the Second Coming will reveal the success of His efforts.

Seven Campaigns

I like to think of the breaking of the seven seals as seven campaigns, with each campaign containing a unique disclosure, process, objective, and result. In a similar vein, politicians conduct political campaigns to win the votes necessary for public office. A political campaign is a laborious process during which candidates must travel often to be seen and heard as much as possible. Politicians make promises, promote their ideas, and ask voters to put their faith in them. The seven seals are seven campaigns which Jesus directs to resolve the sin problem and exonerate the Father's government. Jesus' efforts can be described as campaigns because He is seeking a commitment from each person.

All religious people embrace one of three concepts regarding how they will receive eternal life. These concepts are salvation through works, salvation through grace, and salvation through faith. For example, corporately speaking, Jews, Catholics, Muslims, and Eastern mystics (such as Hindus and Buddhists) embrace salvation through works. Protestants embrace salvation through grace. However, eternal life only comes through faith. Faith is action that stems from conviction. A person exercises faith when he listens to the Holy Spirit and obeys without regard for the consequences. This explains why God has children in every religious system because there are faith-full people within every religious system. Even more, there also are faith-full people within groups of people that deny the existence of God (like Agnostics, Atheists, Communists, and the heathen) or have no knowledge of God.

Chapter 10 – First Seal – Salvation Through Faith Alone

Salvation is not based on a knowledge of God, human works, or God's grace. Contrary to what organized religion teaches, man's salvation is determined by his response to the Holy Spirit (this is faith). This simple fact explains why blaspheming the Holy Spirit is the unpardonable sin.

Now that you understand the idea that human beings embrace one of three routes to eternal life, the Holy Spirit's campaign initiated in 1798 should make a lot of sense as we go forward. To get started, we need to understand the theological climate in Europe in 1798 after 1,260 years of Roman Catholic control.

Origins of Catholic Church Doctrine

The Roman Catholic Church teaches that the pope and/or its priests control access to salvation. If a person is excommunicated from the church, he loses eternal life. If a person wishes to receive eternal life, he must become a part of the church to receive the sacraments of the church. Because there is an interest in ecumenism (cooperation among religious systems), the leaders of the Catholic Church have made overtures regarding the idea that non-Catholics could receive salvation. These declarations are meaningless because the theological views of the church are nonnegotiable. The church holds firmly to a position which they believe is rooted in divine authority. In other words, the Roman Catholic Church believes that in God's sight, it is not one religion among many; it is the only true church of God.

The Church teaches the pope is the infallible successor of Peter and holds the keys to God's kingdom. Consider the following passage and ask yourself if Christ's church is built on those who claim to be Peter's successors: **"When Jesus came to the region of Caesarea Philippi, He asked his disciples, 'Who do people say the Son of Man is?' They replied, 'Some say John the Baptist; others say Elijah; and still others, Jeremiah or one of the prophets.' 'But what about you?' He asked. 'Who do you say I am?' Simon Peter answered, 'You are the Christ, the Son of the living God.' Jesus replied, 'Blessed are you, Simon son of Jonah, for this was not revealed to you by man, but by my Father in Heaven.' 'I tell you that you are Peter, and on this rock I will build my church, and the gates of Hades will not overcome it. I will give you the keys of the kingdom of Heaven; whatever you bind on Earth will be bound in Heaven, and whatever you loose on Earth will be loosed in Heaven.' "** (Matthew 16:13-19)

On this occasion, Jesus queried the disciples about His identity to teach the disciples two impressive lessons. When Peter responded, **"You are the Christ** [the anticipated Messiah]**, the Son of the living God,"** Jesus blessed Peter saying, **"Blessed are you, Simon, son of Jonah."** Notice that Jesus used Peter's formal name because He was about to use Simon's surname to make a profound point. While Peter's affirmation was still lingering in the ears of the disciples, Jesus contrasted Peter's humanity with His divinity.

Speaking to Peter, Jesus said, "I tell you that you are *petros*." (The Greek word *petros* is transliterated "Peter," but it means a small rock or pebble.) Then, Jesus said, "and on this *Petra* [Greek: *petra*, a huge rock] I will build my church." The contrast in the Greek language indicates that Jesus pointed to Himself when He spoke these words. Jesus, not Peter, is the vine and we are the branches. (John 15:5) The Son of God who stood before the disciples in human garb and dusty sandals was the eternal and awesome "I AM," "The *Petra*" of the Old Testament. (Exodus 3:14; Genesis 49:24; Deuteronomy 32:4,15; 1 Samuel 2:2; Psalms 18:31; 1 Corinthians 10:4) When the disciples heard Jesus, they must have shuddered with this reality. Imagine hearing about the God of Israel, the Great Jehovah, "The Rock of the Ages" for all of your life and suddenly, it dawns on you that the Creator of Heaven and Earth Himself is standing before you!

Jesus was preparing His disciples for His departure from Earth. Jesus' testimony that day would greatly increase the disciples' faith in years to come. The Church of Christ would succeed against all odds because it would be founded on "The Rock" and sustained by the eternal power of the Holy Spirit. The distinction between the pebble (*petros*) and The Rock of Ages (*petra*) is unmistakable. It is arrogant to claim that Jesus would build *His* church on someone other than Himself; that Jesus would build His church on mere sinful mortals. This notion is ridiculous and there is no evidence in the New Testament that the disciples regarded Peter as the head or founder of the Christian Church. In fact, Paul reprimanded Peter for improper behavior in Galatians 2:11. Paul also wrote 14 of the 27 books in the New Testament, and James, the half-brother of Jesus, appears to have been selected as the first elder of the church. (Acts 12:17, 15:13, 21:18; 1 Corinthians 5:7; Galatians 1:19).

Then, Jesus taught His disciples a second lesson. He promised to give His followers the keys of the kingdom. Jesus said, **"Whatever you**

Chapter 10 – First Seal – Salvation Through Faith Alone

'loose' or 'bind' on Earth will be loosed or bound in Heaven." The terms, "to bind" or "to loose" indicates having the authority "to approve or disapprove." (Isaiah 22:20-23, Revelation 3:7) The "keys of the kingdom" is a phrase that means "having responsible authority." If you give the keys of your car to a person, he receives the benefit of the car, but he also receives the responsibility to lawfully operate your car. The parallel is that Jesus promised the disciples they would have authority to make the day to day decisions necessary to advance the work of His church and He assured them that He would honor their decisions in Heaven. (See Acts 15 for an example of this.) Of course, Jesus will only honor decisions that are in harmony with the Word of God, are in harmony with the work of the Holy Spirit, and will build up the body of Christ according to His teachings. (Matthew 28:19,20) Notice that Jesus did not give His disciples any authority to determine the eternal destiny of anyone or to change His laws. Jesus did not give His disciples permission to persecute those who were opposed to them. Jesus did not give this authority to men. The Bible clearly states that Jesus Himself judges mankind. He redeemed us with His own blood and His sacrifice for us gives only Him the right to pass judgment on sinners. (John 5:22,23; 2 Corinthians 5:10; Revelation 5:9; Acts 17:31)

This information has been printed so that you can appreciate how and why the early Christian Church morphed into the Roman Catholic Church. After the Roman Catholic Church came to power in A.D. 538, a long winter of darkness settled over Catholics and for 1,260 years anyone who protested "the divine authority" assumed by popes and priests was persecuted.

Martin Luther States Salvation Is Through Faith in Christ

When Martin Luther (1483-1546) nailed his ninety-five theses to the church door in 1517, the Roman Catholic Church was stirred, but not alarmed. Obviously, a priest in Germany could not threaten the mighty Church of Rome! However, Luther's protest against Rome can be compared to Samson's destruction of the Philistine temple. (Judges 16:30) When God gave Samson enough strength to push the main pillars of the Philistine temple out of their places, the temple collapsed. Similarly, when God gave Protestantism enough strength, it pushed the two main pillars of Catholicism (papal authority and the necessity of receiving the sacraments) out of their places and Catholic doctrine was destroyed (in the eyes of Protestants). The Protestants discovered in the Bible that the claims of the pope and priests were false and this explains, in part, the historical conflict that began long ago between Protestants and Catholics.

Protestant historians have conferred the title, "Father of the Protestant Reformation" on John Wycliff (1330-1384) because Wycliff was the first reformer within the Catholic Church to significantly challenge Rome's departure from Bible truth. If Wycliff is the father of Protestantism, then Martin Luther should be given the title "Apostle Paul" of the Reformation. This is because Paul and Luther were highly educated and they stand out in history for having accomplished the same thing. Both men found the exodus from two corrupt religious systems, Judaism and Catholicism, respectively, using the Scripture's authority.

Luther entered the Augustinian monastery at Erfurt in 1505 and he took a vow of obedience, poverty, and chastity in the following year. By 1512, Luther had earned a doctoral degree. In 1515, at the age of 32, he was appointed vicar over eleven Augustinian monasteries. Luther was genuinely zealous in serving the Lord and His church. As a priest, Luther had access to the Bible and the more he read, the more he became concerned about many doctrines the Church upheld.

Eventually, the Holy Spirit opened Luther's eyes and gave him discernment. Even though he loved the Lord and the Church, Luther carefully documented ninety-four issues within the Church that needed reform. When the priest, Tetzel, came to town in 1517 boastfully offering to sell "past, present, and future forgiveness" of all sins for a price, Luther was outraged. Tetzel was selling indulgences to raise money to pay for the construction of St. Peter's Basilica. Selling eternal life for a price was too much. Luther added this behavior to his long list and with a heavy heart and a soul full of disgust, he nailed his ninety-five complaints to the church door in Wittenberg on October 31.

The Church had indoctrinated Luther as a priest. For years, he did not question the idea that Church authority was greater than Bible teachings. However, after comparing Church teachings with the Word of God, Luther realized God's Word must be continually placed above the authority of the Church. Otherwise, man's carnal nature would eventually manipulate and corrupt Jesus' teachings.

The Holy Spirit convicted Luther that mankind is justified before God through faith without the necessity of works and a shocking experi-

Chapter 10 – First Seal – Salvation Through Faith Alone   123

ence confirmed Luther's belief. Between 1512 and 1515, Pope Leo X offered an indulgence (the forgiveness of all sins) to anyone who would climb Pilate's staircase on his knees. Because Luther sincerely wanted freedom from the guilt of sin, he decided to climb the staircase even though he was already struggling with the relationship between faith and works in his heart. While climbing the staircase, he heard a thunderous voice say, **"The just shall live by faith."** (Romans 1:17) It was an epiphany! Suddenly, everything he had been studying in the Bible connected. In a flash, he realized that salvation comes through faith without sacraments or works of penance and he hastily rose to his feet and left the building ashamed.

In April 1521, the church officials in Worms, Germany summoned Luther to defend his radical teachings and behavior. They accused Luther of forty-one errors and gave him sixty days to recant. Of course, the Church could not accept Luther's call for reform because his reformation would weaken the "God given" authority invested in church leaders. When Luther saw that church officials had not even examined his books and that they could not accept the plainest teachings of Scripture, he quit arguing the merits of his case and spoke to the assembly saying, "Here I stand. I can do no other . . . my conscience is captive to the Word of God." Luther was condemned to death, but he escaped with his life.

Even though Luther's call for reformation did not reform the Church, laymen in the church began to accept his call. Laymen had grown weary of the fear and the many burdens which the Church had imposed on them. Luther knew the laymen were trapped in spiritual darkness because they did not have access to the Bible. So, Luther translated the New Testament into the vernacular of the German people in 1522. This was the dawn of a movement that would grow into the Protestant Reformation. Its fuel was Holy Spirit power and its legitimacy was anchored to God's Word. Even though the Church punished anyone caught with a Bible, Luther and his supporters managed to distribute several German copies in the years that followed.

Luther's activities in Germany added to a larger cry for reformation within the Church across Europe. Two hundred eighty-one years after Luther posted his ninety-five theses to the church door at Wittenberg, the Catholic Church was toppled because it would not reform. In 1798, papal power was eliminated and Protestants in Europe could speak freely about salvation through faith in Christ. At last, they could teach and preach without intimidation or the threat of persecution from the Catholic Church. Protestants began to share the good news that salvation was not dependent on church or priest! Salvation came through faith in Jesus alone.

There is nothing more powerful than a truth whose time has come. Remember that the Church of Rome fell because "judgment was pronounced in favor of the saints of the Most High" (Daniel 7:22) and that Jesus was found worthy to receive the Book of Life. On Earth, the gospel of Jesus broke out of the tomb of darkness where it had been sealed for 1,260 years! The Holy Spirit began a mission to reveal that salvation comes through faith in Christ alone.

United States Provided Sanctuary for Protestants

After 1798, God ensured that Protestantism would grow by preparing a new sanctuary where the movement could flourish. The Pilgrims came to America to enjoy religious freedom. Many Lutherans also came to America and they established their first church on Manhattan Island in 1648. Twenty-two years before the papacy fell, the founders of the United States signed the Declaration of Independence in 1776. No one in Philadelphia could have anticipated how the United States of America would develop and accomplish Christ's mission. The book of Revelation describes this phenomenon by saying, **"the Earth helped the woman"** (Revelation 12:16). The Holy Spirit raised the United States by giving it a marvelous Constitution and an amazing Bill of Rights ensuring religious freedom for everyone. Protestant immigrants came to this nation by the millions. Because the United States' population was predominantly Protestant in its early days, Catholic immigrants who settled here were often scorned and mistreated. In fact, Catholics were not elected to hold public office for many years. (The first Catholic president in the U.S. John F. Kennedy, 1960-1963 was elected nearly two centuries after its founding.)

Since 1798, the United States has produced more Christian missionaries, gospel workers, and literature proclaiming "salvation through faith in Jesus Christ" than any other nation in Earth's history. Of course, the Holy Spirit is still pushing "the good news" of salvation through faith in Jesus. He is doing this because Protestantism has mutated and fallen into apostasy because it promotes a false doctrine of salvation through grace.

Chapter 10 – First Seal – Salvation Through Faith Alone

The False Doctrine of Grace – The Implosion of Protestantism

The doctrine of God's grace has been distorted and abused for decades. God's love for sinners is truly amazing and overwhelming. God's grace is a powerful doctrine when it is applied properly, but its power and purpose are spiritually destructive when misunderstood and applied in the wrong way. The problem occurs when people believe that human conduct and behavior have nothing to do with salvation and accept that salvation costs nothing, requires nothing, and demands nothing. If people only believe that God's grace "is sufficient," spiritual decline and atrophy will surely follow.

Sixty-five years after Jesus returned to Heaven, He appeared to the prophet John while he was exiled on Patmos. Jesus had some choice words for the seven churches in Asia Minor and "grace" was not one of them. Jesus harshly identified many behaviors that had infiltrated His church and after He gave the churches stern warnings, He made seven promises. Along with each promise, Jesus gave the assurance of eternal life with the same prerequisite: "To him that overcomes. . . ." The doctrine of grace is distorted and abused when it is used to diminish the necessity and importance of overcoming sin. Do not be deceived. A large crowd attending a megachurch does not necessarily mean many people are overcoming sin. Man's sinful nature is not inclined to overcome sin. Dealing with our sinful natures is a daily struggle that will not end until Jesus removes our carnal nature. Mainline Protestant churches did thrive in the early days and had large crowds and inspirational preachers. In the early days, they believed and taught the importance of overcoming sin. However, when Protestantism removed the Biblical context of grace, it became distorted and abused resulting in the demise of mainline Protestantism.

Three co-dependent doctrines every Christian should understand do not operate or stand alone. I like to compare the doctrines of "Grace, Law and Faith" to a three-legged stool. Each leg has to be sturdy and securely planted for a three-legged stool to perform its duty. If any leg fails, the stool will fail and whatever it supports will fall. Similarly, if these three doctrines are separated from each other or if one is improperly advanced above the other two, the result will be a spiritually toxic experience. These three doctrines *flow* together in a profound way and those who follow Jesus must understand their flow to overcome sin.

Chapter 10 – First Seal – Salvation Through Faith Alone

Because God governs His kingdom by the rule of law, He puts His laws within His children's hearts and minds when He creates them. His laws are righteous, comprehensive, and eternal because He is love. God never changes and has previously considered and prepared for every situation. When Adam and Eve violated His law, God's grace became necessary. Adam and Eve were not defiant and sinned due to Lucifer's predatory efforts, so God extended grace to Adam and Eve (and their offspring) by staying their execution. Remember, anyone eating of the Tree of the Knowledge of Good and Evil was to be executed on the very day he sinned. (Genesis 2:17)

When Adam and Eve sinned, they changed and were not in natural harmony with God's laws. Sin immediately transformed them from being selfless to being selfish. Because the curse of sin is a spiritual cancer, rebellion and selfishness have contaminated every person. *Because the cancer of sin began with Adam and Eve and it has been passed on to their offspring, because all human beings have sinned, because the wages of sin is death, God extended grace to Adam and Eve and their offspring. This grace is called "life."* God's grace has several dimensions. For example, God has graciously given human beings a span of life; years to mature so we can comprehend His love and choose to either walk in His ways or not. God Himself has graciously provided atonement for our sins and made it possible, through the indwelling power of the Holy Spirit, to overcome any sin. Finally, God has graciously given us the assurance that He will save everyone who fights "the good fight of faith."

God has a high ideal and a special purpose for every person, and He gives the gift of the Holy Spirit to every person. God also requires that we trust in His infinite wisdom and obey the laws of His universe. He requires every sinner to trust Him because it is only through faith in God's care and wisdom that we can stay on the path of righteousness. *The doctrine of faith teaches us that faith means obeying the dictates of the Holy Spirit without regard for the consequences.* (Hebrews 11) God has promised that He will take care of all circumstances *if* we trust and obey Him. (Romans 8:28) Therefore, when we are tempted to do wrong we can overcome the temptation by asking God for the desire to do right as well as the strength and courage to stay on track. This is how sinners obtain victory and transformation through faith. When God hears our cry for help, He immediately sends the power we ask for! (Romans 6:14, 1 John 1:9-2:1)

Chapter 10 – First Seal – Salvation Through Faith Alone

At first, Romans is difficult to read and understand because Paul seems to contradict himself with every other verse. For centuries, Bible expositors have exploited these "apparent contradictions" to appease man's sinful nature. (2 Peter 3:16) However, read the book of Romans a few times and you will begin to understand the problems Paul was addressing. Paul addresses two toxic conditions affecting early Christians in Rome. The first condition was legalism (Jewish converts to Christianity were captives of this toxic experience). The second condition was a distortion of grace (Gentile converts to Christianity were captives of this toxic experience). These opposing problems explain why Paul seems to contradict himself. He was trying to get Jewish converts out of the ditch of legalism while trying to get Gentile converts out of the other ditch of distorted grace.

Ironically, Paul's summary can be found in the middle of the book, Romans 7 and 8! Obeying God's law will not produce salvation and believing that salvation has nothing to do with human behavior because God's grace is sufficient is fiction. If we allow our sinful desires to control us and we justify our transgressions, we do not have faith in God. The fruit of faith is seen in overcoming.

If we continue to do things that we know are wrong, we do not love God. (1 John 2:4-6) Jesus said no one can serve two masters. Informed Christians know that sinners cannot overcome sin on their own. (Jeremiah 13:23) Revelation 20 says God will annihilate many people at the end of the age, because a God of love does not offer grace to defiant sinners. God's kingdom is governed by laws, so He has given us grace as sinners, even though we are naturally rebellious toward His laws. He offers us His grace for sinners in three ways:

1. **Time.** God delayed the immediate annihilation of Adam, Eve, and consequently, their offspring. He has given us life and a span of years to grow up so that we can discover and know Jesus if we want Him.

2. **Sacrifice.** God Himself provided a perfect sacrifice at Calvary so that our guilt might be removed from us and transferred to Heaven's altar.

3. **Deposit.** God has given us faith to make it possible to overcome sin. He has also sent us the Holy Spirit to draw us to Himself. He has promised to transform our hearts and minds, which is only possible through the indwelling power of the Holy Spirit.

Chapter 10 – First Seal – Salvation Through Faith Alone

The following anecdote illustrates the doctrine of grace. A college teacher assigned a term paper. He told the students the paper would represent 75% of their grade. He assigned a due date of Monday with no exceptions. (The teacher declared the law.) John and two classmates were hurt in an auto accident (through no fault of their own) five days before the term paper was due. They were released from the hospital two days before the due date, but the recovering students could not meet the deadline. The students contacted the teacher and asked for grace. Given their circumstances, the teacher said he would accept their submission by Wednesday noon (grace was given). The injured students struggled to meet the deadline (they believed the teacher would do as promised, burnt some midnight oil) and all three passed the course.

In this illustration, the teacher gave the three students grace (an extension of time) because the teacher cared enough to help the students. He wanted to see his students complete the course even though they knew the due date six weeks earlier. The injured students accepted the teacher's grace and after putting forth extra effort, they met the deadline and the requirement for the course. They were grateful for the grace they had received and their efforts (works) reflected their appreciation.

God's grace does require a human response. He has saved us through faith because He has given us grace in the form of time, sacrifice, and deposit. Many Protestants believe that grace cannot be called grace if overcoming sin is required (works), but God's grace exists because God's laws have penalties. We show God that we appreciate His amazing grace by putting faith in Him and obeying His commands. If the teacher had told the injured students they did not have to submit the term paper and he would still give them each A's, he would not have been fair to the other students. This dispensation of grace would not be appropriate and would have threatened the accreditation of the institution. In other words, it would be academic deception to give passing grades to students when there is no evidence the students met academic requirements. During a peer review by his colleagues, most likely the teacher's extension of grace would be viewed as unauthorized use of authority to defeat course requirements and the teacher's actions would not be justified.

The Bible does not teach that God saves us by a dispensation of grace; instead, the Bible teaches that God made salvation possible because He extended grace to all sinners. The doctrine of grace is a story of

Chapter 10 – First Seal – Salvation Through Faith Alone

overwhelming love because God has taken every initiative necessary to save sinners. On the other hand, when the doctrine of grace is distorted and abused, it causes harm to individuals and ultimately, denominations. If an individual advances the concept of grace without recognizing that it is also necessary to overcome sin, God is not honored and the other two doctrines of Law and Faith are minimized. Salvation does not come through grace. Instead, grace makes God's *offer of* salvation possible. Salvation comes through faith in God. Christ's life is a flawless example of this truth: Jesus cried out in the Garden, **"not my will, but yours be done."** (Luke 22:42) Unfortunately, Protestants have promoted a distorted doctrine of grace today, so I think it is fitting that we thoughtfully consider Jesus' words, **"However, when the Son of Man comes, will he find *faith* on the Earth?"** (Luke 18:8, emphasis mine)

Summary

The breaking of the first seal in 1798 resulted in the emancipation and empowerment of the Protestant movement. After the papacy fell, Protestants in Europe could proclaim salvation through faith in Jesus without intimidation or persecution from the Church of Rome. Millions of Protestants immigrated to the shores of the United States. The first seal was a great start in the revelation of Jesus, but we are now more than 200 years into this campaign, so we see the Holy Spirit is almost at the point of starting all over! Christianity has embraced salvation through works or grace and faith in God has grown faint.

Chapter 11
Second Seal – Bible Translated/Distributed

"When the Lamb opened the second seal, I heard the second living creature say, 'Come [and see my action]!' Then another horse came out, a fiery red one. Its rider was given power to take peace from the Earth and to make men slay each other. To him was given a large sword." (Revelation 6:3,4, insertion mine)

Seal #2   Red Horse – 1800 – The Bible Translated and Distributed

I believe Jesus broke the second seal around the year 1800. At that time, Jesus gave the Holy Spirit the "sword" of Truth and sent Him to Earth on a campaign to enlighten the world. The face of the second living creature looks like an ox (Revelation 4:7) because the endeavor would take strength and endurance. In a spiritual context, when Jesus' teachings and demands become clear, human resistance becomes more hostile and defiant unless the Holy Spirit changes the heart. The Jews killed Jesus because He exposed and condemned false religion. Bible prophecy predicts a day when wicked people will kill (or attempt to kill) the saints because the saints will expose and condemn false religion. Jesus warned His disciples that the carnal heart would respond to His teachings by saying, **"Do not suppose that I have come to bring peace to the Earth. I did not come to bring peace, but a sword."** (Matthew 10:34)

Sometimes, we have to use parallel passages in the Bible to clarify other passages. Since the second seal is somewhat cryptic, consider Jesus' words, **"All this I have told you so that you will not go astray. They will put you out of the synagogue; in fact, a time is coming when anyone who kills you will think he is offering a service to God. They will do such things because they have not known the Father or me. I have told you this, so that when the time comes you will remember that I warned you."** (John 16:1-4) Jesus made the comment that religious people would persecute and kill His disciples because He wanted His disciples to understand the power and nature of false religion.

Remember the statement, when a man who is honestly mistaken hears the truth, he will either quit being mistaken or cease being honest. When religious people are confronted with divine truth, they react in one of two ways. They either rejoice and submit or they become angry and hostile. During the Great Tribulation, the saints will be persecuted and put to death because of their loyalty to the Word of God. (Revelation 6:9-11;13:5-7) Therefore, the campaign of the second seal must relate to the death of many saints after 1798 because the Bible says, **"Its rider was given power to take peace from the Earth and to make men slay each other."**

John wrote about the final days of Earth's history, **"I saw that the woman** [the great whore, Babylon the Great] **was drunk with the blood of the saints, the blood of those who bore testimony to Jesus. When I saw her, I was greatly astonished."** (Revelation 17:6, insertion mine) Why were they killed? **"When he opened the fifth seal, I saw under the altar the souls of those who had been slain because of the word of God and the testimony they had maintained."** (Revelation 6:9) The primary issue that puts the Word of God into direct conflict with the followers of the Antichrist relates to worship. **"And** [the Antichrist] **caused all who refused to worship the image to be killed."** (Revelation 13:15, insertion mine) The Antichrist and his followers will kill many of those who worship and obey God, and amazingly, the wicked will think they are doing God a service by killing the saints! Keep this thought in mind as we continue to examine the second seal.

The Large Sword of the Second Seal

The apostle Paul writes the Word of God is sharper than "a double-edged sword." (Hebrews 4:12; Ephesians 6:17) When God's people present the truth about His will with power and authority, openly rebuking sinful behavior, and exposing evil motives and deeds, rebellious people will be furious because the Bible insults their arrogance and behavior. Remember, King Herod killed John the Baptist, the greatest of the prophets, (Matthew 11:11) for telling King Herod that he had sinned by taking his brother's wife. (Mark 6:18) Today, every sinner has a bit of King Herod's arrogance in his heart. If you had sovereign authority and power, you would be tempted to kill someone who publicly insulted and humiliated you, revealing your sins.

Chapter 11 – Second Seal – Bible Translated/Distributed

Consider the political leaders in all countries today. Evil doers will go to great lengths to avoid the embarrassment and humiliation that comes from having their deeds exposed to the light of truth. The book of Revelation predicts that many, if not all of the 144,000, will be killed during the Great Tribulation because of the testimony they deliver. (Revelation 16:4-7) In this sense, the sword of truth will cut both ways. When the Bible insults defiant sinners, political leaders will respond by punishing the messengers of God. Both the leaders and God's messengers get hurt in the process because the sword of truth cuts on both sides.

The world is developing enormous inertia, resistance, and hatred toward Christians. This growth is to be expected because Paul says the carnal heart is hostile toward God and His laws. (Romans 8:5-8) No one naturally wants to surrender to God's higher authority and this is where the Holy Spirit comes in. He is always working, trying to have us submit to God's Word. This is not an easy task because our sinful nature is naturally opposed to God's will and it is always difficult to go against the ways of unconverted friends and family. (1 Peter 4:4) Jesus said, **"This is the verdict: Light** [the truth about the will of God] **has come into the world, but men loved darkness instead of light because their deeds were evil. Everyone who does evil hates the light, and will not come into the light for fear that his deeds will be exposed. But whoever lives by the truth** [those who love truth] **comes into the light, so that it may be seen plainly that what he has done** [the progress he has made] **has been done through God** [the ministry of the Holy Spirit]**."** (John 3:19-21, insertions mine)

Even though Martin Luther rediscovered the doctrine of salvation through faith in Jesus soon after he nailed his 95 complaints to the church door in 1515, Protestantism was not free to proclaim the gospel of Jesus until 1798. After General Berthier imprisoned the pope and damaged the Church of Rome in 1798, Protestantism quickly became a significant Christian force in the world. As explained previously, I believe the first seal was broken in 1798. So, the second seal must have been opened shortly thereafter, or about the year 1800. When Jesus broke the second seal, He sent the Holy Spirit out of Heaven's temple on an amazing, even phenomenal, campaign to translate and distribute the Bible (the sword of truth).

The Holy Spirit motivated Protestants to quickly form Bible Societies throughout Europe and the United States with impressive results. The

British and Foreign Bible Society was founded (1804), the Basel Bible Society was founded (1804), the Berlin (later Prussian) Bible Society was founded (1805), the Pennsylvania Bible Society was founded (1808), the Connecticut Bible Society was founded (1809), the Massachusetts Bible Society was founded (1809), the International Bible Society was founded (1809), the Bible Society of India was founded (1811), the Russian Bible Society was founded (1812), the Swedish Bible Society was founded (1814), the Netherlands Bible Society was founded (1814), the Icelandic Bible Society was founded (1815), the Norwegian Bible Society was founded (1816), the American Bible Society was founded (1816), the Bible Society in Australia was founded (1817), and the Protestant Biblical Society of Paris was founded (1818).

The task of translating and distributing the Bible has been labor intensive and very expensive. Many Protestants gave sacrificially to see the Bible translated in multiple languages. The Bible (or portions of it) now exists in more than 2,572 languages and dialects. Since 1908, Gideons International has distributed about 1.7 billion Bibles. Since 1942, Wycliffe Bible translators have helped to complete more than 700 translations. This enormous undertaking, spanning the globe, was not the result of human prowess. The Holy Spirit gave this campaign its strength and success. For two hundred years, no book has outsold the Bible and had its exposure and global distribution.

Prior to the fall of the papacy in 1798, only a few people in Europe owned a Bible. This was either due to the expense, or in some countries, the Church forbade the possession of a Bible. Today, this context seems so foreign. Even the Catholic Church now publishes Bibles, albeit in the archaic Douay Version. I believe the opening of the second seal provided the impetus for this marvelous transition from a few Bibles to the sudden appearance of millions of Bibles after 1800. From 1800 to 1844, the Bible (or portions of it) was translated into approximately 112 languages. By 1944, the number of translations exceeded one thousand. Today, the number of translations exceeds 1,500. As people began to read the Bible, they had varying ideas about what Jesus taught in the Bible. Nineteenth century Protestants were a diverse group of people from the many nations of Europe and the United States. After 1798, Jesus used this diversity and the leadership of godly people to fracture Protestantism into several distinctive denominations.

Protestant America Discovers Two Doctrines

Remember that when the meaning of salvation through faith in Jesus is separated from Law, Grace, and Faith, the assurance of salvation becomes a "theological fantasy." This altered view of salvation may be wonderful to believe, but it is practically worthless for dealing with the temptations and trials of the human experience. In the early nineteenth century, Jesus used the Holy Spirit to stimulate the Bible societies, translation, printing, and distribution and share the doctrine of "salvation through faith alone." The Bible is a treasure trove of 66 books and it takes considerable time and effort to become familiar with its gems of truth. Jesus has commissioned the Holy Spirit to guide us into all truth (John 16:13), so the Holy Spirit gives God's Word special attraction. The Bible becomes interesting to everyone who wants to know more about God.

During the nineteenth century, some Protestants discovered two new Bible doctrines, "soul sleep" and "the obligatory nature of the Ten Commandments." Although mainstream Protestantism in Europe and the United States did not embrace these two doctrines, many people began to believe these doctrines and God's Word became brighter. Remember, truth is always true, regardless of who believes it or rejects it, and the fulfillment of prophecy reveals who had the truth!

Dr. Edward White (1819-1898), a Congregationalist minister in Britain, is credited with uncovering (or discovering) the doctrine of soul sleep. His discovery began when he rejected John Calvin's (1509-1564) view of predestination. Calvin taught that only a predetermined number of people could be saved and the rest were doomed to suffer in eternal hell. Dr. White argued that God *alone* is immortal (1 Timothy 6:15,16) therefore, man's soul cannot be immortal. Since the soul is subject to death, the souls of sinners cannot be tormented forever. At that time, a few Protestants accepted White's views and the doctrine of "soul sleep" was added to the "fringe" of Protestantism's theological fabric.

The basic idea behind soul sleep is that when a person dies, he is not judged nor does he go to his eternal reward. Instead, he "sleeps," that is, he has no awareness or intelligence while in the grave. At the appointed time, each dead person is judged according to the record of his life. The judgment of mankind will be completed before the Second

Coming. When Jesus appears at the Second Coming, the Lord will resurrect the righteous dead to meet Him in the air (1 Thessalonians 4:16,17) and the Lord will slay the wicked who are still alive at that time. (Revelation 19:19-21) At the end of the thousand years mentioned in Revelation 20, the Lord will resurrect the wicked dead of all ages to meet their Maker in a great white throne judgment scene. (Revelation 20:12) After Jesus informs the wicked of His judgment decision, He will sentence the wicked to suffer for their cruelty to others. The Lord will then punish them with fire and annihilate them because their souls are mortal. (Ezekiel 18:4) Protestantism, in general, has rejected this doctrine even though it is one of the five essential doctrines needed to understand the book of Revelation. Most Protestants today believe, as Catholics do, that at death, people either go to Heaven (paradise) or they burn in Hell for eternity.

Another essential doctrine took root in the United States during the nineteenth century. The doctrine of the perpetuity of the Ten Commandments also came from England. This doctrine teaches that God requires man to obey all Ten Commandments, including observing the seventh day Sabbath (the fourth commandment). To many Protestants, observing the fourth commandment, unlike the other nine commandments, seems contradictory to the doctrine of salvation through faith in Jesus.

In 1664, Stephen Mumford, a member of the Bell Lane Seventh Day Baptist Church in London, came to Rhode Island. Because he could not find any Seventh Day Baptists, he worshiped with Sunday keeping Baptists for a while. Eventually, five Baptist families adopted Mumford's view that the Ten Commandments were obligatory and the Seventh Day Baptist Church in the United States began in 1671. By 1802, there were twenty churches with two thousand members in the United States. Increasing numbers of immigrants were arriving in America each month. Bibles were available and affordable and the Baptist church was a respected Protestant denomination, so interest in the seventh day Sabbath continued to grow. However, Sunday-keeping Baptists were strongly opposed (and remain opposed) to the idea that Jesus requires mankind to observe the fourth commandment.

Summary

When we consider that as a part of the first seal, Jesus was found worthy and inaugurated in 1798 and that Protestants were freed to believe that salvation came through Jesus shortly thereafter, we can understand how the second seal followed shortly after 1798. So, the second seal appears to have been broken around 1800 with the immediate establishment of Bible societies in Europe and the United States. The large sword of truth that the Holy Spirit carried throughout the Earth represents the Bible, the only book that authoritatively reveals Jesus' teachings. Of course, Jesus' teachings reveal the Father's will; this is why Jesus is called "The Word." Ultimately, the saints will experience deadly consequences during the Great Tribulation due to Bible (the great sword of truth) translation and distribution. The doctrines of "salvation through faith in Jesus," "soul sleep," and "the obligatory nature of the Ten Commandments," including observing our Creator's seventh day Sabbath rest will all play crucial roles in coming days.

Chapter 12
Third Seal – Judgment of the Dead

"When the Lamb opened the third seal, I heard the third living creature say, 'Come!' I looked, and there before me was a black horse! Its rider was holding a pair of scales in his hand. Then I heard what sounded like a voice among the four living creatures, saying, A quart of wheat for a day's wages, and three quarts of barley for a day's wages, and do not damage the oil and the wine!' " (Revelation 6:5,6)

Seal #3   Black Horse – 1844 – The Judgment of the Dead

Before we proceed with this study on the third seal, I would like you to consider that the third seal concerns judging the dead and the fourth seal concerns judging the living. These two seals are extremely important and reveal dimensions of Jesus that are infinitely wonderful. The third seal is more difficult to explain than any of the other six, because it requires a person to understand two essential Bible doctrines as well as two apocalyptic prophecies from the book of Daniel. If you are interested in a comprehensive study on these doctrines, please see Chapters 11 through 14 in my book, *Jesus: The Alpha and The Omega*. If you also wish to examine the two apocalyptic prophecies that position the third seal in 1844, please see Chapters 4 and 6 in my book, *Daniel: Unlocked for the Final Generation*. PDF versions of both books can be found here: *https://www.wake-up.org/find-articles-by-topic/*

The third living creature that spoke to John had a face like that of a man. (Revelation 4:7) This face is perfect for this campaign. You may recall that the other three faces of the Holy Spirit in Revelation 4 are faces of animals (a lion, an ox and an eagle) and the one feature that separates mankind from animals is that man has the ability to reason. Mankind also has a brain that can consider ideas and remember details, he can exercise intelligent choice and he has free will to act according to his will.

The scales in the rider's hand indicated judgment. From Babylonian days, scales were used to signify judgment. (Daniel 5:27) Before John's day, Egyptian, Greek, and Roman cultures incorporated the idea of a woman dispensing justice. Later, Rome used the symbol of a blindfolded woman holding a pair of scales to represent judgment (a goddess named Justitia). Today, courthouses often incorporate statues of "Lady Justice" holding scales in one hand and a sword in the other. The blindfold over her eyes indicates she pays no heed to personal status. Everyone in her court is judged without bias. The scales in her left hand represent measurement. She measures the strength or weakness of each case on its merits. The double-edged sword in her right hand represents justice which the court must implement for plaintiff or defendant.

More than 600 years earlier, Daniel saw the judgment of the dead begin. He wrote, **"the court was seated and the books were opened."** (Daniel 7:10) King Solomon saw the judgment of the dead, **"For God will bring every deed into judgment, including every hidden thing, whether it is good or evil."** (Ecclesiastes 12:14) Paul also knew that judgment day was coming, but he did not know when it would occur. (The date would not be revealed until centuries after his death.) Paul wrote: **"For we must all appear before the judgment seat of Christ, that each one may receive what is due him for the things done while in the body, whether good or bad."** (2 Corinthians 5:10) The judgment of the dead merges the inauguration of Jesus, the doctrine of "soul sleep," and the doctrine of "parallel temples" into one comprehensive subject. Of course, if a person does not understand the doctrines of soul sleep or parallel temples, breaking the third seal in 1844 is meaningless. We will spend some time establishing the basis for the doctrines of parallel temples and soul sleep in the next part of this chapter.

In the third seal, Jesus sent the Holy Spirit from Heaven to Earth to begin a new campaign. His mission was to inform Bible students that the time had come for Jesus to judge the dead. Jesus commissioned the Holy Spirit to reveal that Jesus had opened the books of records and started his investigation of each person's thoughts, motives, words, and actions. After a thorough investigation, Jesus declares a verdict of either eternal life or eternal death.

The Doctrine of Parallel Temples

When God delivered Israel out of Egypt, He gave Moses a set of plans. These plans included details concerning the construction of His temple and instructions on how services were to be performed in the temple. (Hebrews 8:1-5) God gave Moses very intricate directions because God

Chapter 12 – Third Seal – Judgment of the Dead

planned for earthly temple services to provide important details about similar processes occurring in Heaven's temple. So, God designed a skit, a set of processes that people could view and study, which would allow finite beings to understand His ways. God designed the earthly temple and its services to parallel similar processes in Heaven. For this reason, the doctrine of parallel temples is similar to the "Heaven Earth Linkage Law." God established this elaborate system so that people could begin to understand His terms and conditions for salvation. In other words, any ideas about salvation that do not align with the processes God designed in the earthly temple services are false.

Before Jesus created Earth, the Father set a date, near to the end of the world, when Jesus would begin "cleansing" Heaven's temple. Jesus needs to "cleanse" the temple in Heaven of the record of sin because Heaven's temple operates as "a holding tank" for sin. Please consider the following statement to appreciate how this works: God does not forgive sin, but He has a method whereby sinners can be freed from sin's guilt and sinners can receive Christ's righteousness. Both elements, freedom from sin's guilt and Christ's righteousness are necessary for salvation. When Adam and Eve sinned, God's law said they were guilty of sin and the law condemned them to death. They also lost God's righteousness which they wore (as garments of light). For sinners to be saved, a guilty person must be freed from sin's guilt and have God's righteousness restored. Unfortunately, many Christians do not understand this.

God designed a process to free a person of sin's guilt and restore His righteousness to the sinner. This process allows the guilt of a repentant and faithful sinner to be *transferred* to an altar. When the earthly temple was built, this altar was called "the Altar of Burnt Offering." To transfer his guilt, the sinner needed to obtain and present a perfect lamb at the Altar of Burnt Offering. The only possible way for the sinner to receive freedom from guilt and God's righteousness was through the perfect life and death of the lamb. After the sinner confessed his sins by placing his hands on the innocent head of the lamb, he slit the lamb's throat and took the lamb's life. The attending priest at the altar captured some of the lamb's blood in a cup, dipped a branch of hyssop into the cup, and sprinkled the lamb's blood on the four horns of the altar. That blood served as a record of the sinner's sin and at that point, the Altar of Burnt Offering was defiled by sin.

Chapter 12 – Third Seal – Judgment of the Dead

This daily process in the earthly temple teaches three important points. First, the plan of salvation is not based on the "erase theory." God does not whitewash or erase sin. Instead, He created a legitimate way to set a repentant sinner free from sin's penalty while preserving the record of sin in the temple (on the altar). Second, when the sinner killed the lamb and *transferred* his guilt to the altar by the blood of the lamb, the sinner instantly received the lamb's righteousness. The lamb had never sinned, so in God's sight it was innocent, not under the penalty for sin. When the sinner received the lamb's righteousness, this means that in God's sight, the sinner was totally justified and in God's eyes, it was as though the sinner had never sinned. Third, once a year, on the Day of Atonement, the high priest performed a ceremony that cleansed the temple and its altars of the accumulated guilt. The guilt that was previously stored on the horns of the altars was transferred to the scapegoat's head. Again, this transfer required a perfect sacrifice (the Lord's goat) to die. At the end of this service on the Day of Atonement, the earthly temple was "cleansed" and all repentant sinners received the lamb's righteousness.

A coin always has two sides and likewise, I understand the coin of salvation to have two sides. One side concerns removing our guilt and the other side concerns our need for Christ's righteousness. When we understand both sides of this coin, we see how the Father, the Son, and the Holy Spirit have made it possible to save sinners. The Father so loved the world that He created a plan of salvation. Jesus so loved sinners that He came to Earth to do something that no human has been able to do. First, Jesus faced and overcame every temptation so that he could give repentant sinners His righteousness. Second, Jesus came to give His eternal life to repentant sinners. Jesus was willing to cease to exist forever so that He could transfer His eternal life to every repentant sinner. No demonstration of love will ever match the humility and love that Christ expressed and this is why the Father decreed that Jesus Christ will be fully revealed! Finally, the Holy Spirit loves sinners so much that He can hardly bring Himself to walk away from us, even when we are defiant. The Holy Spirit does His best to bring us to repentance, transform us, make us thirsty and hungry for truth and righteousness, and sanctify us so that He can draw us closer to the Father and Jesus. He gives us strength and victory over sin whenever we ask. He does His best to lead us into all truth, giving us precious

Chapter 12 – Third Seal – Judgment of the Dead

insights into the Father's character, will, and plans. Even with all the Father has done for us, it is nearly impossible for Him to sway the free will of rebellious sinners.

One final point regarding parallel temples is that there is no justification for sin. This means that if a person chooses to sin, he is guilty of sin because he made the choice to disobey God. Every sinner must die unless he is willing to repent, forsake his sins, and put his faith in Jesus as his Savior. Because God wisely chose to allow Lucifer and his followers to live after they sinned, the whole universe now sees (after thousands of years) what the curse of sin ultimately does to angels as well as human beings. Sin's curse turns every sinner into a predator. Lucifer preyed on his friends – innocent angels. Lucifer preyed on Eve. Eve tempted Adam and sinners have been preying on one another ever since. Even Adam and Eve's first born son, Cain, preyed on his brother Abel. Because Lucifer sinned first and all sin in the universe can be traced back to him, Lucifer is the universe's "predator-in-chief." This explains how the earthly temple was finally cleansed on the Day of Atonement. All of the accumulated guilt was transferred from the temple to the head of the scapegoat which represents Lucifer, the originator of sin. This annual process in the earthly temple points forward to a day when Jesus will transfer the saint's guilt to Lucifer's head. When that day arrives, Heaven's temple will be cleansed. The process will be completed.

The Doctrine of Soul Sleep

We first have to understand the doctrine of soul sleep before we can understand Jesus' judgment of the dead. The doctrine of soul sleep teaches that when a person dies, he does not immediately go to Heaven or Hell. This doctrine teaches that a person knows nothing after death and has no awareness or intelligence. (Ecclesiastes 9:5) The person simply ceases to exist with the only thing remaining is the record made by recording angels. Since the person has no consciousness, all spiritists and mediums are either pretending or communicating with demons. (Leviticus 19:31; 20:6) The doctrine of soul sleep teaches that Jesus will resurrect those judged to be righteous to meet Him in the air at the Second Coming. (1 Thessalonians 4:16,17) The people judged to be wicked will remain in their graves until Jesus resurrects them at the end of the thousand years. (Revelation 20:5,6)

Chapter 12 – Third Seal – Judgment of the Dead

The Promise of Wages

When Jesus broke the third seal, He sent the Holy Spirit to the world on an educational campaign. As the Holy Spirit prepared to leave the throne room, Jesus said, "A quart of wheat for a day's *wages*, and three quarts of barley for a day's *wages*, and do not damage the oil and the wine!" Jesus promised wages, in the form of "good" food, to those who will enter God's service to educate others about the judgment of the dead.

The Old Testament has a very good parallel concerning the use of wheat, barley, oil, and wine as wages! King Solomon offered Hiram, king of Tyre, an enormous quantity of food if Hiram's servants would gather materials to construct the Lord's temple in Jerusalem. **"I will give your servants, the woodsmen who cut the timber, twenty thousand cors of ground wheat** [125,000 bushels]**, twenty thousand cors of barley** [125,000 bushels]**, twenty thousand baths of wine** [115,000 gallons] **and twenty thousand baths of olive oil** [115,000 gallons]**."** (2 Chronicles 2:10, insertions mine) Solomon offered Hiram food because at that time food had a greater value than silver or gold. Solomon did not have the needed building materials, but he did have "good food" to compensate for building the Lord's enormous temple in Jerusalem. As you think about this, do not forget that at various times in human history, food has been the currency of choice between nations.

The parallel between Solomon and the promise of wages in the third seal is that since 1844, Jesus has been offering wages to those who are willing to build up the knowledge of His ministry in Heaven's temple. The Bible is a very comprehensive book and God's ways are vast. Teaching God's Word, if done properly, is not a simple or easy task. I can testify from personal experience that this work has been the most difficult assignment I have ever had. Jesus gave an offer of wages when he broke the third seal because He wants the world to know that He is judging dead people and He will judge living people soon. Jesus wants the news spread everywhere and He is willing to pay wages to anyone willing to carry the news!

William Miller (1782-1849)

An interesting sequence of events occurred in the United States just before the third seal was broken. The story began on a Sunday morning in 1816, when the Holy Spirit changed the heart of William Miller. Captain Miller was a 34-year old army officer who had settled in Low

Chapter 12 – Third Seal – Judgment of the Dead

Hampton, New York, after retiring from military service. At the time, Miller was a self-proclaimed deist. (Deists believe in a Supreme Being, but they deny the Bible is inspired and their view of God is contrary to the Bible.) However, Miller had two uncles who were Baptist preachers, and even though he was not a church member, he dutifully attended services at the Hampton Baptist Church with his believing wife whenever his uncle, Elisha, was preaching.

Because Miller did not attend church when his uncle was absent, a few members of the church thought Captain Miller might be persuaded to attend church more regularly if he were asked to participate. So, they asked him to read a selected sermon from *Proudfit's Practical Sermons* the next time his itinerant uncle was absent. To their surprise, Miller agreed. A few weeks later, they called Miller to read the sermon one Sunday morning. About halfway through the sermon on Isaiah 53, Miller was suddenly overcome with a personal realization of what he was reading. Isaiah's predictions about Christ's suffering for our sins caused Miller to stop mid-sermon and begin weeping. He buried his face in his hands and humbly sat down. Many in the audience wept, too. The Holy Spirit moved powerfully on that wonderful morning and, from that day forward, William Miller was a changed man. He became a born again believer in Christ and joined the Baptist Church. After Miller's conversion, he began to study the Bible intensely. Two years later, in 1818, Miller concluded the book of Daniel revealed that Jesus would return to Earth "around 1843." For several years, Miller kept this matter to himself because he thought he was the only person who believed Jesus was returning in 1843.

Fifteen years after becoming a born again Christian, Miller began to feel the Holy Spirit calling him to share his discoveries in the Bible. Miller's nephew invited him to speak to a small church group in August 1831 and this initiated Miller's "lay ministry." Miller's views on the Second Coming were unusual and word of his findings spread. People who heard Miller speak respected him even though he was not highly educated. Miller was a very bright person, a keen thinker, well organized in his thoughts, thorough in his research and most of all, humble.

In the early nineteenth century, New England Baptist churches were loosely organized and independent of one another. The churches were isolated and had no electronic communication, so ministers in some areas could accept Miller's views without causing a problem for the Baptist denomination in general. Because Miller was a layman and his early efforts were confined to a small geographical area in New York, opposition to Miller's ministry was not significant in the beginning. In addition to this, Protestants in New England were quite open to new ideas from the Bible. There was deep respect and interest in the Bible in those days. Remember, the Declaration of Independence was only 55 years old when Miller began to preach. In 1833, a small group of Baptist ministers licensed Miller so he could preach in surrounding Baptist churches.

An event occurring on November 13, 1833 suddenly transformed Miller's obscure ministry into a public phenomenon. That night, New England experienced the most remarkable meteoric shower people had ever witnessed. In New England and portions of Europe, people saw tens of thousands of meteorites falling. It looked as though the whole sky was falling! New Englanders panicked and many thought the world was ending. This spectacular event catapulted interest in Miller's message to a much larger stage and Miller's seventeen years of study on Bible prophecy had prepared him for this dramatic moment. When it became evident that Miller was unusually qualified and informed on the books of Daniel and Revelation, a group of about 40 ministers (half of whom were Baptists) recognized Miller's unique ministry in 1835 by granting him a license to speak in their affiliated churches. This impressive meteorite shower overcame denominational barriers so that Baptists and non-Baptists were interested to hear what a self-taught Baptist preacher had to say.

William Miller has had few peers in early American history and people considered him the "Billy Graham" of his day. Of course, as Miller's popularity grew, so did resistance. At the height of Miller's ministry, historians calculate the Millerites (as his followers were often called) numbered between fifty and one hundred thousand people. By 1844, Miller estimated that he had personally delivered 4,500 lectures on Bible prophecy to 500,000 people. This was a remarkable feat considering that he was about 50 years old when he began preaching, most of his travel was on horseback, and he spoke to audiences without the support of a public address system. When Jesus did not appear in 1843 (which Miller corrected to 1844), Miller's credibility was ruined and he went to his grave five years later bearing the shame and stigma of a "false prophet."

Chapter 12 – Third Seal – Judgment of the Dead

Shortly after the bitter disappointment of 1844, Miller responded to his critics saying, "I have never courted the smiles of the proud, nor quailed when the world frowned. I shall not now purchase their favor; nor shall I go beyond duty to tempt their hate. I shall never seek my life at their hands; nor shrink I hope, from losing it, if God in his good providence so orders." (The Prophetic Faith of Our Fathers, by LeRoy Edwin Froom, Volume IV, page 683) William Miller died in 1849, broken in health and a pauper. He had "bet the farm" on Jesus' Second Coming and spent everything he owned in an effort to educate people about the good news of Christ's return. Miller died as he lived, a man of faith, trusting in Jesus as his Savior. I have no doubt that Jesus will resurrect him with the righteous at the Second Coming. He was never able to understand where he had gone wrong.

Miller's Logic

Miller believed in 1833 that Daniel 8:14 pointed to the Second Coming in 1843, so he interpreted the meteorite shower to be a prophetic sign meaning Jesus would appear in about ten years. He had no doubt that the falling stars were a fulfillment of Revelation 6:13. Consider the basis for his logic:

The breaking of the sixth seal defines a sequence of events that climax with Jesus appearing in the clouds of Heaven. These events include a great earthquake, the darkening of the sun, the falling of the stars, and Jesus' appearing, in this order. (Revelation 6:12-14) Appealing to recent history, Miller reminded his listeners of the Lisbon, Portugal earthquake on November 1, 1755 where 60,000 people perished. This, he claimed, fulfilled the great earthquake in Revelation 6:12. Some New Englanders remembered "the dark day" of May 19, 1780. By noon on that day, the sun became so dark that a person could not see a white sheet of paper in front of his face. Later that day, the moon appeared and it was blood red. The animals even came in from the field around noon because of the darkness. There is historical evidence that suggests this darkness was caused by a massive volcano eruption in Mexico. When Miller considered the dates of the great earthquake (1755), the dark day (1790), and the falling of the stars (1833) during a period of 78 years, he concluded the sixth seal had been broken. Therefore, according to Miller, Jesus' second coming had to be the next event because Revelation 6:14, the next verse after the falling of the stars, begins to describe Jesus appearing in clouds of glory.

To make the breaking of the sixth seal even more timely and believable, Miller then demonstrated from the book of Daniel how the 2,300 evenings and mornings in Daniel 8:14 terminated in 1843. The dates seemed to properly align and many sincere Protestants embraced Miller's message. Several influential pastors joined Miller and the Millerite movement formed. As Miller's teachings grew in popularity, mainstream Protestant churches circled the wagons by expelling people from their churches for "denying the faith once delivered to the saints."

When the spring of 1843 passed and Jesus did not appear, the Millerites poured over their calculations and found a simple mistake. They had overlooked one year. Because calendar years are not counted on a mathematical scale, the transition from B.C. dating to A.D. dating requires adding an extra year because there is no zero year. So, the 1843 date was corrected to 1844 and 1844 became the terminus of the 2,300 years of Daniel 8:14. The hopes of the Millerites were renewed and, more important, they had one more year to spread the doctrine of an imminent Second Coming. But the spring and fall of 1844 came and went without a Second Coming. Jesus did not appear and the Millerite movement imploded in bitter disappointment. The Millerite fiasco caused many Protestant churches, particularly Baptists, to disdain study and interpretation of prophecy.

Millerites Conclude Heavenly Cleansing of Sanctuary

After the Millerite movement collapsed, many Millerites renounced their faith in God or sheepishly returned to their churches, but a few Millerites did not give up. They returned to their Bibles to try and figure out what went wrong and soon, they discovered the problem. Miller had interpreted the cleansing of the sanctuary in Daniel 8:14 to mean the cleansing of Earth. Miller thought Earth would be purified of wicked people in 1844. After carefully comparing the books of Hebrews, Leviticus, and Daniel, these Millerites concluded that Miller's view on the 2,300 years was correct, but the sanctuary to be cleansed was the true temple which is in Heaven. (Leviticus 16; Hebrews 8 and 9) In other words, they concluded that Jesus began cleansing Heaven's temple in 1844.

Looking back, I conclude that Miller's ministry and disappointment served two important purposes. First, Miller brought attention to Daniel 8:14 in a way that no one else had done. Second, the doctrine of parallel temples was discovered because of Miller's disappointment.

Chapter 12 – Third Seal – Judgment of the Dead 149

The Holy Spirit achieved an important victory through a bitter failure. After the Millerite movement imploded, there were people on Earth who understood that Jesus had begun to cleanse Heaven's temple and remarkably, all of this information came out of the Bible.

Mainstream Protestants were pleased when the Millerite movement disappeared, but out of the ashes of Miller's disappointment, a new church body formed that would become known as the Seventh-day Adventist Church. This church group organized about twenty years after the disappointment (1863); the same year that astronomer Hubert Newton figured out why the meteorite shower occurred in November 1833. Every thirty-three years, Earth passes through the same clump of space debris and this produces the shooting stars. Some years the number of shooting stars is few and other years the number is great.

Although William Miller died in 1849 without understanding why Jesus had not appeared and even though the Seventh-day Adventist church does not properly understand the books of Daniel and Revelation, their stories are germane to the breaking of the third seal. The Holy Spirit raised up a humble Baptist preacher to draw attention to 1844 and He used Seventh Day Adventists to draw attention to the judgment of the dead. (2 Corinthians 5:10; Daniel 8:14) This is not surprising. The Holy Spirit used a Catholic monk (Martin Luther) to draw attention to the essential doctrine of justification through faith alone. (Romans 1:17)

Consider the historical process: God broke the power of the Catholic Church in 1798. Just a few years previously, God had opened a new frontier in 1776 called the United States of America. Uniquely, this nation had a constitution providing separation between church and state. The doctrine of salvation through faith in Christ had blossomed. The Holy Spirit driven Bible translation and distribution was going strong. The Holy Spirit found a willing man in William Miller in 1816 and the Spirit empowered Miller for 15 years to proclaim a Bible truth whose time had come. Even though many of Miller's conclusions were faulty, he correctly understood the 2,300 days in Daniel 8:14 ended in the spring of 1844 and my studies affirm the validity of his claim. I am also convinced the Holy Spirit raised the Seventh-day Adventist Church out of the ashes of Miller's implosion. God wanted these people to bring together five essential Bible doctrines in a systematic way. Seventh Day Adventists compiled Luther's discovery of salvation through faith in Jesus, the Congregationalist view of soul sleep, the Seventh Day Baptist view on the observance of God's seventh day Sabbath, Miller's views on the Second Coming, and they discovered the doctrine of parallel temples.

Adventists carefully merged these five doctrines into a harmonious system of understanding. As church bodies go, they have done well. The church claims to have nearly twenty million members today. But the Seventh Day Adventist church, like all Protestant churches, has stumbled because it has not been willing to follow the advancing light of truth. This is a true paradox. Even though Protestant churches will form around a truth whose time has come, they seem incapable of moving beyond their beginning when the Holy Spirit provides additional truth. In this sense, Seventh-day Adventists have followed in the footsteps of all Protestant churches. None of them have been able to move forward with advancing light. Of course they respond to this charge saying that they have "the light" or they are walking "in the light" and everyone else is in darkness, but the truth about their prophetic poverty will only be revealed when they admit their understanding of God's Word is inadequate. This painful awakening is about to occur. The fourth seal will do the job!

Summary

Four key points need to be emphasized as we conclude this section on the breaking of the third seal. First, a person cannot reach the intended meaning of the third seal without some understanding of the inauguration of Jesus in 1798, the doctrine of soul sleep, and the operation of parallel temples.

Second, history reveals that the advancement of truth always comes with a high price and most people are unwilling to pay the price. It is much more comfortable to remain within the social and religious comforts of fellowship than to follow the Spirit into the desert of rejection where often, you are alone with God. The Bible represents people as sheep for good reason. They prefer to flock together. They also tend to follow their leaders (political and religious) without thinking or thoroughly studying matters out for themselves. Consider all the religious thought that Hindus, Moslems, Catholics, Jews, Protestants, atheists and pagans believe today. All of these different ideas about God came from spiritual leaders who are as blind as the people they guide. (Matthew 23:16)

Chapter 12 – Third Seal – Judgment of the Dead   151

Third, people are capable of believing anything. Man's diversity proves that religious systems have nothing to do with eternal truth. Even though Catholics and Protestants insist their views come directly from Scripture, a cursory study of Scripture can demonstrate otherwise. Truth is not determined by a majority vote or acceptance. Thoughtfully consider these amazing words: "Truth is not what I believe. Truth is not even what I know. Truth is fact. I may not believe it. I may not know it. That does not change it. It is there nevertheless, waiting to be discovered and believed. Truth does not depend on the unsettled and changing opinions of men. It was truth before it was believed. It remains truth whether it is believed or not. Reason does not originate or create it. It merely discovers it. Consequently, reason is not a source. Truth goes back beyond reason. Others would have us believe that the church is the source of authority, particularly in matters of theology. They are wrong. The church is the product of truth. It does not originate it. It came into being by accepting divine revelation. It is not the source of that revelation. Truth goes beyond the church, it is antecedent to it." (When a Man Dies, Carlyle B. Haynes (1882-1958); p.5)

Finally, Jesus broke the third seal in 1844. Because the Heaven Earth Linkage Law says there are corresponding events on Earth with events in Heaven, the unique ministry of William Miller and the subsequent discovery of the doctrine of parallel temples affirms that Jesus began cleansing Heaven's temple that year.

One last thought: The first thing Jesus did after He began His public ministry on Earth was to cleanse the temple in Jerusalem. **"To those who sold doves He said, Get these out of here! How dare you turn my Father's house into a market!' . . . Then the Jews demanded of him, 'What miraculous sign can you show us to prove your authority to do all this?' Jesus answered them, 'Destroy this temple, and I will raise it again in three days.' The Jews replied, 'It has taken forty-six years to build this temple, and you are going to raise it in three days?' "** (John 2:16-19) Jesus cleansed the Earthly temple after forty-six years of construction, and there is forty-six years between the time that Jesus received the Book of Life and began breaking the seals in 1798 to the time He began cleansing Heaven's temple in 1844.

Do not forget. If you are interested in a comprehensive study on soul sleep and God's use for parallel temples, please see Chapters 11 through 14 in my book, *Jesus: The Alpha and The Omega*. If you also wish to carefully examine the two apocalyptic prophecies that position the third seal in 1844, please see Chapters 4 and 6 in my book, *Daniel: Unlocked for the Final Generation*. PDF versions of both books can be freely downloaded here: *https://www.wake-up.org/find-articles-by-topic/*)

Chapter 13
Fourth Seal – Judgment of the Living

> "When the Lamb opened the fourth seal, I heard the voice of the fourth living creature say, 'Come!' I looked, and there before me was a pale horse! Its rider was named Death, and Hades was following close behind him. They were given power over a fourth of the Earth to kill by sword, famine and plague, and by the wild beasts of the Earth." (Revelation 6:7,8)

Seal #4 - Pale Horse – Coming Soon – The Judgment of the Living

When Jesus breaks the fourth seal, the Holy Spirit will leave Heaven's temple and begin a campaign of horrific death and destruction which is beyond our ability to comprehend.

The fourth living creature has a face of an eagle. (Revelation 4:7) Eagles are birds of prey and are predators. Very few animals notice the swift and silent approach of a diving eagle. This face signifies sudden destruction. **"While people are saying, 'Peace and safety,' destruction will come on them *suddenly,* as labor pains on a pregnant woman, and they will not escape."** (1 Thessalonians 5:3, italics mine) Notice God's use of parallel language when He was about to destroy Moab for its wickedness, He said to Jeremiah: **"This is what the Lord says: 'Look! An eagle is swooping down** [to devour, to destroy]**, spreading its wings over Moab.'"** (Jeremiah 48:40, insertion mine)

The words in the text, "Death" and the grave (Greek: *hades*) following "close behind," personify the mission which the Holy Spirit "faces" when Jesus breaks the fourth seal. This combination means a fourth of Earth's population will be killed and buried on a global scale not seen since Noah's flood. God will display His sovereign authority to Earth's final generation when the Holy Spirit leaves Heaven's temple to carry out His mission. The breaking of the fourth seal also means that Judgment Day, a distressing time during which God will judge the living, has begun.

Chapter 13 – Fourth Seal – Judgment of the Living

The Holy Spirit – Executioner of God's Wrath

Jesus said, **"The Spirit gives life; the flesh counts for nothing."** (John 6:63) Because the Holy Spirit gives life, it seems contradictory that the Holy Spirit is given the name "Death." It is also difficult to think the Holy Spirit is implementing God's wrath since He is called "The Comforter" in the KJV or the "The Counselor" in the NIV. Christians tend to think the Holy Spirit is the conduit for love, joy, peace, patience, kindness, goodness, faithfulness, gentleness, and self-control. (Galatians 5:22,23) Therefore, it is difficult for a Bible student to associate the Holy Spirit with God's wrath.

The problem with our genteel view of the Holy Spirit is that it produces a limited view of God. The Holy Spirit is no different in nature and character than Jesus and the Father. All three of them were in perfect unison when God destroyed the world in Noah's day, burned Sodom and Gomorrah, and destroyed Jerusalem with the Babylonians and later, with the Romans. The Holy Spirit has the same powers and prerogatives as the Father and Son.

At times, the Holy Spirit has enabled people to do incredible things. For example, Samson's great strength came from the Holy Spirit's indwelling power. **"The Spirit of the Lord came upon him [Samson] in power so that he tore the lion apart with his bare hands as he might have torn a young goat."** (Judges 14:6) **"Then the Spirit of the Lord came upon him [Samson] in power. He went down to Ashkelon, struck down thirty of their men, stripped them of their belongings and gave their clothes to those who had explained the riddle."** (Judges 14:19)

Shortly after Jesus ascended to Heaven, the Holy Spirit surprisingly killed a husband and wife in Jerusalem for lying. This event caused early Christians to have a great deal of respect for the Holy Spirit. Here is the story: **"Now a man named Ananias, together with his wife Sapphira, also sold a piece of property. With his wife's full knowledge he kept back part of the money for himself, but brought the rest and put it at the apostles' feet. Then Peter said, 'Ananias, how is it that Satan has so filled your heart that *you have lied to the Holy Spirit* and have kept for yourself some of the money you received for the land? Did not it belong to you before it was sold? And after it was sold, was not the money at your disposal? What made you think of doing such a thing? You

Chapter 13 – Fourth Seal – Judgment of the Living

have not lied to men but *to God.*' When Ananias heard this, he fell down and died. And great fear seized all who heard what had happened. Then the young men came forward, wrapped up his body, and carried him out and buried him. About three hours later his wife came in, not knowing what had happened. Peter asked her, 'Tell me, is this the price you and Ananias got for the land?' 'Yes,' she said, 'that is the price.' Peter said to her, 'How could you agree *to test the Spirit of the Lord*? Look! The feet of the men who buried your husband are at the door, and they will carry you out also.' At that moment she fell down at his feet and died. Then the young men came in and, finding her dead, carried her out and buried her beside her husband. Great fear seized the whole church and all who heard about these events." (Acts 5:1-11, italics mine)

Judgment Day Is Coming!

Judgment day will begin for people who are alive at the time the fourth seal is opened. **"For He [the Father] has set a day when he will judge the world with justice by the man he has appointed. He has given proof of this to all men by raising him from the dead."** (Acts 17:31, insertion mine) God will perform astonishing signs and wonders in the heavens and on Earth to get our attention. Then, four horrific events will occur on Earth. The first event is a firestorm that will burn a third of the Earth and then two huge asteroid impacts will follow. The impacts will be civilization threatening. Finally, there will be many volcano eruptions and darkness will cover the Earth.

God's four deadly disasters will end life on Earth as we presently know it. He will mortally wound Earth's ecosystems and Earth will not recover. This will cause global famine and the clergy and laymen of the world's religious systems will be totally unprepared. The world's political leaders will not know what to do other than implement martial law. Every infrastructure created by man will implode. God's coming wrath is more encompassing and distressing than words can express. Every person on Earth will be dramatically affected. I believe almost two billion people will die during a very short period of time. God's wrath will be so extensive, so pronounced, so overwhelming, and so overreaching that many survivors will be afraid to even speak because they might further offend a very angry God. God will silence mankind's arrogance and impudence toward God and each other. The fourth seal will be deadly and serious. Jesus will halt the ways and thoughts of mankind to inform us that the time has come for Him to judge and sentence the living.

When God uses His four catastrophes to hammer the Earth, He will force the survivors to realize the reality of an angry God and the reach and power of His sovereign authority. His wrath will terrorize the whole world and in the process, He will accomplish two purposes: First, the quantity of death involved will create a whole new reality. God will put the entire world on notice that He, Jesus Christ, is Almighty God, the Ruler of Earth, and the Judge of Mankind. When you consider that over two-thirds of Earth's population does not believe that Jesus is Deity, God's wrath will be a bitter surprise. Second, while Earth's inhabitants are reeling from the destruction of everything they once trusted, Jesus will issue demands through His servants, the 144,000. All who put their faith in Jesus and obey His demands "shall not perish, but have everlasting life!"

The Great Tribulation will last 1,335 days. (Daniel 12:12) During this time, God's wrath will come in two waves. I anticipate the first wave of *seven first* plagues will last about 1,265 days and the second wave of *seven last* plagues will last about 70 days. The seven first plagues will be dreadful, but Jesus will announce a generous offer during that time. The 144,000 will proclaim that Jesus will save any sinner who desires eternal life if the sinner places his faith in Jesus and obeys His commandments. Tragically, billions of people will refuse the offer and will remain defiant. Ultimately, they will blaspheme the Holy Spirit and commit the unpardonable sin. When everyone has made a decision, Jesus will bring Judgment Day to a close and He will destroy everyone who refused salvation during the seven last plagues.

Jesus will accomplish many things during the fourth seal that He could not accomplish earlier. For example, His "acts of God" will humble the living so they will hear and intelligently consider the Creator's demands as well as His offer of salvation. Jesus will remove religious blinders and expose the foolishness of false gods. The 144,000 will speak with penetrating Holy Spirit power and clarity and millions of people will be saved! The Father deliberately designed this series of events before Jesus created the world. Remember, the Father ordained the revelation of Jesus. During the Great Tribulation the Father wants everyone to hear and receive the truth about His Son and be saved. (2 Peter 3:9)

Chapter 13 – Fourth Seal – Judgment of the Living

Three Types of Wrath

Advocates of a pre-tribulation rapture believe "the church" will escape the Great Tribulation. They typically combine the information from 1 Thessalonians 5:9, Romans 5:9 and Revelation 3:10 to support this claim. Unfortunately, the first two texts do not address escaping the Great Tribulation. Instead, they address avoiding God's wrath (the penalty for sin) which is eternal death. Understand that there are three types of wrath in the Bible and the distinction between them is crucial if we wish to understand the punitive judgments that occur during the fourth seal. After reviewing the types of God's wrath, we will consider the information from Revelation 3:10.

1. The Wrath of Law

The Bible defines the *wrath of law* as the fruit or consequence that comes from doing wrong. If we violate a physical or moral law, there are consequences. Paul wrote, **"Because** [the violation of] **law brings wrath. And where there is no law there is no transgression."** (Romans 4:15, insertion mine) Notice how physical and moral laws work. If we violate the laws of health and eat too much on a regular basis, we will suffer for it. If we violate a moral law and are caught committing adultery, we will suffer the wrath of law (social consequences) and the innocents (the spouse, children, families involved) will also suffer the wrath of law as well. The Bible says, **"Do not be deceived: God cannot be mocked. A man reaps what he sows. The one who sows to please his sinful nature, from that nature will reap destruction; the one who sows to please the Spirit, from the Spirit will reap eternal life."** (Galatians 6:7,8) Doing wrong by violating the law brings the consequences of the law's wrath which are sorrow, suffering, pain, and death.

2. Wrath as the Penalty for Sin

When Jesus created Adam and Eve, He immediately placed them under the obligation of this law: God said, **"But of the tree of the knowledge of good and evil, thou shalt not eat of it: for in the day that thou eatest thereof thou shalt surely die."** (Genesis 2:17, KJV) This law meant that God would execute Adam and Eve on the very day they sinned because the penalty for sin is sudden death by execution. God stayed the demand of this law and permitted Adam and Eve to live because Jesus offered to die in their place. However, God will not stay the wrath of the sudden death law indefinitely. God's final act in resolving the sin problem will be to execute all people who refused to embrace the Savior. God will send fire down from Heaven to execute the wicked at the end of the 1,000 years because the penalty for sin is death by execution. In Old Testament times, each time a sacrificial lamb was executed, God provided an illustrative lesson of the penalty for sin. The layman or the priest *slaughtered* the lamb on an altar and it did not die of natural causes. Even more, Jesus Himself was executed on the cross for our sins. (1 Thessalonians 2:14,15) He died this way because the penalty for sin is death by execution.

3. Wrath in the Form of Redemptive and/or Destructive Judgments

If a nation arouses God's anger with degenerate and decadent behavior, He will punish that nation with redemptive judgments. If that nation continues in defiant rebellion, God will punish that nation with totally destructive judgments. Jesus told Israel, **"But if you will not listen to me and carry out all these commands, and if you reject my decrees and abhor my laws and fail to carry out all my commands and so violate my covenant, then I will do this to you: I will bring upon you sudden terror, wasting diseases and fever that will destroy your sight and drain away your life. You will plant seed in vain, because your enemies will eat it."** (Leviticus 26:14-16)

For centuries Jesus patiently tried to get Israel to accomplish the purposes for which He delivered them out of Egypt, but due to Israel's rebellion, Jesus sent the nation into Babylonian captivity in 605 B.C. Babylon's first siege of Jerusalem and capture of Israel's finest young men did not change Israel's attitude or behavior. So, Jesus sent king Nebuchadnezzar a second time against Jerusalem in 598 B.C., but there was still no change of heart. Finally, Jesus told Ezekiel: **"For this is what the Sovereign Lord says: How much worse will it be when I send against Jerusalem my four dreadful judgments sword and famine and wild beasts and plague – to kill its men and their animals! Yet there will be some survivors – sons and daughters who will be brought out of it. They will come to you, and when you see their conduct and their actions, you will be consoled regarding the disaster I have brought upon Jerusalem – every disaster I have brought upon it."** (Ezekiel 14:21,22) According to His word, God sent King Nebuchadnezzar against Jerusalem

Chapter 13 – Fourth Seal – Judgment of the Living

in 586 B.C. and this time the king totally destroyed the temple and the city. When God's redemptive judgments do not produce repentance and reformation, His wrath escalates to total destruction. God caused global destruction in Noah's day because He gave the world 120 years of probation and there was no improvement. Global destruction is coming again because God has given Protestants more than 200 years to spread the gospel and the world today mirrors the world in Noah's day.

We have examined three types of wrath. Through Jesus, sinners can escape the penalty for sin, but no one can escape the wrath that comes from violating a physical or moral law. No sinner can escape God's punitive judgments unless he is not at the location of the people who God intends to punish. Noah did not escape the flood; he survived the flood. Lot did not escape God's fiery wrath on Sodom and Gomorrah; he survived the fire by leaving home and forfeiting everything he owned. Daniel did not escape God's punitive wrath on Jerusalem; he lost his family and was taken to Babylon as a captive. Nine of the twelve apostles were martyred for their faith in Jesus! Make no mistake, the Bible says the saints will be on Earth during the Great Tribulation: **"He [the beast] was given power to make war against *the saints* and to conquer them. And he [the beast] was given authority over every tribe, people, language and nation... I saw that the woman was drunk with the blood of *the saints,* the blood of those who bore testimony to Jesus. When I saw her, I was greatly astonished."** (Revelation 13:7; 17:6, italics mine)

The Living Are Judged

Jesus will ensure that every survivor hears about His generous offer of salvation after He breaks the fourth seal! Jesus Himself will speak through the 144,000 and everyone will hear "the testimony of Jesus!" The Bible teaches that salvation comes through faith alone and ever since Jesus opened the first seal in 1798, the Holy Spirit has been advancing this message throughout the world. It is only by placing the entire world in a dire situation that Jesus will give the survivors a chance to live by faith regardless of religious heritage or background. The judgment of the living involves four steps:

First: **Enlightenment** – Each survivor will hear God's demands.
Second: Decision – Each survivor will thoughtfully consider God's demands and then decide his course of action.

Third: **Testing** – Persecution will test the decision of each person who chooses to put faith in God.

Fourth: **Sealing** – God will reward those passing the test of faith, obeying Him without regard for the consequences, with the same awesome transformation he gave to the 144,000. A few days before the Great Tribulation begins, God will select the 144,000 and their sinful natures will be removed. Jesus will make the 144,000 into mirrors of Himself (the only person who lived without sinning). When Jesus sees a person enduring persecution because of his faith, Jesus will judge that person. He will remove the sinner's sinful nature and the doorway to sin will be sealed. Suddenly, Jesus will set prostitutes, like Rahab, and demon possessed people, such as Mary Magdalene, free! Through their faith, Jesus will judge and transform all sinners. People that Jesus has sealed will no longer have any interest or attraction for sin. They will be like Adam and Eve before the fall, having no proclivity for sin!

God has designed a plan and persecution of His people has always been part of that plan. When we enter the Great Tribulation, God will place everyone in this position. People who choose to obey God's demands have to live by faith because they will eventually lose everything, including the right to buy and sell. The devil and his agencies will do everything possible to scare, torment, and abuse people so that they will give up their faith in God. Jesus told His persecuted followers at Philadelphia, **"Since you have kept my command to endure patiently, I will also keep you from the hour of trial that is going to come upon the whole world to test those who live on the Earth."** (Revelation 3:10) Jesus pointed forward to an hour of trial that is coming upon the whole world and its purpose is **"to test those who live on the Earth."** Advocates of a pre-tribulation rapture often use this verse to indicate the saints will escape "from" the hour of trial. The Greek preposition *'ek* can be translated to mean "from the hour of trial," but it can also be translated to mean "during the hour of trial."

The fatal problem of the pre-tribulation rapture theory is that God is required to judge the people of Earth *prior* to the rapture, otherwise, Jesus would not be able to determine who should be raptured and who should not. So, if Jesus judges the whole world prior to the rapture, He would not need to judge the whole world *after* the rapture. The Bible

Chapter 13 – Fourth Seal – Judgment of the Living

does not support the idea that Jesus judges the whole world twice. Jesus is going to test everyone living on Earth at the same time. In effect, Jesus told His suffering saints in Philadelphia, "I know you are weary from years of persecution and I am aware of all the things that you have patiently endured for my sake, but do not be overcome with discouragement. I have sustained you thus far and I will continue to sustain you *during* the hour of trial that is coming upon the world."

God Allows Persecution

Even though it may be hard to understand, God does have a reason for allowing the saints to be persecuted. Consider this scenario: After God has silenced the world with his four catastrophes, the 144,000 will tell the survivors that Jesus Christ is the Creator of Heaven and Earth. Jesus has given the world notice of His judgment and soon return. All people who wish to be a part of Jesus' coming kingdom must repent of their sins and put their faith in Him. The 144,000 will also tell the world that after creating the world in six days, Jesus rested and made the seventh day of the week holy. (Exodus 20:8-11) Jesus now requires everyone to rest from labor on *His* holy day which is Saturday, the seventh day of the week. Obviously, this will be very difficult for Catholics, Protestants, Muslims, Hindus, Buddhists, and Atheists to accept.

The 144,000 will also explain that all human beings are condemned to death because all have sinned and the penalty for sin is death. The *only* way to eternal life is through faith in Jesus. Obviously, this will be difficult for Jews, Atheists, Hindus and Muslims to accept. The 144,000 will also tell the survivors that Jesus has paid the price for every repentant sinner with His own blood and He will return to Earth soon and gather the redeemed at the end of the Great Tribulation. Many of the world's survivors will scorn the 144,000 and the information they share.

The political and religious leaders of the world will respond to the 144,000's testimony with indignation and blasphemy. They will create a global government, called Babylon, trying to appease God so that He will cease His wrath. Of course, Babylon will do everything possible to make it impossible to observe God's Sabbath. In Muslim countries, Babylon will make laws to enforce Friday observance. In Catholic and Protestant countries, Babylon will make laws to enforce Sunday observance. In Israel, Babylon will make laws to enforce Saturday observance, but Israel will not embrace Jesus Christ as the Creator of Heaven and Earth! This shows that merely resting on God's Sabbath will not save a person. God does not require anyone to worship the Sabbath, instead He calls everyone to worship the Creator on His holy Sabbath day.

The devil will use Babylon to persecute everyone who puts faith in Jesus and the Creator's Sabbath will become a very inflammatory issue. Notice what the Bible says about Babylon (represented in the book of Revelation as a beast): **"He [the beast] opened his mouth to blaspheme God, and to slander His name and His dwelling place and those who live in Heaven. He was given power** *to make war against the saints and to conquer them.* **And he was given authority over every tribe, people, language and nation."** (Revelation 13:6,7, insertion and italics mine)

This is how Jesus will judge the living. Before Jesus created the world, the Father ordained that Jesus would judge the survivors during the last days of Earth's history. Because the Father foreknew the political, cultural, and religious diversity of mankind, He leveled the playing field by aligning the time of judgment with the four global disasters. Remember, Jesus does not save a person because he is a Hindu, Jew, Muslim, Catholic, or Protestant. God only saves a person by his faith which is doing whatever God commands without regard for the consequences. (Hebrews 11) During the Great Tribulation, God will abolish all religious systems because He must separate survivors of the four cataclysmic events from their religious heritage to see who will live by faith.

In a sense, the coming test mirrors Noah's day. For 120 years, Noah worked and preached that God was going to use a flood to destroy the whole world. Noah built the ark and then the antediluvians condemned themselves, by refusing to believe. They put no faith in God's message or his messenger. Jesus said, **"For in the days before the flood, people were eating and drinking, marrying and giving in marriage, up to the day Noah entered the ark; and they knew nothing about what would happen until the flood came and took them all away. That is how it will be at the coming of the Son of Man."** (Matthew 24:38,39)

Today, our world is full of antagonistic cultures, religions, and gospels. Long ago, the Father used His foreknowledge to devise a way to cut through our religious and political gridlock with "justifiable" judgments (disasters) to humble and silence the survivors. Furthermore, the

Chapter 13 – Fourth Seal – Judgment of the Living

Father will give the eternal gospel credibility by using the Holy Spirit to select, seal, and empower 144,000 people just *before* His judgments begin. The first four judgments will create a great theological vacuum. This vacuum is because the world's clergy do not properly understand the Bible (especially the books of Daniel and Revelation), God's wrath (the seven trumpets and the seven bowls), and God's end-time plan and purpose. Therefore, the religious leaders, as well as the laymen, will have an overwhelming surprise. People will quickly see that their religious leaders do not actually know God or His Word. Knowing God is not the same thing as knowing the framework of a religious system. God will use death and destruction to break religious paradigms. When God humbles the people of Earth and replaces cultural and religious bias, they will listen to a gospel they have not heard before. God will use this temporary vacuum to propel the eternal gospel throughout the world swiftly with little resistance. Man's resistance will come later.

God Is Looking for Honest Hearted People

God's method for judging people from every walk of life illumines a profound fact. Anyone who conscientiously does the good that he knows he should do is honest-hearted. Each time a person's knowledge of "good" expands, God challenges our honesty again. As attorney Richard J. Humpal once said, "When a man who is honestly mistaken hears the truth, he will either quit being mistaken or cease being honest."

God is constantly challenging our faith to see if we would be happy in an environment where advancing knowledge of eternal truth never ends. An honest-hearted person will embrace God's truth regardless of the consequences because he loves God and His truth. A truth-loving person, even if he died having only 1% truth, would be happy for eternity with God and the holy angels. This is because his attitude toward God is right and will continue as his knowledge of God's truth forever expands. Jesus said, **"But whoever lives by the truth comes** [keeps on coming] **into the light, so that it may be seen plainly that what he has** [learned and] **done has been done through God** [God's power]." (John 3:21, insertions mine) The eternal gospel is so simple a child can understand it. (Revelation 14:6,7) The gospel commands all created beings to worship our Creator, Jesus Christ, and Jesus has made it clear in the Ten Commandments that His holy day is Saturday, the seventh day of the week. The 144,000 servants will proclaim this simple gospel throughout the world with great power and authority for 1,260 days. The Holy Spirit will torment each person to convict them of sin, righteousness, and judgment to make sure they know that the 144,000's testimony is true! (John 16:8; Revelation 14:11) The honest in heart will respond to this enlightenment just like steel responds to a magnet's pull and making a decision about the Holy Spirit-filled message will separate the sheep from the goats!

God is love and Jesus is more than fair! Jesus will judge the survivors according to our faith. Each person will decide whether to embrace the eternal gospel and obey the conviction of the Holy Spirit when the price for doing so demands a sacrifice. This coming process will prove to the watching angels that anyone who loves truth and lives up to what he knows to be right and true is safe to redeem for eternity. An honest-hearted person thirsts, seeks, and welcomes more truth. Jesus said, **"Blessed are those who hunger and thirst for righteousness, for they will be filled."** (Matthew 5:6)

Summary

We have now examined all four horsemen of Revelation 6 and they reveal a very interesting progression. The first campaign began with a message to the world: Salvation through faith in Jesus. The second campaign began with Bible societies translating and distributing the Bible around the world so that people could learn Jesus' teachings. The third campaign began with a message that Jesus had started cleansing Heaven's temple by judging the dead. The fourth campaign will be a mission of wrath that will kill 25% of the world's population. This coming display of God's wrath will provide the means for the 144,000 to share the eternal gospel with people who survive these cataclysmic events. Their response to the gospel will determine their eternal destiny.

The stage is set. Earth's cup of iniquity is overflowing and its people do not anticipate that they are about to be participants in a drama. God is holding back the "four winds" of His wrath until the time He has determined. Soon, Jesus will select and seal the 144,000 (Revelation 7:1-4) and God's wrath will begin. Jesus will speak through His servants and the survivors must consider a gospel that is contrary to everything they currently believe. The Bible says that amazingly, there will be an innumerable group of people who will pass a test of faith, embrace Jesus' testimony, and be saved. (Revelation 7:9-14)

Chapter 14
Fifth Seal – Believers Martyred

"When He opened the fifth seal, I saw under the altar the souls of those who had been slain because of the word of God and the testimony they had maintained. They called out in a loud voice, 'How long, Sovereign Lord, holy and true, until you judge the inhabitants of the Earth and avenge our blood?' Then each of them was given a white robe, and they were told to wait a little longer, until the number of their fellow servants and brothers who were to be killed as they had been was completed." (Revelation 6:9-11)

Seal #5 – Martyrdom – The Faith of Jesus Demonstrated

When the fifth seal is broken, there will be a period of time when the saints will be martyred. This makes the fifth seal very sobering, but once you understand God's purpose for the martyrdom and His promise to give a martyr's faith to His saints, this coming martyrdom should not be feared. There are things worse than "sleeping" through the remainder of the Great Tribulation. According to my calculation, Jesus will open the fifth seal about 1,039 days into the Great Tribulation and the martyrdom that follows will last about seven months.

The fifth seal declares that circumstances are coming when the human race will be severely tested. The saints will choose something more precious than life. Those loyal to God and His Word will choose death rather than submit to Lucifer's demands. The saints will do this because their faith in God will trump their love for life. The Bible says, **"They overcame him** [the devil] **by the blood of the Lamb and by the word of their testimony; they did not love their lives so much as to shrink from death."** (Revelation 12:11, insertion mine)

A person gets to a place in his life where being loyal to God is more important than life itself through small steps, from one faith experience to the next. **"For therein** [within the gospel of Christ] **is the righteousness of God revealed from faith to faith: as it is written, The just shall live by faith."** (Romans 1:17, KJV, insertion mine) Living from one faith experience to the next is contrary to human nature. This is why Jesus rebuked the church at Laodicea. **"You say, 'I am rich; I have acquired wealth and do not need a thing.' But you do not realize that you are wretched, pitiful, poor, blind and naked. I counsel you to buy from me gold refined in the fire** [multiple faith experiences when trust in God is purified by significant tests]**, so you can become rich; and white clothes to wear, so you can cover your shameful nakedness; and salve to put on your eyes, so you can see. Those whom I love I rebuke and discipline. So be earnest, and repent. Here I am! I stand at the door and knock. If anyone hears my voice and opens the door, I will come in and eat with him, and he with me. To him who overcomes, I will give the right to sit with me on my throne, just as I overcame and sat down with my Father on his throne."** (Revelation 3:17-21, insertion mine)

Martyrdom Is Justified

The fact that God's people have been persecuted through the ages is no accident. Hostility toward God's people was put in motion on the day that Adam and Eve sinned. When Jesus came to Earth to meet with the guilty pair, I believe Jesus built the first altar and killed the first sacrificial lamb to demonstrate a profound truth about the nature and price of salvation. His actions pointed forward to a day when the Father would produce the altar, provide the sacrifice, and slay the Lamb of God. I believe Jesus told Adam and Eve that He would become the sacrificial lamb. He explained that He would have to die so Adam and Eve could return to Eden. I am sure they wept at such a thought. The devil was summoned to this meeting and Jesus spoke directly to Lucifer saying, **"And I will put enmity** [opposition, hostility, hatred] **between you and the woman, and between your offspring and hers; He** [the sacrificial Lamb] **will crush your head, and you will strike his heel."** (Genesis 3:15, insertions mine) Then, Jesus took the skin from the sacrificial lamb and clothed Adam and Eve. (Genesis 3:21) Little did Adam and Eve realize that the promised enmity would lead to the murder of their second son.

I am sure there are many divine reasons why the saints will be martyred. By the time the fifth seal is broken, most of God's saints will have endured two years of horrible tribulation and persecution. In this sense, martyrdom is merciful because it ends the travail. Notice how John's words apply to the fifth seal: **"This** [martyrdom] **calls for patient endurance on the part of the saints who obey God's**

Chapter 14 – Fifth Seal – Believers Martyred

commandments and remain faithful to Jesus. Then I heard a voice from Heaven say, 'Write: Blessed are the dead who die in the Lord from now on.' 'Yes,' says the Spirit, 'they will rest from their labor, for their deeds will follow them.' " (Revelation 14:13, insertion mine) From God's point of view, death is inconsequential. For the saints, death is a temporary "resting place." The martyred saints will simply "sleep through" the remaining days of the Great Tribulation. Jesus will call them back to life when He arrives to take His children home.

Consider the phrase **"Blessed are the dead who die in the Lord from now on?"** The reason why the Bible says "Blessed are the *dead* who die . . . " instead of "Blessed are the *living* who die in the Lord . . . " is found in this verse: **"If anyone** [any saint] **is to go into captivity, into captivity he will go. If anyone** [any saint] **is to be killed with the sword, with the sword he will be killed. This calls for patient endurance and faithfulness on the part of the saints."** (Revelation 13:10, insertions mine) This verse indicates that when the Great Tribulation begins, God has already determined the experience and journey for each of His children. God does this to free will beings because when a person gives His heart and soul to the Lord, "to go, to be, and to do all that the Lord commands," that person voluntarily places himself at the Lord's disposal. As an example, when a person joins the military, that person voluntarily places himself at the disposal of his commander. Millions of soldiers have died because they surrendered their will and destiny to the will of their commander. Likewise, Jesus, our Commander-in-Chief, has a purpose for each of His saints and those destined for death need not to be afraid. Jesus will grant a martyr's faith when it is needed and the martyr will not flinch.

The phrase, **"Blessed are the dead who die in the Lord from now on"** references a specific moment in time. The Bible says **"from now on."** When Jesus breaks the fifth seal and the martyrdom begins, He will especially bless these faith-full martyrs. **"Then each of them was given a white robe."** (Revelation 6:11) Do not confuse this gift with *the promise* of a white robe. During the fifth seal, through the martyrs, Jesus will reveal *the faith of Jesus* (that is, the relationship which Jesus and the Father had when Jesus was on Earth) to the world. When Jesus was transfigured on the mount, the Bible says, **"There he was transfigured before them. His face shone like the sun, and his clothes became as white as the light."** (Matthew 17:2) I believe

Jesus will transfigure the martyrs right before the eyes of their enemies. Notice what happened when Stephen, the first Christian martyr was executed: **"All who were sitting in the Sanhedrin looked intently at Stephen, and they saw that his face was** [illumined, bright] **like the face of an angel."** (Acts 6:15, insertion mine)

A second reason why the saints will be martyred during the fifth seal pertains to saving people who, thus far during the Great Tribulation, have remained defiant toward God. I calculate that the time remaining to receive salvation is short, about seven months after Jesus breaks the fifth seal. Jesus is not willing that any person should perish, so He will use the martyrdom of His saints (along with the glory that each martyr displays) to arouse, if possible, the sensibilities of wicked people. If you recall, Stephen's testimony and demeanor deeply affected Saul of Tarsus (who held Stephen's coat while he was being stoned). The most powerful testimony for truth that a saint can give occurs when a person like Stephen, full of grace, peace, and joy, willingly and fearlessly lays down his life for His Lord. Therefore, the Lord permits many saints to be martyred so that He might save some of the defiant wicked. This is God's love for sinners! You might think that allowing millions of saints to be martyred to save a few wicked people is unfair, but remember that Jesus willingly laid down His life for each of us. John 3:16 says the Father so loved this world that He even gave up Jesus!

Finally, Jesus allows His saints to be martyred to demonstrate the difference between faith and presumption. Faith loves God and upholds God's Word at all cost. Faith humbly submits to God's demands without regard for the consequences. Faith says the commands of the Creator are greater than the desires of the created. Conversely, presumption believes in God, but it justifies rebellion against God's commands to avoid the consequences. The behaviors of Cain and Abel demonstrate the difference between faith and presumption. Both men built altars to worship God. Abel obeyed the Lord's command by bringing a lamb from his flock. Cain presumed God would accept his offering of fruit. The sinner uses presumption in an attempt to justify his rebellion. Faith occurs when we obey God's command and the price for so doing is significant. Presumption is hostile to faith, and ultimately, presumption attempts to justify the destruction of the faithful.

Chapter 14 – Fifth Seal – Believers Martyred

The Meaning of "Faith in Christ" Badly Distorted Today

The devil has managed to turn "faith in Christ" into "presumptions about Christ." Today, many religious leaders are teaching fables as truth and laymen have deceived themselves into thinking that God is pleased with their actions. (See Isaiah 1-4 for a review of this ever-persistent problem.) The fruit that comes from religious presumption is decadence and blasphemy. The devil's deceptions are clever. He is also a master of gradualism and introduces intellectual concepts that lead to compromises because he knows that over time, any drift from a plain "thus saith the Lord" will bring consequences.

For example, United States' citizens have been wrestling with the abortion issue for forty years and the United States is just as divided today on the subject as when the controversy started. Unfortunately, hardly anyone is addressing the sinful, immoral behavior that produces unwanted babies. There is so much silence about the evils of sexual promiscuity. Immoral behavior is glamorized in television and movies and the media is consumed with nudity and sexual immorality. Sex sells. The devil knows that once an immoral couple conceives, tough choices lie ahead for everyone involved. Something has to be done with the fruit of promiscuity. So, the controversy moves away from the cause of the problem to dealing with the consequences of sinful behavior and there is no solution for sin!

An intellectual assent to truth cannot withstand the purifying fires of persecution. Jesus willingly went to His death because of the faith He exercised in His Father each day. When Jesus arrived at the Garden of Gethsemane, His faith in His Father was strong. Jesus asked the Father to remove the cup of martyrdom from His lips, but it was the Father's will that Jesus die and Jesus accepted His Father's will. Similarly, many martyrs will pray for deliverance, but they will submit to death because it is Jesus' will. This is why the Bible says, **"This calls for patient endurance and faithfulness on the part of the saints."** (Revelation 13:10)

The Identity of the Altar

"I saw under the altar the souls of those who had been slain because of the Word of God and the testimony they had maintained." (Revelation 6:9) John saw the souls of martyrs located under

Chapter 14 – Fifth Seal – Believers Martyred

an altar in Heaven when Jesus broke the fifth seal. The altar mentioned in the fifth seal refers to the bronze Altar of Burnt Offering. You may recall, this altar was located in the courtyard of the Earthly tabernacle (Exodus 40:6), while the golden Altar of Incense was located inside the tabernacle, near the veil. (Exodus 40:5; Leviticus 16:12) Since the golden Altar of Incense is specifically mentioned in Revelation 8:3, this has led some people to assume the altar mentioned in the fifth seal is also the golden Altar of Incense. But we discover the true identity of the altar by comparing it with the Altar of Burnt Offering in the earthly temple. (Hebrews 8:1-5) Notice this text: **"Present your burnt offerings on the altar of the Lord your God, both the meat and the blood. The blood of your sacrifices must be poured beside the altar of the Lord your God, but you may eat the meat."** (Deuteronomy 12:27, See also Leviticus 5:9; 8:15.) This text indicates that the priest was to pour the blood of animal sacrifices into a container beneath the Altar of Burnt Offering in the earthly temple. At the end of each day, the blood was taken outside the camp and buried. In the earthly temple, all sacrifices were offered on the Altar of Burnt Offering and no animal was sacrificed on the Altar of Incense. Therefore, no blood was stored beside or near the earthly Altar of Incense. Because blood is only used with the Altar of Burnt Offering on Earth, references to blood on the altar during the fifth seal obviously must refer to the Heavenly bronze Altar of Burnt Offering.

The souls of the martyrs were represented to John as being underneath the Altar of Burnt Offering because their blood represents human sacrifices for the cause of Christ. The Bible says they were slain because of their faithfulness to the Word of God and the testimony they maintained. Remember the campaign to translate and distribute the Bible that began with the second seal. A large sword, the sword of truth, was placed in the rider's hand and Bible translation and distribution would eventually cause men to kill each other. If we properly put these pieces together, we find that the breaking of the fifth seal is the fulfilling of the second seal. The Bible says the souls under the altar were slain because of *the Word of God*.

During the Great Tribulation, God will have people who stand on the Bible and the Bible alone as the basis for their faith in God. Ironically, a time is coming when people on Earth will regard everyone who obeys God's Word to be God's enemy because Lucifer will appear on Earth and masquerade as Almighty God. (See Appendix B for a discussion on this topic.) Because the saints will refuse to worship this glorious imposter of Jesus, the devil will insist "God's enemies" be killed. **"He [the devil] was given power [from God] to give breath [life] to the image of the first beast [a theocracy], so that it could speak [and make laws] and cause all who refused to worship the image to be killed."** (Revelation 13:15, insertions mine) Jesus warned His disciples, **"All this I have told you so that you will not go astray. They will put you out of the synagogue; in fact, a time is coming when anyone who kills you will think he is offering a service to God. They will do such things because they have not known the Father or me. I have told you this, so that when the time comes you will remember that I warned you."** (John 16:1-4)

The Problem with a Pre-Tribulation Rapture

The fifth seal presents a problem for people who believe in a pre-tribulation rapture. Advocates of a pre-tribulation rapture believe that they are worthy of escaping the suffering of the Great Tribulation because they "believe in Christ." This is a foolish idea. James wrote, **"You believe that there is one God. Good! Even the demons believe that – and shudder."** (James 2:19) Believing there is a God is one thing, but obeying God's commands even to the point of death is quite another.

Currently, a large part of the world does not know about Jesus. Many people who have heard about Jesus reject the idea that He is Deity, the Creator of everything in Heaven and on Earth. (Colossians 1:16) Earth's population is exploding faster than the gospel can travel. This means billions of people have not thoughtfully considered that Jesus will soon return, destroy Earth, and establish His eternal kingdom. Even worse, billions of people cannot consider such a gospel because they are prisoners of culture, language, religion, and ignorance. These poor people should not be punished and persecuted for years while raptured saints are safe and secure, playing their harps in Heaven. It would not be fair for Jesus to torment all of the unsaved with a Great Tribulation and also maintain that Christians are responsible for proclaiming and demonstrating the gospel to the unsaved. (Matthew 28:19,20)

Who has the greater guilt: The unsaved who could not hear the gospel because Christians did not come to their village, or Christians who chose a fine paying job at home instead of traveling to remote villages to share the gospel? The "great escape" (pre-tribulation rapture) is only plausible when presumption has displaced faith in Christ. If Jesus, our Lord and Master, came to Earth to suffer and die for us, His servants should do no less for Him. Jesus said, **"Remember the words I spoke to you: No servant is greater than his master.' If they persecuted me, they will persecute you also. If they obeyed my teaching, they will obey yours also. They will treat you this way because of my name, for they do not know the One who sent me."** (John 15:20,21)

Souls under the Altar / Doctrine of Soul Sleep

Many Christians use the fifth seal to prove the doctrine of soul sleep is a bogus doctrine. However, we have to remember the elements that Jesus revealed to John are representations instead of realities when we study the book of Revelation. For example, the Lamb having seven horns and seven eyes can only be Jesus. The four living creatures riding four horses that go into all the Earth can only be the Holy Spirit. The angel king of the Abyss that commands millions of locusts can only be Lucifer and his angels.

God showed John the souls of martyrs under the Altar of Burnt Offering in Heaven because they represent people who were "sacrificed" on the altar to save other people. Similarly, priests in the tabernacle collected blood from sacrifices in a jar below the Altar of Burnt Offering. The doctrine of soul sleep teaches that when a person dies, his soul ceases to exist. **"For every living soul belongs to me, the father as well as the son – both alike belong to me. The soul who sins is the one who will die."** (Ezekiel 18:4) When Jesus judges the dead, He examines each life record and determines each person's eternal destiny. So, all dead people are awaiting a resurrection, either the first resurrection when Jesus returns at the second coming or the second resurrection at the end of the 1,000 years. (John 6:39,40; 1 Thessalonians 4:16-18; Revelation 20:5) The souls of Abel, Stephen, Paul, and millions of other martyrs are not located under the Altar of Burnt Offering in Heaven. Dead souls are not burning in Hell, either. Furthermore, the fifth seal has yet to be opened so the souls of those martyred during the fifth seal should not be confused with people who have been martyred through the ages. The souls under the Altar are a representation; they represent people who will die for Jesus after He breaks the fifth seal.

An apocalyptic prophecy rule that I use is "Apocalyptic language can be literal, symbolic, or analogous. To reach the intended meaning of

Chapter 14 – Fifth Seal – Believers Martyred

apocalyptic prophecy, the student must consider: (a) the context, (b) the use of parallel language elsewhere in the Bible, and (c) relevant statements in the Bible which define the symbol if an element is thought to be symbolic." This rule mandates that we consider parallel language as demonstrated in the following passage: **"Now Cain said to his brother Abel, 'Let's go out to the field.' And while they were in the field, Cain attacked his brother Abel and killed him. Then the Lord said to Cain, 'Where is your brother Abel?' 'I do not know,' he replied. 'Am I my brother's keeper?' The Lord said, 'What have you done? Listen! Your brother's blood cries out to me from the ground.' "** (Genesis 4:8-10) Of course, Abel's blood was not talking to God, but Abel's innocent blood that was spilled spoke volumes to God! God saw Abel's blood on the ground and its presence cried out for justice. Therefore, the Lord punished Cain for the murder of his brother. (Genesis 4:11-16)

This is the point of the fifth seal. John saw souls under the altar and their location under the altar meant they were sacrifices for the cause of Christ. Like Abel's blood, the blood of these martyrs cried out in a loud voice for relief and revenge saying, **" 'How long, Sovereign Lord, holy and true, until you judge the inhabitants of the Earth and avenge our blood?'** [Then, God told the martyrs,] **. . . to wait a little longer, until the number of their fellow servants and brothers who were to be killed as they had been was completed."** (Revelation 6:10,11, insertion mine)

God gave us the knowledge of the fifth seal in advance so that when the martyrdom begins, we can know that Jesus is faithfully following the Father's plan. Jesus is intimately aware of each martyr's situation and He is meticulously counting the quantity of martyrs sacrificed. Long ago, the Father set a specific number of saints that He would sacrifice to save wicked people who will wake up at the last minute and come to their senses.

The Setting for the Fifth Seal

To better appreciate the fifth seal, consider the setting on Earth when martyrdom begins. About two and a half years after the Great Tribulation begins, God will send a fifth judgment (also called the fifth trumpet) to impact Earth. He will release Lucifer, the devil, and his angels, from the Abyss (the spirit world). (Please see Appendix B.) At this point in time, almost everyone will have heard Jesus' gospel (the terms and conditions of salvation), but many people will have refused to love the truth and be saved. This is why God will release the devil.

When the Lord releases the devil and his angels from the spirit world, they will appear physically all over Earth. The devil will masquerade as Almighty God and millions of the devil's angels will join him. Jesus permits the devil to do this because the wicked have thus far, rejected Christ's authority. Paul wrote about this event saying, **"They perish because they refused to love the truth and so be saved. For this reason God sends them a powerful delusion so that they will believe the lie and so that all will be condemned who have not believed the truth but have delighted in wickedness."** (2 Thessalonians 2:10-12)

When people refuse to obey the eternal gospel and worship Jesus and refuse to submit to Christ's authority after the 144,000 has presented the clearest evidences of His will, and defiantly refuse to accept the Holy Spirit's urging, there is nothing that Jesus can do to save people. So Jesus releases the Antichrist – Lucifer, "the destroyer" – from the Abyss. (Revelation 9:1,11) The devil's physical presence, with power and radiance, changes everything on Earth. Human beings will have only two choices: Obey God or obey Lucifer. No other options exist. The devil's physical appearing will force *undecided* people to make a firm decision. When the devil commands people to worship him, the question in their minds will be who will defy him? Thus, the conflict between Christ and the Antichrist will narrow down to the same question that Elijah asked Israel on Mt. Carmel: **"How long will you waver between two opinions?"** (1 Kings 18:21)

About five months before Jesus breaks the fifth seal, the devil will appear and his angels will torment the people who refuse to worship Lucifer, but they are not allowed to kill a single person. **"They** [Lucifer's angels] **were not given power to kill them, but only to torture them for five months. And the agony they suffered was like that of the sting of a scorpion when it strikes a man. During those days men will seek death, but will not find it; they will long to die, but death will elude them."** (Revelation 9:5,6, insertion mine) For five months, the devil will intimidate and torture people into submission. Then, Jesus breaks the fifth seal and the sixth trumpet judgment arrives simultaneously. Most of the people on Earth will have made

Chapter 14 – Fifth Seal – Believers Martyred

their decision whether to worship Christ or the Antichrist, but a few wicked people will remain undecided.

When the sixth trumpet sounds, the devil will set up a worldwide theocracy. He will rule the world as King of kings and Lord of lords. Jesus will allow four powerful demons to be released to move on the hearts and emotions of wicked people. The devil will attempt to kill everyone who refuses to obey and worship him. Lucifer's forces will kill two groups of people; those who rebel against Lucifer's authority and the saints who refuse to worship the devil. This is when the martyrdom of the fifth seal occurs: **"And the four angels who had been kept ready for this very hour and day and month and year were released to kill a third of mankind. The number of the mounted troops was two hundred million. I heard their number."** (Revelation 9:15,16)

There are a few profound issues we should consider. First, the Father foreknows the number of martyrs that will be required to save the most people. When the last person on Earth chooses to make his decision for Christ, the martyrdom stops and the seventh trumpet sounds. **"But at that time your people – everyone whose name is found written in the Book** [of Life] **will be delivered** [from martyrdom]." (Daniel 12:1, insertions mine) Jesus will declare: **"Let him who does wrong continue to do wrong; let him who is vile continue to be vile; let him who does right continue to do right; and let him who is holy continue to be holy."** (Revelation 22:11)

The second issue is even more profound. It is hard to comprehend that millions of saints will be martyred to benefit a few people who will choose salvation at the last minute. For example, if ten million saints are sacrificed to produce ten converts to Christ during the last moments of grace, then Jesus considers the sacrifice worth it. This shows the value that Jesus places on each human being. When God's children begin to understand that ten million martyrs are worth as few as ten converts to Jesus, we faintly begin to realize what the Father gave the world when He gave us Jesus. Jesus' sacrifice is of greater value than the sum total of the human race! **"God so loved the world that he gave his one and only Son, that whoever believes in him shall not perish but have eternal life. For God did not send his Son into the world to condemn the world, but to save the world through Him."** (John 3:16,17)

There is a third profound issue that we should consider. After killing one-third of the human race, the devil gains the dominion over mankind he has wanted from the day that Adam and Eve sinned. Jesus allows the devil to kill one-third of mankind so that for a short time, the universe can watch a very powerful sinner lacking infinite love, wisdom, and knowledge operate a government. God's created beings will study the strong contrast between Lucifer's governance and God's governance throughout eternity.

The martyrs cried out to the Lord in a loud voice, **"How long, Sovereign Lord, holy and true, until you judge the inhabitants of the Earth and avenge our blood?"** (Revelation 6:10) The devil's injustice against the saints will be bitter and day after day, the martyrs will cry out for deliverance. However, God tells the martyrs to wait until the number assigned for martyrdom is completed: **"Then each of them [the martyrs] was given a white robe, and they were told to wait a little longer."** (Revelation 6:11)

When the last wicked person surrenders his life to Jesus, the door of mercy closes. The seventh trumpet will sound and the seven bowls will begin. The seven bowls contain the seven last plagues which Jesus will impose on the wicked. He will avenge the torture and persecution of His saints by making the enemies of righteousness and truth pay double. Each person who participates in the persecution and torture of God's children will suffer twice as much as the pain he inflicted. **"Give back to her** [the whore, Lucifer's government] **as she has given; pay her back double for what she has done. Mix her a double portion from her own cup."** (Revelation 18:6)

Summary

Our examination of the fifth seal concludes with the discovery that faith in Jesus means a complete surrender to His will. We must be willing "to go, to be, and to do" all that Jesus commands at any cost, even death. Following Jesus and living by faith is so contrary to our fallen nature. No one likes pain or naturally likes to love his enemies. No one likes to live a selfless life, but Jesus died for us, while we were His enemies. (Romans 5:10) It is difficult to stand alone for what is right, but Jesus stood alone in Pilate's judgment hall for us. (Matthew 27) It is difficult to be completely honest and true, but Jesus came from Heaven and withstood endless scorn to reveal the truth about the Fa-

Chapter 14 – Fifth Seal – Believers Martyred

ther. (John 17) It is difficult to be submissive to the leading of the Holy Spirit, but Jesus was tempted in all points as we are without sinning. (Hebrews 4:15) It is so hard to be different when the pressure builds to "go along to get along." (Matthew 7:13) Living by faith is the most difficult experience known to the human race. Living in presumption is so much easier. Ancient Israel, the Catholic Church, and Protestantism failed due to presumption. When a majority of people in any religious organization displaces faith with presumption, that religious system becomes a house of darkness. (Matthew 23:27)

The gospel of Jesus is far more than an intellectual assent to truth, instead it reveals our true position and condition before God. Jesus' gospel reveals our need for a Savior and through the gospel, he offers us power to be an overcomer. Accepting Jesus' gospel in our lives seems to require the impossible, but we can overcome sin through the power of Christ. In fact, the fifth seal teaches that many will overcome their love for life through faith! Through faith, we can do all kinds of things. **"I can do everything through him who gives me strength."** (Philippians 4:13) Paul also wrote, **"I am not ashamed of the gospel, because it is the power of God for the salvation of everyone who believes: first for the Jew, then for the Gentile. For in the gospel a righteousness from God is revealed, a righteousness that is by faith from first to last, just as it is written: The righteous will live by faith.' "** (Romans 1:16-17) The gospel of Jesus reveals that He gives us grace and strength to do the impossible if we are willing to submit to God's will! (2 Corinthians 12:9) In fact, Jesus will give us strength and peace when the time comes to go to our death for Christ if that is God's will for us. (Revelation 13:10) Jesus saved us by His faith and He will save us by our faith!

The study of the fifth seal has allowed us to examine the sharp difference between faith and presumption. The drama of martyrdom completes the story. By understanding the fifth seal, we are now in an excellent position to understand the message that came when Jesus broke the first seal. Now, we see where faith in Jesus will take us. The fifth seal allows us to see "around the bend." We can see why Jesus needs people who will put complete faith in Him so He can use our life and our death (if/as necessary), to save those around us! The fifth seal illumines the meaning of salvific faith and unmasks the deception of presumption. People who live by faith are partakers of divine power! **"For everyone** born of God overcomes the world. This is the victory that has overcome the world, even our faith. Who is it that overcomes the world? Only he who believes that Jesus is the Son of God." (1 John 5:4,5)

Chapter 15
Sixth Seal – Second Coming

"I watched as he opened the sixth seal. There was a great earthquake. The Sun turned black like sackcloth made of goat hair, the whole moon turned blood red, and the stars in the sky fell to Earth, as late figs drop from a fig tree when shaken by a strong wind. The sky receded like a scroll, rolling up, and every mountain and island was removed from its place. Then the kings of the earth, the princes, the generals, the rich, the mighty, and every slave and every free man hid in caves and among the rocks of the mountains. They called to the mountains and the rocks, 'Fall on us and hide us from the face of him who sits on the throne and from the wrath of the Lamb! For the great day of their wrath has come, and who can stand?' " (Revelation 6:12-17)

Seal #6 – The Victory – The Glory of Jesus Exposed

The sixth seal includes a show of divine power, brilliance, and glory that would dwarf the simultaneous detonation of all the world's atomic bombs. When Jesus appears at the Second Coming, He arrives to rescue the righteous and destroy the wicked. Jesus will throw the false prophet (Lucifer) and his crisis government (called Babylon, the beast of Revelation 13:1) alive into a lake of burning sulfur. **"The two of them were thrown alive into the fiery lake of burning sulfur."** (Revelation 19:20)

When Lucifer comes out of the spirit world into the physical world, he will have a special body. Jesus will consume this body completely with fire when he and the wicked who participated in his government are burned up. Currently, Lucifer and his angels live in a spiritual dimension (called the Abyss), but this dimension will change at the fifth trumpet. God will give Lucifer a visible body so that he and his angels can appear physically on Earth. Jesus will destroy Lucifer's visible body at the Second Coming and this will return Lucifer to living in the Abyss, or the spirit world. (Revelation 9:1-3; 20:1-3) Meanwhile, Jesus will destroy the rest of the wicked at the Second Coming with a single command. They will not be burned up. **"The rest of them** [the wicked] **were killed with the sword that came out of the mouth of the rider on the horse, and all the birds gorged themselves on their flesh."** (Revelation 19:21)

Two distinct groups of people will see Jesus appear. The population of Earth at that time will be quite small compared to Earth's current population. Jesus' precious saints that remain alive, clothed with tattered rags, will tremble at His majesty and grandeur as He approaches Earth. They will cry out, **"Surely this is our God; we trusted in him, and he saved us. This is the Lord, we trusted in Him; let us rejoice and be glad in His salvation."** (Isaiah 25:9) A much larger group of people will also tremble at Jesus' majesty and grandeur, but their trembling will not be joyful. This group of people are captives of fear. They fear justice, exposure, death, and righteousness. **"Then the kings of the Earth, the princes, the generals, the rich, the mighty, and every slave and every free man hid in caves and among the rocks of the mountains. They called to the mountains and the rocks, Fall on us and hide us from the face of him who sits on the throne and from the wrath of the Lamb! For the great day of their wrath has come, and who can stand?"** (Revelation 6:15)

I believe Jesus will appear over a period of ten days. The first sign that He will appear will be a small cloud in the eastern sky. (Revelation 16:12) As He comes closer to Earth, the cloud will grow larger and the sky will become more violent until the Rider on the white horse and His army fill the whole sky, from horizon to horizon. **"For as lightning that comes from the east is visible even in the west, so will be the coming of the Son of Man."** (Matthew 24:27) The lightning and thunder within this approaching cloud of glory will grow in intensity until the armies of Earth are paralyzed with fear. **"Every heart will melt and every hand go limp; every spirit will become faint and every knee become as weak as water."** (Ezekiel 21:7) The Second Coming of Jesus will not be a local event. **"Look, He is coming with the clouds, and every eye will see Him, even those who pierced Him; and all the peoples of the Earth will mourn because of Him. So shall it be! Amen."** (Revelation 1:7)

Because Earth rotates on its axis in a counterclockwise direction, any object approaching Earth from space will appear first in the eastern sky. As Earth rotates beneath this swelling cloud of glory, the people

Chapter 15 – Sixth Seal – Second Coming

of Earth will have several days to see Jesus as He approaches. **"At that time the sign of the Son of Man will appear in the sky, and all the nations of the Earth will mourn. They will see the Son of Man coming on the clouds of the sky, with power and great glory."** (Matthew 24:30) **"Blessed is the one who waits for and reaches the end of the 1,335 days** [for he shall see the arrival of Jesus]**."** (Daniel 12:12, insertion mine)

The Great Day of the Lord

King David wrote about the Lord's return saying, **"The Earth trembled and quaked, and the foundations of the mountains shook; they trembled because He was angry. Smoke rose from His nostrils; consuming fire came from His mouth, burning coals blazed out of it. He parted the Heavens and came down; dark clouds were under His feet. He mounted the cherubim and flew; He soared on the wings of the wind. He made darkness his covering, His canopy around him – the dark rain clouds of the sky. Out of the brightness of His presence clouds advanced, with hailstones and bolts of lightning."** (Psalms 18:7-12) Joel also wrote about the great day of the Lord's appearing saying, **"The Lord thunders at the head of His army; His forces are beyond number, and mighty are those who obey His command. The day of the Lord is great; it is dreadful. Who can endure it?"** (Joel 2:11)

When Jesus breaks the sixth seal, Revelation 6:12 indicates there will be a great earthquake. This global earthquake will cause Earth to begin shaking with violent tremors. This earthquake will grow in intensity and disaster, ultimately making islands disappear and leveling the mountains! **"No earthquake like it has ever occurred since man has been on Earth, so tremendous was the quake. . . . Every island fled away and the mountains could not be found."** (Revelation 16:18,20) As this earthquake breaks Earth's crust, Jesus will resurrect a special group of selected people. He will fulfill the promise He made two thousand years ago to resurrect the people who participated in His crucifixion. When Jesus awakes the chief priests and religious rulers from their sleep, their terror and anxiety will be indescribable. When they see the Righteous One they condemned as a blasphemer now sitting beside the Father who lives in unapproachable light, they will be filled with shame and self-loathing. Jesus and the high priest had a conversation on Friday morning, April 7, A.D. 30. **"The high priest said to Him, 'I charge you under oath by the** living God: Tell us if you are the Christ, the Son of God.' 'Yes, it is as you say,' Jesus replied. 'But I say to all of you: In the future you will see the Son of Man sitting at the right hand of the Mighty One and coming on the clouds of Heaven.'" (Matthew 26:63,64) Jesus will even resurrect the Roman soldiers who pierced His body and divided His garments to see the majesty of "The Lamb of God." (Revelation 1:7)

The Father Comes with Jesus

Many people overlook the fact that the Father comes to Earth with Jesus at the second coming! Both the Father and the Son are visible on that day because no one has given more for our redemption than the Father and the Son. Remember what Jesus said to the high priest, **"In the future you will see the Son of Man sitting at the right hand of the Mighty One and coming on the clouds of Heaven."** (Matthew 26:64) Compare this verse with the cry of the wicked, **"They** [the wicked] **called to the mountains and the rocks, 'Fall on us and hide us from [a] the face of Him who sits on the throne** [the Father] **and from the wrath of the Lamb** [the Son]! **For the great day of their** [notice the plural] **wrath has come, and who can stand?"** (Revelation 6:16,17, insertions mine) Also, consider this verse: **"The sixth angel poured out his bowl on the great river Euphrates, and its water was dried up to prepare the way for the kings** [notice the plural] **from the East."** (Revelation 16:12, insertion mine)

Jesus told His accusers that He would be sitting at the right hand of the Father and coming on the clouds of Heaven. Since the Father and the Son are approaching Earth from space and we know they will appear in the east, so it is not difficult to conclude that they are "the Kings from the east." The Father and the Son will appear in a light that will be brighter than a welder's arc. The righteous will tremble with awe and respect, but the wicked will run for cover faster than cockroaches hiding from daylight. Jesus' glory at the Second Coming will eclipse the powerful display of authority that He demonstrated on Mount Sinai. **"When the people saw the thunder and lightning and heard the trumpet** [voice] **and saw the mountain in smoke, they trembled with fear. They stayed at a distance and said to Moses, Speak to us yourself and we will listen. But do not have God speak to us or we will die."'** (Exodus 20:18,19, insertion mine)

Chapter 15 – Sixth Seal – Second Coming

Saints Rescued

Jesus' Second Coming will be marked with power, glory, redemption, and destruction. Jesus will reveal God's wrath against sin and sinners in a never-to-be-forgotten display of sovereign power. Jesus will also reveal God's unfailing love for people who put their faith in Him. I believe Jesus will gather the righteous from Earth to meet Him in the air *after* He has destroyed the wicked with the sharp sword that comes out of His mouth. On Day 1334 of the Great Tribulation, Jesus will put the wicked to death and the righteous will see the wicked people destroyed. **"Only with thine eyes shalt thou behold and see the reward of the wicked."** (Psalms 91:8, KJV) Then, on Day 1335, Jesus will rescue the righteous. **"Blessed is the one who waits for and reaches the end of the 1,335 days. 'As for you [Daniel], go your way till the end. You will rest [in death], and then at the end of the [1335] days you will rise to receive your allotted inheritance.'"** (Daniel 12:12,13) Jesus will raise the dead in Christ to life and then the saints who have managed to survive until the last day will meet in a joyous gathering. The saints will meet together with the Lord in the air. (1 Thessalonians 4:16,17) Perhaps the saints will repeat this song many times. **"They held harps given them by God and sang the song of Moses the servant of God and the song of the Lamb: Great and marvelous are your deeds, Lord God Almighty. Just and true are your ways, King of the ages. Who will not fear you, O Lord, and bring glory to your name? For you alone are holy. All nations will come and worship before you, for your righteous acts have been revealed.'"** (Revelation 15:2-4)

Let us review what Jesus faced when he was here on Earth. He endured false arrest, accusations of blasphemy, torture, humiliation, and death at the hands of wicked men. He experienced subjection and the second death (the penalty for sin) at the hands of the Father. Because Jesus went through these experiences without sinning, He alone is worthy to exonerate the Father's government and redeem man! At the Second Coming, Jesus will show Himself to be Almighty God. He was elevated to this position in 1798 when He was found worthy to receive the Book of Life. There is no one like Him. The Second Coming will be a great epiphany. Jesus, His Eternal Majesty, King of kings and Lord of lords, and the King of Everlasting Glory will be revealed. When we examine Jesus' love, life, and victory over sin, we realize there is no one in the universe like Him. The Father wants the universe to know that Jesus is not a lesser God than Himself so He has implemented a plan to reveal everything about Jesus. What a gracious and generous Father! The members of the Godhead have no jealousy for highest honor. Jesus has the same attributes as the Father and the Father will be delighted with the revelation of Jesus!

The Process of the Second Coming

I like to think of the Second Coming as an inaugural process that takes 1,335 days to complete. The first segment consists of "seven first plagues" and the last segment consists of "seven last plagues."

The Great Tribulation

Many people use Jesus' statement, **"No one knows about that day or hour, not even the angels in heaven, nor the Son, but only the Father."** (Matthew 24:36) to prove that no one knows the day or hour of Christ's return. However, once the Great Tribulation begins, the date of Christ's return will no longer be a secret because Jesus has given us a comprehensive timetable of end time events in the books of Daniel and Revelation. There are eighteen prophetic time periods in the seventeen apocalyptic prophecies in these two books. God provided information about Jesus' return so when the Great Tribulation begins, we will be able to start a countdown clock for His appearing. God has generously given us a countdown clock so that His children will not lose hope!

The book of Revelation outlines five displays of divine power that will occur three times. The first display will mark the beginning of the Great Tribulation:

1. Flashes of lightning
2. Mysterious voices saying things
3. Peals of thunder
4. Global earthquake
5. Fiery hail

Look at the chart on the next page and identify three instances of the letter "X." (Revelation 8:5, 11:19, 16:18)

The first X marks the breaking of the fourth seal. The five physical events will confirm Jesus' sovereignty throughout Earth. The first X marks the point when (a) Jesus' begins to judge the living, (b) the Great

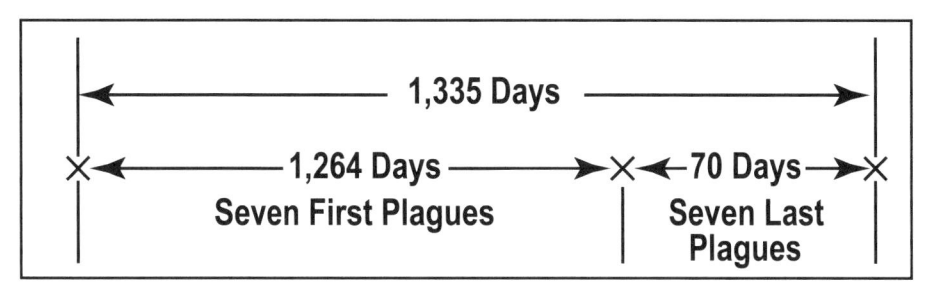

Chapter 15 – Sixth Seal – Second Coming

```
|←————————— 1,335 Days ——————————→|
X|←——— 1,264 Days ———→X←70 Days→|X
 |   Seven First Plagues    |  Seven Last   |
 |                          |    Plagues    |
```

Tribulation begins, and (c) the seven trumpets (seven first plagues) begin. These Devine manifestations will cause all mankind to take notice.

Christ's second display of divine power occurs 1,264 days later. The second X marks the point when (a) Judgment Day ends and (b) the seven bowls (seven last plagues) begin. These events will indicate that Jesus has terminated His intercession for sinners. He has judged mankind and determined who will receive eternal life and who will be destroyed.

The last X marks Jesus' Second Coming. The same five Devine manifestations will be displayed at the Second Coming with much greater intensity and Jesus will end life on Earth. He will slay the wicked by fire or sword and He will take the righteous to Heaven. Jesus will also send Lucifer and his angels back to the abyss (spirit world). No life will exist on Earth for one thousand years so the planet can receive its Sabbath rest; it will be the seventh millennium.

"See, the day of the Lord is coming a cruel day, with wrath and fierce anger – to make the land desolate and destroy the sinners within it. The stars of heaven and their constellations will not show their light. The rising sun will be darkened and the moon will not give its light. I will punish the world for its evil, the wicked for their sins. I will put an end to the arrogance of the haughty and will humble the pride of the ruthless." (Isaiah 13:9-11)

Summary

When Jesus breaks the sixth seal, He will reveal His divine glory that belongs to Him. He will come in the clouds with the Father and they will display unmatched power and authority that words cannot express. Jesus will destroy His enemies and rescue His children. Earth will truly be His footstool. Let us review the process by which Jesus is completely revealed.

Chapter 15 – Sixth Seal – Second Coming

Before sin began in Heaven, Jesus identified closely with the angels by living among them in the form of an angel. His name was Michael, the archangel. (See Appendix A.) Lucifer was the highest and most beautiful of all created beings, but he became jealous of Michael. Lucifer coveted the worship and adoration that belonged to "ordinary looking" Michael. Lucifer became anti-Christ because of jealousy. Over time, one third of the angels listened to Lucifer's lies and deceptions and joined in his rebellion.

Jesus shielded the glory that belonged to Him from view when He lived among the angels. He lived among them as a companion. (Hebrews 1:9) Thousands of years later, when Jesus came to Earth to live among us in the form of a man, His glory was shrouded from view. A few people received Him as Messiah, but most people rejected Him. **"He came to that which was his own, but his own did not receive Him."** (John 1:11) Jesus looked like a very ordinary man with nothing attractive about Him. (Isaiah 53:2) The Father wants all beings to know who Jesus really is so He ordained that Jesus be revealed in seven steps called the seven seals. During the Great Tribulation, Jesus will shroud His glory from mankind until He physically appears at the Second Coming. Jesus does not want His subjects worshiping His power, position, or glory! He does not want to be a superstar or an icon! Jesus wants to live among His created beings so that we can know and love God. When Jesus breaks the sixth seal, God will reveal that Jesus has the same glory and authority as the Father. This explains how and why the Father has put everything in Heaven and on Earth under Jesus' control! (Ephesians 1:9,10)

Artists often depict Jesus on the cross wearing a loincloth because it would be too offensive to show what really happened. The Romans stripped criminals of all their clothing so that their shame would haunt them in the life hereafter. Jesus was willing to bear our shame. He was disrobed and publicly humiliated because He loved us enough to die in our place. Ironically, Jesus will be disrobed once again, but this time, there will be no shame! We will see Jesus for who He is – Almighty God. **"For to us a child is born, to us a son is given, and the government will be on His shoulders. And He will be called Wonderful Counselor, Mighty God, Everlasting Father, Prince of Peace."** (Isaiah 9:6) **"Who is He, this King of glory? The Lord Almighty – He is the King of glory."** (Psalms 24:10) The breaking of the sixth seal extraordinarily reveals the glory of Jesus.

Chapter 16
Seventh Seal – Book of Life Opened

"When he opened the seventh seal, there was silence in Heaven for about half an hour." (Revelation 8:1)

Seal #7 – The Revelation of Jesus Completed – The Deity of Jesus Exposed

Unless a person understands that each series of apocalyptic prophecies progresses in chronological order, he might conclude the seventh seal occurs before the seven trumpets. On the other hand, if a person understands the sixth seal to be Jesus' second coming, he might wonder why the seventh seal would be broken *after* Jesus' second coming. The confusion arises because the book of Revelation disconnects the seventh seal from the previous six seals. Revelation 6 describes the first six seals and Revelation 7 gives the story of the 144,000. Then, the seventh seal is found in Revelation 8! God gives an interesting solution to this question because He is deliberate and purposeful in everything He does!

Apocalyptic prophecy is chronological in nature. Each apocalyptic prophecy has a beginning and ending point in time and events occur in the order given. We see this pattern repeated without exception in Daniel and Revelation seventeen times. This pattern in apocalyptic prophecy resolves many questions. For example, when we study the metal man in Daniel 2, it is easy to identify the chronology. Similarly, when we study the four beasts and the little horn in Daniel 7, we can easily identify the chronology of events. Then in Revelation 6, we can easily identify that the seals occur in chronological order. Jesus was found worthy to receive the Book of Life in 1798, then He broke each seal in chronological order. However, the chronology of each apocalyptic prophecy is not always easy to see.

The first apocalyptic prophecy in Revelation begins with Revelation 4:1 (the beginning point in time for this prophecy is 1798) and the chronological order of this prophecy ends with the sixth seal. The sixth seal is Jesus' second coming in Revelation 6:17 (this is the ending point in time for this prophecy). We know the chronological order of the seven seals prophecy ends with the sixth seal because Revelation 7:1, the next verse after Revelation 6:17, cannot occur after Jesus' second coming.

Chapter 16 – Seventh Seal – Book of Life Opened

So, the chronological order in Revelation is broken at Revelation 7:1 and this forces a new prophecy to begin. In other words, the 144,000 cannot be selected and sealed (the story in Revelation 7) after the kings and generals of the Earth hide in the caves and cry out for the mountains to fall on them (the sixth seal). Therefore, the second prophecy in Revelation begins with Revelation 7:1 and the third prophecy in Revelation regarding the seven trumpets begins with Revelation 8:2. Please take a moment and study the chart below to see how these prophecies align.

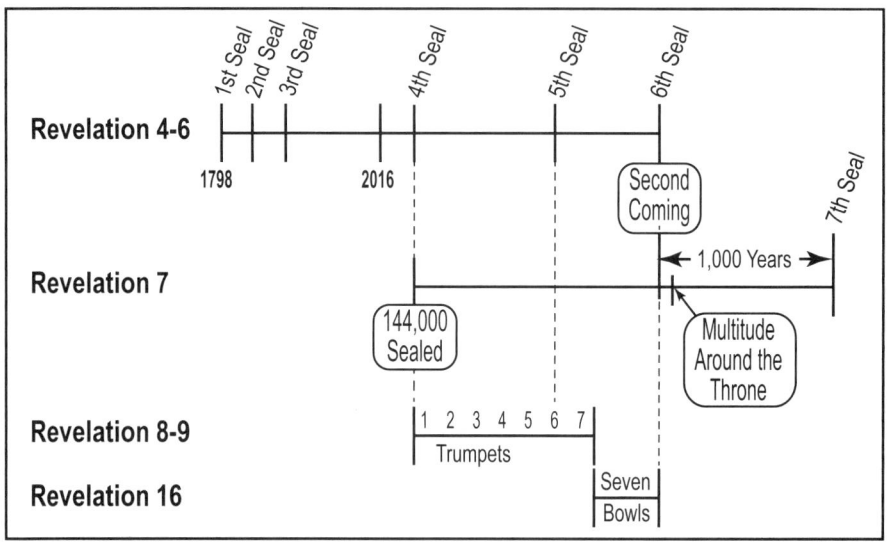

[Chart showing timeline with Revelation 4-6 (1st-6th Seals from 1798, 2016, through Second Coming, 7th Seal after 1,000 Years), Revelation 7 (144,000 Sealed, Multitude Around the Throne), Revelation 8-9 (Trumpets 1-7), Revelation 16 (Seven Bowls)]

Relationships between Revelation's Prophecies

The prophet John did not divide the book of Revelation into chapters and verses. Centuries after John wrote Revelation, scholars divided the Bible into chapters and verses for reference and study and they did not know what to do with the one sentence describing the seventh seal. This sentence does not appear to fit within Revelation 7 which deals with the 144,000 and the numberless multitude and it does not appear to have anything to do with the seven trumpets. Since they could not move the sentence to the end of Revelation 6 so that the seventh seal would follow after the sixth seal, they decided to make this one sentence the first verse in Revelation 8. (To their credit, they did not tamper or alter the order of the text that John wrote! They did not move this one short sentence from its all-important location!)

Please notice that the second prophecy in Revelation (Revelation 7:1 through 8:1) is in chronological order. There are three events in this prophecy.

Chapter 16 – Seventh Seal – Book of Life Opened

A. Jesus selects and seals the 144,000 just before the fourth seal is broken (Revelation 7:1-4)
B. Jesus saves a numberless multitude during the Great Tribulation and takes them to Heaven at the Second Coming. John saw them standing before the throne in Heaven. (Revelation 7:9-14)
C. Jesus breaks the seventh seal. Silence in Heaven. (Revelation 8:1)

Now that you see the chronological order, the explanation of why Jesus breaks the seventh seal 1,000 years after the sixth seal at the end of the millennium might surprise you. Consider these four steps:

1. The Lamb's Book of Life is separate and distinct from the other books in Heaven.
2. The Bible says the Book of Life is opened once, at the end of the one thousand years. **"And I saw the dead, great and small, standing before the throne, and books were opened. Another book was opened, which is the Book of Life. The dead were judged according to what they had done as recorded in the books."** (Revelation 20:12)
3. The Lamb's Book of Life is the book sealed with seven seals. Therefore, the Book of Life can only be opened when the seventh seal is broken.
4. Because the second prophecy in Revelation is given to us in chronological order, the seventh seal can only be broken open *after* the numberless multitude have been taken to Heaven and are seen standing around the throne. Consider the timing in this verse: **"After this I looked and there before me was a great multitude that no one could count, from every nation, tribe, people and language, standing before the throne and in front of the Lamb. They were wearing white robes and were holding palm branches in their hands. . . . Then one of the elders asked me, 'These in white robes – who are they, and where did they come from?' I answered, 'Sir, you know.' And he said, 'These are they who have come out of the great tribulation; they have washed their robes and made them white in the blood of the Lamb.' "** (Revelation 7:9,13,14)

The saints described in verses 9-14 are not the saints from all of the ages. The saints in Revelation 7:9-14 will come out of great tribulation and they will stand around the throne indicating there will be a huge harvest of souls at the end of the world! After this event, John saw the seventh seal opened. (Revelation 8:1). This forces the timing of the seventh seal to the end of the 1,000 years because the Lamb's Book of Life is only opened at the end of the 1,000 years. Once Jesus breaks the seventh seal, everything the Father wrote in the Book of Life will be exposed. For the first time in the history of the universe, the Father will permit everyone to see this solemn fact: **"If anyone's name was not found written in the Book of Life, he was thrown into the lake of fire."** (Revelation 20:15)

Great White Throne Judgment

At the end of the thousand years the holy city, New Jerusalem, will descend from Heaven with all of the saints inside. (Revelation 21:2) After the city comes to rest, the wicked will come to life from their graves. (Revelation 20:5) The wicked, from Cain on down to the Second Coming will number in the tens of billions. Remember that most of these people did not see the Second Coming because they were asleep in their graves. On this day of resurrection, two great classes of people will be present. The saints, a thousand years older, but free of the aging process and any deformity, will see the wicked's miserable and degenerate condition. The wicked will rise from their graves just as they went in. The wicked will be astonished as they study the gleaming walls of New Jerusalem. They will see family members, friends, and individuals who they regarded as poor, weak, unsophisticated, and uneducated. Generals, kings, presidents, scholars, statesmen, tycoons, religious leaders, and greedy employers will be found standing outside the city. (Matthew 7:14; 19:24)

Jesus will resurrect the wicked for three reasons:

1. Jesus will confront each wicked person with the result of His investigation. Jesus will have a personal face to face meeting with each created being. This will be possible through the ministry of the Holy Spirit. Jesus will do this because He loved every wicked person and He wants every wicked person to know that He personally investigated and weighed the conduct of each sinner's life. Jesus wants every wicked person to know exactly why He could not grant him eternal life. To put His investigation and decision beyond controversy, Jesus will open the books of records and present the evidence to each person. Each wicked person will see the record of his life. Each wicked person will see the unvarnished truth just as God saw it. **"For God will bring every deed into judgment, including every hidden thing, whether it is good**

Chapter 16 – Seventh Seal – Book of Life Opened   191

or evil." (Ecclesiastes 12:14) **"For we must all appear before the judgment seat of Christ, that each one may receive what is due him for the things done while in the body, whether good or bad."** (2 Corinthians 5:10) Jesus will deny eternal life to the wicked because they have blasphemed the Holy Spirit and rejected God's voice in their hearts. (Matthew 12:31,32) After reviewing the evidence and hearing Jesus' decision, the wicked will kneel down and confess, **"In the Lord alone are righteousness and strength."** (Isaiah 45:24) Unlike Esau, who regretted selling his birthright for a dish of food, the hearts of the wicked will not be changed. (Hebrews 12:17)

2. Jesus will resurrect the wicked so that they can provide restitution. During the millennium, the saints will have reigned with Jesus. This means that the saints will sit in judgment with the Judge of Mankind. They will be required to go over the records of the wicked and determine the amount of restitution each wicked person must pay. **"Do you not know that the saints will judge the world? And if you are to judge the world, are you not competent to judge trivial cases? Do you not know that we will judge angels? How much more the things of this life!"** (1 Corinthians 6:2,3) **"I saw thrones on which were seated those who had been given authority to judge. And I saw the souls of those who had been beheaded because of their testimony for Jesus and because of the word of God."** (Revelation 20:4)

This may shock some people, but the golden rule is ironclad and it cannot be violated. As you did unto others, the same will be done unto you, with additional penalties. Jesus said, **"For in the same way you judge others, you will be judged, and with the measure you use, it will be measured to you."** (Matthew 7:2) The doctrine of restitution is a marvelous study. Basically, it teaches that whenever we do wrong, God requires that we make every effort to restore the damage and make it right. If we refuse to make things right, God will see to it that restitution is extracted from us at the appointed time, even if we are unwilling to repay. This is why Paul wrote, **"Do not take revenge, my friends, but leave room for God's wrath, for it is written: 'It is mine to avenge; I will repay,' says the Lord."** (Romans 12:19) During the millennium, the saints, many of whom were victims of crimes and predatory behavior, will determine the amount of suffering which their wicked assailants must repay and God will extract restitution from them in a lake of burning sulfur. In many cases, the wicked will burn and suffer according to the decisions made by their victims. God's law demands it.

Contrary to what most Christians believe today, God does not forgive or ignore sin, instead he transfers the guilt of our sin away from us. In God's economy, sin always requires atonement. Only after the wicked have totally paid restitution will they be allowed to perish. Many wicked people have committed horrible crimes and gone to their grave thinking they got away with murder. They will be surprised when they learn they have been awakened from the sleep of death to provide restitution for their deeds by suffering. The saints will also pass judgment on Lucifer and each demon. Jesus will completely expose the culpability of Lucifer and his demons and the saints will judge them during the millennium. In the end, justice will be served. The wrath of law will be satisfied.

3. The third reason that God will resurrect the wicked at the end of the 1,000 years is because Jesus breaks the seventh seal! This will be the only moment in the history of the universe when everyone whom God has given life will be alive. Billions of people and angels will be present. The wicked will be outside the Holy city with Lucifer and his angels, and the saints will be positioned inside the city with all of the angels of God. What a meeting! At this point in time, Jesus has something to say to everyone (literally to everyone who has ever lived).

I understand that Jesus will break the seventh seal and every being will look into the sky at what appears like a movie screen for about half an hour. A giant movie will play on this screen and everyone will see who Jesus fully is. The Father has ordained that Jesus would only be revealed when every creature stands before Him. Jesus will show angels and humans alike that He is an Eternal God, a member of the eternal Trinity, and possesses every attribute of the Father. Jesus is responsible for the creation of everyone at the meeting and that He was not willing that anyone should perish. He will explain that He was willing to die for any angel or human being before He created them. Jesus will reveal His love for God's children to every being that draws breath. This touching revelation will take half an hour. Everyone will begin to understand the depth and magnitude of God's love and that Jesus is fully God. Everyone

Chapter 16 – Seventh Seal – Book of Life Opened   193

will see scenes from the Creation, the Fall, the Redemption, and the Restoration and everyone will be humbled into bowing before the most powerful force in the universe: Divine Love.

After Jesus breaks the seventh seal and the half hour presentation ends, He will then show everyone what the Father knew from the beginning. Jesus will show that the books of records and the Book of Life are identical. The choices of angels and humans alike were recorded as they happened and even though the Father foreknew the rise and price of sin, He authorized the creation of life anyway. (Hebrews 1:2) After the Book of Life has been opened, Jesus will confirm seven eternal truths before the assembled host:

1. **The Father** has perfect foreknowledge. He will not, under any circumstances, use His foreknowledge to manipulate the choices and affections of His children. He treats and respects His finite children on the basis of infinite love.

2. **The Father** is love. Even though He foreknew the rise of sin and the staggering price of redemption, He chose to have children and gave them freedom anyway.

3. **The Father** gives free will and the power of choice to His children. Even though He foreknew which individuals would be saved and which would not, He gave everyone the freedom to love and obey Him or to hate and rebel against Him.

4. **The Father's** ways are not deemed righteous because He declares Himself to be righteous. Instead, God's ways are deemed righteous because He has demonstrated perfect righteousness during the presence of sin and rebellion. The Book of Life will prove that the Godhead only uses omnipotence, omniscience, and omnipresence to ensure the eternal rule of the law of love throughout an expanding universe. The Godhead does not use these incredible powers to maintain an elevated position in the universe.

5. **The Father** is unbelievably humble and selfless. Jesus is a perfect mirror of the Father. Jesus was willing to forfeit His eternal existence so that Adam and Eve and their offspring might have the possibility of recovering all that was lost through sin. The Father would have done the same thing if He served the universe as the Creator.

6. **The Father's** government is based on the eternal principles of righteousness and justice. Because the Father lives within the boundaries of unchangeable laws, only God could save sinners. The plan of salvation required perfect blood to transfer the sinner's guilt to the scapegoat. A perfect life was required to restore the righteousness that sinners need. Jesus met and satisfied both requirements.

7. **The Father** ordained long ago after the knowledge of good and evil has become universal, people redeemed from the penalty of sin will use their experience and influence to thwart sin if another event should arise.

When the whole universe sees these seven truths, the saints will fall on their faces saying over and over, "God is too good and too great to describe."

What a Savior! Jesus will exonerate the Father's government and redeem sinners from their sins! What a God! The angels will rejoice at this revelation of Jesus as they see the contents of the Book of Life. Everyone who will be there will know that the Father has revealed His beautiful and selfless character through Jesus. The saints and angels will fall on their faces before Jesus praising Him for His goodness and generosity. Saints and the angels of God will declare again and again that worthy is the Lamb! The Godhead can be totally trusted. The Godhead is worthy of nonnegotiable faith.

The Dark Side

As saints and angels of God rejoice over the contents of the Book of Life, Lucifer, his demons and the wicked multitude will be moved to anger. They cannot blame anyone but themselves for their hopeless position outside the city. They cannot do anything to save themselves from the suffering that they are about to receive. As they gaze on the glorious holy city and the rejoicing saints inside, they feel darkness, jealousy, and despair. Their hatred for God rises and Lucifer seizes the moment. He assumes command and marshals the mighty host to make war against Jesus, inspiring them to take the city by force. The nature of false religion is to do whatever it takes to save self: **"They marched across the breadth of the Earth and surrounded the camp of God's people, the city He loves. But fire came down from Heaven and devoured them. And the devil, who deceived them, was thrown into the lake of burning sulfur, where the beast and the false prophet had been thrown. They will be tormented day**

Chapter 16 – Seventh Seal – Book of Life Opened

and night for ever and ever." (Revelation 20:9,10) This torment, which the wicked receive day and night forever and ever, reflects the demands of restitution. The wicked will suffer until their debt is paid in full. **"But the cowardly, the unbelieving, the vile, the murderers, the sexually immoral, those who practice magic arts, the idolaters and all liars their place will be in the fiery lake of burning sulfur. This is the second death."** (Revelation 21:8)

"Surely the day is coming; it will burn like a furnace. All the arrogant and every evildoer will be stubble, and that day that is coming will set them on fire," says the Lord Almighty. 'Not a root or a branch will be left to them. But for you who revere my name, the sun of righteousness will rise with healing in its wings. And you will go out and leap like calves released from the stall. Then you will trample down the wicked; they will be ashes under the soles of your feet on the day when I do these things,' says the Lord Almighty." (Malachi 4:1-3)

When Jesus completely annihilates the wicked, He will create a new Heaven and a new Earth. (Revelation 21:5) Then, after using his creative abilities, Jesus will do something even greater! **"Then the end will come, when He hands over the kingdom to God the Father after He has destroyed all dominion, authority and power. For He must reign until He has put all his enemies under his feet. The last enemy to be destroyed is death."** (1 Corinthians 15:24-26) Amazingly, Jesus will give His great authority as Almighty God to the Father so that the Father can be everything. Jesus will relinquish the throne and return to living among His created beings as one of us. This action reveals the true nature and character of God. **God is love.** Let's shout it: GOD IS LOVE!

Summary

This book has been lengthy, but I hope you have found the information helpful. The next time you read it through, the entire story will make more sense because you will know the end from the beginning. The story of the seven seals is inspiring and I am very grateful for the opportunity to share the results of my investigation with you. The first apocalyptic prophccy in the book of Revelation is dedicated to the seven seals because there is no grander topic than the revealing of all that Jesus fully is. He is worthy to receive worship, praise, honor, strength, glory, wisdom, and power. Even in our wildest dreams, no angel or

Chapter 16 – Seventh Seal – Book of Life Opened

man could have invented a God with the awesome attributes of Jesus! Even though He is more than we can possibly understand, we can love Him with all of our hearts.

The Father wrote the Book of Life before Jesus created life. The Father prerecorded the history of angels and humans and then sealed the book with seven seals so that no one could view the contents of the book until the appropriate time. In 1798, Jesus was found worthy to receive the book and begin breaking the seals. When Jesus breaks each seal, a new revelation about Him occurs:

Seal 1: The salvation of Jesus
Seal 2: The teachings of Jesus
Seal 3: The judgment bar of Jesus
Seal 4: The authority of Jesus
Seal 5: The faith of Jesus
Seal 6: The glory of Jesus
Seal 7: The Deity of Jesus

We are now waiting for Jesus to break the fourth seal. This seal marks the beginning of the Great Tribulation. The stage is set and the hour is almost here for Earth's final curtain. For six thousand years, Earth has been a theater of conflict between good and evil. The drama of sin is almost over. We are very close to the Second Coming. The next revelation of Jesus will be awful and awesome at the same time. A great declaration of His sovereign powers will soon occur. (Remember the five physical phenomena?)

At the end of the seventh millennium, the drama of sin will close when the seventh seal is broken and Jesus exposes the contents of the Book of Life. Because the Book of Life will be found to be identical with the books of record, the Father will silence the charge that He used His foreknowledge to manipulate the choices of His children and the outcome of events for eternity. The universe will see that even though God knows everything and has all power, He can be explicitly trusted to respect the power of choice that He grants to each of His children. When Jesus breaks the seventh seal, every question about the Father's integrity, character, and government will be resolved because an open Book of Life and the books of records will say everything that needs to be said.

Appendix A
Monotheism versus Tritheism

The Bible teaches that Jesus Christ is a separate, distinct, coeternal member of Deity. Jesus is not the Father and the Father is not Jesus. Both deities are separate persons having separate wills. Jesus said, **"For I have come down from heaven not to do my will but to do the will of him who sent me."** (John 6:38) Jesus and the Father are equals in substance. The Father calls Jesus, "God." **"But about the Son He** [the Father] **says, 'Your throne, O God, will last for ever and ever, and righteousness will be the scepter of your kingdom. You have loved righteousness and hated wickedness; therefore God** [Jesus]**, your God** [the Father]**, has set you above your companions by anointing you with the oil of joy.' He also says, 'In the beginning, O Lord, you laid the foundations of the Earth, and the Heavens are the work of your hands. They will perish, but you remain; they will all wear out like a garment.' "** (Hebrews 1:8-11, insertions mine)

The apostle Paul clearly equates and separates the Deity of Jesus from the Deity of the Father: **"Your attitude should be the same as that of Christ Jesus: Who, being in very nature God, did not consider equality with God something to be grasped, but made Himself nothing, taking the very nature of a servant, being made in human likeness. And being found in appearance as a man, He humbled himself and became obedient to death – even death on a cross! Therefore God** [the Father] **exalted Him** [Jesus] **to the highest place and gave Him the name that is above every name, that at the name of Jesus every knee should bow, in Heaven and on Earth and under the Earth, and every tongue confess that Jesus Christ is Lord, to the glory of God the Father."** (Philippians 2:5-11, insertions mine)

By definition, if you can accept the idea that the Father is not Jesus and both persons are Deity you are a polytheist. Do not be alarmed. The Bible teaches tritheism. The Bible teaches there are three and only three Gods who are united in love. All other gods are false. (Exodus 20:3; Isaiah 44:6) In the Old Testament, the three Gods seem to be one God. Then, in the New Testament we begin to see there are three Gods. Finally, in the book of Revelation we can confirm there are three separate, distinct, coeternal Gods. Because the three Gods are so closely united, they appear as one God. Because Jesus is the Word, the voice of God, He often uses a singular voice because they are one in purpose, plan, and action. Honoring one of them is the same as worshiping all three. (John 5:22,23; Matthew 12:31,32; Matthew 28:19)

The Bible teaches the Holy Spirit is a God. He is a separate, distinct, coeternal member of Deity. The Holy Spirit has a will of His own. The Holy Spirit is not the Father or Jesus. The Holy Spirit can hear and speak on His own. He is equal with the Father and Jesus in substance. There has been a great deal of controversy over the nature of the Godhead and I hope this study will resolve some difficult questions.

Three Gods in One

Three separate members of Deity functioning as one God can be compared to a husband and wife (two separate individuals) functioning as one flesh. (Genesis 2:24; Matthew 19:6) Many Christians believe in God the Father, God the Son, and God the Holy Spirit without thinking through what they really believe. Many Christians reject tritheism (three Gods) without first considering what they are rejecting. They believe the Bible teaches monotheism, that is, there is one God who manifests Himself as three persons. Therefore, they reason that if a person worships Jesus or the Holy Spirit, he is actually worshiping the Father because the Father is in Jesus and the Father is in the Holy Spirit and all together, these three persons are the Father. The question of whether there are three separate coeternal Gods or one God manifesting Himself as one person dates back to the beginning of the Christian church.

The Nature of Jesus in Church History

During Christ's ministry on Earth, the Pharisees found Jesus' teachings to be blasphemous because Jesus claimed to be the Son of God and this logically made Him an equal with God. (See John 5:18.) The Pharisees were incensed because Judaism is strictly a "one God" religion. Naturally, Judaism rejects the possibility of three separate coeternal Gods and Judaism also rejects the possibility of a Godhead where one God manifests Himself as three persons. Therefore, Jesus seriously challenged Israel's monotheistic tradition when he began His miracle working ministry in A.D. 27.

Appendix A – Monotheism Versus Tritheism 199

The first converts to Christ's teachings were Jews (His disciples). During His ministry, the number of Jewish believers grew, but still remained a small percentage of the population. Then, a few days after His ascension, 3,000 Jews were baptized into Christ at Pentecost. (Acts 2) As the number of Jewish converts swelled, they became divided over the nature of Jesus. Some Jewish converts believed that Jesus was a separate God, separate and distinct from the Father. Others believed that God created Jesus, and still others believed that Jesus was an incarnation of the Father. Years later, after Paul converted to Christianity, Gentiles joined the Christian Church in increasing numbers and seeds of a stubborn controversy began to sprout. Gentiles generally came from polytheistic backgrounds and arguments between monotheistic biased Jews and polytheistic biased Gentiles began over the nature of Jesus and the Godhead. The core of their argument was whether Christians should be monotheistic or tritheistic.

Conflict over the nature of Jesus and the Godhead roiled the church for several centuries and many ideas and divisions followed. During the fifth and sixth centuries A.D., the church at Rome gained religious and political powers. Once the Catholic church held sufficient standing within the Holy Roman Empire, the church moved to "forever settle and end" the argument over the nature of Jesus and the Godhead. The Eleventh Synod of Toledo (in Spain) in A.D. 675 formally declared the Church's position on the Trinity. In brief, church leaders said: "We confess and we believe that the holy and indescribable Trinity, Father, Son, and Holy Spirit is one only God in His nature, a single substance, a single nature, a single majesty and power. . . . The three are one, as a nature, that is, not as person. Nevertheless, these three persons are not to be considered separable, since we believe that no one of them existed or at any time effected anything before the other, after the other, or without the other." (Source: Fr. John A. Hardon, S.J., Catholic Doctrine on the Holy Trinity)

With this declaration, the Roman Catholic Church modified the strict monotheism of the Jews. Abbot Joachim (1135-1202) was an influential monk who promoted the idea that the Trinity was made up of three separate, distinct Gods. Because Joachim was widely respected as a priest, his views gained some traction. After his death, the church silenced Joachim's teaching during the Fourth Lateran Council (1251). The council affirmed that there is one God, manifested in the Bible as three persons. Nearly 200 years later, at the huge Council of Florence

(1445), the church reaffirmed monotheism: The Trinity is One God who manifests Himself as three persons. Like the Jews, the Church maintained there was one God, but He manifested Himself as three persons. This position remains unchanged and many Protestant Churches embrace this understanding today.

Conflicts between Bible Texts

Sometimes, the Bible presents a topic that seems to have opposing properties. For example, the Bible indicates in one place that Hell will burn forever and in another place, that Hell will not burn forever. When the Bible presents an *apparent conflict*, a controversy can occur because people will typically sample *some* of the evidence and reach a premature conclusion. Human nature loves to magnify what it wants to believe and diminish the importance of what it does not understand or want to believe. The doctrine of the Godhead has been controversial for centuries because the Bible *appears* to present conflicting things on this topic. However, to seekers of truth, an *apparent conflict* in the Bible is an invitation for careful and thorough study because mature Christians know there is no internal conflict within God's Word. The Godhead is true and changeless and the Word of God accurately reflects their character. Therefore, an *apparent conflict* in the Bible means there is a lofty solution that, when found, will harmoniously encompass all the apparent conflicts. *The Bible has to make sense just as it reads or it cannot speak for itself.* With this premise in mind, please consider the following seven issues:

1. If the Catholic position on the Trinity, "one God manifesting Himself as three persons" is valid, how can one God have two wills? Did Jesus petition another manifestation of Himself in the Garden? **"Father, if you are willing, take this cup from me;** *yet not my will, but yours be done.***"** (Luke 22:42, italics mine)

2. Did the Father send a manifestation of Himself to Earth or did He send another Deity who had a will of His own, a Deity who was separate and distinct from Himself? Jesus told the Jews, **"For I have come down from Heaven** *not to do My will but to do the will of Him who sent Me.***"** (John 6:38, italics mine)

3. Did the Father speak about His love for Himself when Jesus was baptized or did the Father speak about His love for another member of Deity? **"Then a cloud appeared and enveloped them, and**

Appendix A – Monotheism Versus Tritheism

a voice came from the cloud: *'This is my Son, whom I love. Listen to him!'* " (Mark 9:7, italics mine)

4. During His final moments on the cross, did Jesus cry out to another manifestation of Himself with a question? **"And at the ninth hour Jesus cried out in a loud voice, 'Eloi, Eloi, lama sabachthani?' – which means, 'My God, my God,** *why have You forsaken me?'* **"** (Mark 15:34, insertion mine)

5. Paul said that God the Father raised Jesus from the dead. Did the Father raise up a manifestation of Himself or did the Father restore life to a member of Deity who willingly gave up His eternal life so that sinners could have it? **"Paul, an apostle, (not of men, neither by man, but by Jesus Christ, and** *God the Father, who raised Him from the dead.***)"** (Galatians 1:1, italics mine)

6. Jesus says that He was once dead and is now alive forever more. (Revelation 1:18) If Jesus is a separate member of Deity who willingly gave up His eternal life so that sinners could have it, the price of our redemption exceeds calculation. On the other hand, if Jesus is a mere manifestation of the Father, God's sacrifice for our sins amounts to just suffering. Said another way, if the penalty for sin is death, God did not pay the penalty for our sins because God Himself could not die (cease to exist) on the cross and then resurrect Himself.

7. Finally, if there is one God who manifests Himself as three persons, why did the Father search through the whole universe only to determine that another manifestation of Himself (Jesus) was worthy to receive the book sealed with seven seals? (See Revelation 5.) This prophetic story highlights the core issue between the doctrine of monotheism (one God) and tritheism (three Gods). If the Father found Himself worthy to take the book sealed with seven seals, what is the point of His search of the universe only to give Himself the book which He wrote? If monotheism is true and there is only one God, then Revelation 5 becomes a divine sham and we know this is not possible! **"Let God be true and every man a liar."** (Romans 3:4) God is honest and always above any hint of reproach.

When considering the previous seven issues, the idea of one God manifesting Himself as three persons creates many logical and textual problems for which there are no solutions. *The greatest problem I have with Jewish monotheism and the Catholic Church's modification of that monotheism is that the Bible is put into a position where it cannot be understood just as it reads.*

If a Bible student is willing to consider the idea that the Godhead (the Trinity) is made up of three separate Gods who are united as one Deity, serving creation as one God in purpose, plan, and action, the entire Bible will make perfect sense *just as it reads*. When people reach or support conclusions built on religious bias, insufficient samples, inadequate knowledge, or maligned opinions, these conclusions create many insurmountable problems and questions resulting in confusion and more division.

What Difference Does One God or Three Gods Make?

If the Godhead functions as one in purpose, plan and action, what difference does it ultimately make if there is one God or three separate Gods? Let me emphasize why I believe this topic is important by listing four reasons:

First, when people know the truth about the Godhead, the Bible will make sense, *just as it reads*. This is extremely important. *Every truth is a stepping stone for understanding greater truth.* For example, Paul says the Father is **"King of kings and Lord of lords."** (1 Timothy 6:15) However, when Jesus appears at the Second Coming, John saw Jesus wearing the title, **"King of kings and Lord of lords."** (Revelation 19:16) Can the Father and the Son be the same person or is there more to the story? Chapter 5 of this book reveals that Jesus was found worthy in 1798 to receive sovereign power from the Father and to take over God's throne. In essence, the Father gave His throne and power to Jesus and this is how Jesus became "King of kings and Lord of lords." Paul tells us that once Jesus has accomplished everything that needs to be done, Jesus will return the sovereign power and throne to the Father. (1 Corinthians 15:25-28) This means the Father has chosen to end the sin problem with a profound revelation. At the end of sin's drama, the Father will reveal that Jesus is His equal in every way even though Jesus will not sit on the throne throughout eternity! (For further study on this topic, please see Prophecies 3 and 6 in my book, *Jesus' Final Victory*.)

There is a second reason why a proper understanding of the Godhead is important. The behavior of three separate but equal deities is defining. Three separate Gods living in perfect harmony defines what love is and

Appendix A – Monotheism Versus Tritheism

is not to all observers. Every moment, they live and function according to the laws of love, thus their lives are a comprehensive demonstration, a living laboratory for all creation to study.

There is a third reason why a proper understanding of the Godhead is important. If we understand that Jesus is Deity, a separate, distinct coeternal member of the Godhead, then the enormous price which our salvation required is shocking. Think about this: A coeternal member of the Godhead was willing to cease to exist forever so that we might have His eternal life. Because Jesus was willing to forfeit His life for sinners and was willing to fulfill the Father's will perfectly for our salvation, the Father, by His own authority, raised Jesus from the dead so that He could later exalt Jesus as His equal! This is important to know because the character of Jesus perfectly mirrors the character of the Father. This is why Jesus said, **"Anyone who has seen me has seen the Father."** (John 14:9)

There is a fourth reason for properly understanding the nature of the Godhead. The presence of three independent members of Deity and an expanding universe of created beings having free will requires a very wise government. Three Gods and billions of people having the power of choice could not harmoniously live together without a government based on love. This is why monotheism is a deficient doctrine. If there is only one God as Judaism claims or one God having three manifestations as Catholicism claims, then love becomes a doctrine (or a theory) instead of a living demonstration. If God does not have to live and love as His subjects do, then love becomes whatever God determines love will be. When there is tritheism, the Godhead is not in a position to make up what love will or will not be. When three equals have to live and function as one God, the universe has the privilege of seeing love demonstrated!

If Lucifer and his followers had to wait for "a manifestation of God" to die on the cross in A.D. 30 to see what love is, their complaints against God before the Earth was created could be justified. If there is only one God, there is no example of love to emulate and no definition of love other than what God says. Conversely, if there are three distinct, separate, coeternal members of the Godhead who have their own wills, their daily submission to each other is a divine example which created beings can study and emulate throughout eternity. *God never asks His children to do or experience something that He has not first experienced.*

The Deity of Jesus

Now that we have briefly examined some church history and mildly challenged two forms of monotheism, we need to dig a little deeper into the Bible to see if Jesus is in fact, a coeternal, separate, and distinct Deity independent of the Father. We need to know if the Bible teaches polytheism at a minimum and tritheism as a maximum. Please examine the following passages and consider my response to each one:

Psalms 45:7 "[The Father said to the Son,] **You love righteousness and hate wickedness; therefore God, your God, has set you above your companions by anointing you with the oil of joy.**" (Paul repeats Psalms 45:7 in his letter to Jewish believers to affirm that Jesus is a God who was set above His companions. At a point in time, God the Father elevated Jesus above the angels. See Hebrews 1:8-11.)

> Comment: This verse, twice repeated in Scripture, confuses many Christians because they either reject or do not know that Jesus once lived among the angels as one of them. Before coming to Earth, Michael was the archangel. For the purpose of discussion, consider this: Before Jesus lived on Earth in the form of a man, Jesus lived in Heaven in the form of an angel. Similarly, many people did not know that Jesus was God when He was on Earth and many of the angels did not, at first, know that Michael was God. (For further discussion on this issue, please see Chapters 1-3 in my book, *Jesus: The Alpha and The Omega* and Prophecy 12 in my book, *Jesus' Final Victory*.) When sin occurred on Earth, Michael offered to give His eternal life for sinners and the Father responded with the words written in Psalms 45:7. The Father openly declared Michael to be "God" before the angels and this is how Michael was elevated above His companions. This is one of the wonderful things about the Godhead. They do not lord their awesome powers over their subjects. Love does not permit it! Returning to the reason for discussing this text, this text indicates polytheism, which is one member of Deity speaking to another member of Deity, calling Him, "God."

Philippians 2:6, Colossians 2:9 "[Jesus] **Who, being in very nature God, did not consider equality with God something to be grasped ... For in Christ all the fullness of the Deity lives in bodily form.**"

> Comment: Because Jewish converts to Christianity often stumbled and struggled with the Deity of Jesus, Paul was forced to confront the monotheism of Judaism regularly. Wishing to clear the air on

Appendix A – Monotheism Versus Tritheism

this topic, Paul wrote to the churches in Philippi and Collossae saying, (a) Jesus was "God in His very nature" and (b) "in Christ's body, all the fullness of Deity lives." Paul was adamant that Jesus is Deity like the Father. Jesus also said that He should be honored (worshiped) even as the Father is honored. (John 5:22,23) If the Father and the Son were not equals, Jesus' words would have been blasphemous and this is precisely how the Jews interpreted His words. (See the following text.)

John 5:18 **"For this reason the Jews tried all the harder to kill Him; not only was He breaking the Sabbath, but He was even calling God his own Father, making himself equal with God."**

Comment: The Jews were fiercely loyal to "one God" and because of this, they "tried all the harder to kill Jesus" when He called God His Father. To better appreciate their hatred for Jesus, please consider this backdrop:

The devil is a master at creating lies and counterfeits. For example, the Bible says that Jesus created the world in six days. But the devil has led many educated and intelligent people to believe that the world and everything in it evolved over billions of years. Jesus made the seventh day holy at the end of Creation week and the devil has either created competing holy days (Friday for Moslems and Sunday for Christians) or anti-Semitism (to disparage the "Jewish Sabbath"). The Bible teaches that salvation comes through faith in Christ, but the devil has led billions of people into thinking they can obtain salvation through sacraments, merits, or good works (self-righteousness). For every good thing that God has said or created, the devil has created a lie or a counterfeit. This is particularly true regarding the Godhead. After Noah's flood, at the Tower of Babel, God divided the world. The devil seized this development by leading mankind into the darkness of superstition and counterfeit polytheism. The devil did this to obscure the truth about the Godhead. The devil led the ancients to believe there were many gods, each of them competing for supremacy. (Greek mythology is a good example of counterfeit polytheism.)

Lucifer's counterfeit polytheism was apparent at the time of Abraham when the Egyptians worshiped a number of gods. Four hundred years later, many of Abraham's descendants worshiped the gods [notice the word is plural] of the Egyptians. The biblical account confirms this practice: **"When the people saw that Moses was so long in coming down from the mountain, they gathered around Aaron and said, 'Come, make us gods who will go before us. As for this fellow Moses who brought us up out of Egypt, we don't know what has happened to him.'"** (Exodus 32:1) I am sure that you remember that Aaron made a golden calf which probably represented Apis, a powerful "bull god" which the Egyptians worshiped in hopes of having the military might of a "divine bull in a china closet."

When Jesus spoke to the Israelites at Mt. Sinai, He spoke to them in the singular because Jesus spoke on behalf of a united Deity. Therefore, the first commandment says, **"I am the Lord your God, who brought you out of Egypt, out of the land of slavery. You shall have no other gods before Me."** (Exodus 20:2,3)

Given their polytheistic experience in Egypt, the Jews understood the first commandment to mean the gods of the Egyptians were nothing because there was only one God, the God who had delivered them from Egypt. However, their simplistic understanding of the Godhead eventually set them up for a fatal mistake. Their narrow understanding of the first commandment gave them a reason and the authority to reject Jesus as another God fifteen hundred years later. Ironically, the Jews never discovered that the God who they called Jehovah for fifteen hundred years was Jesus Christ Himself. When Jesus claimed that God was His Father, they understood Jesus to claim equality with the Father which made them so angry they tried "all the harder to kill Him."

This brings us to an important point. If a person wishes to properly understand the doctrine of the Godhead, he has to search the Bible with timeliness in mind. In other words, a Bible student has to be aware of a divine process called "progressive revelation." Progressive revelation means that over time, more about the subject is revealed. The book of Genesis introduces the Godhead in the first verse by using the Hebrew word *elohiym* (*elohiym* indicates plural Gods) and sixty-five books later, the book of Revelation brings this topic to a profound climax. The book of Revelation is called, "The Revelation of Jesus Christ" because at the end of sin's drama, Jesus will be revealed to the universe as a distinct, separate, coeternal equal with the Father. Of course, Jews and Christians through the ages did not understand the Godhead because the book of Daniel

Appendix A – Monotheism Versus Tritheism

was sealed up until the time of the end. (Daniel 12:9) Now that Daniel has been unsealed and the rules of interpretation have been discovered, Revelation's story unfolds to reveal the truth about the Godhead. For the first time in Earth's history, we can understand all sixty-six books in the Bible. They are in perfect harmony *just as they read.*

Here are three examples of progressive revelation: The Lord said to Moses, "I [Jesus] **appeared to Abraham, to Isaac and to Jacob as God Almighty, but by my name the Lord** [Jehovah – eternal God] *I did not make myself known to them.*" (Exodus 6:3, italics and insertions mine)

Paul wrote: "**Now to Him who is able to establish you by my gospel and the proclamation of Jesus Christ, according to the revelation of the mystery hidden for long ages past, but** *now revealed and made known through the prophetic writings* **by the command of the eternal God, so that all nations might believe and obey Him.**" (Romans 16:25,26, italics mine)

Peter wrote: "He [Jesus] **was chosen** [by the Father] **before the creation of the world, but was revealed** [to us] **in these last times for your sake.**" (1 Peter 1:20, insertions mine)

We can begin to understand progressive revelation when we study the relationship of monotheism with the first commandment. When Jesus spoke from Mt. Sinai, He spoke in the singular because the Godhead is singular in purpose, plan, and action. The first commandment declares the oneness of the Godhead. **"I am the Lord your God. . . . you shall have no other Gods before Me."** (Exodus 20:2,3) We know that Jesus spoke for the Godhead because He used the plural for God (*elohiym*) when He said, **"I am the Lord your God."** Speaking in the singular, Jesus counteracted the gross polytheism which permeated the world at the time. Remember, the Father does not have a problem with Jesus speaking in the singular because worshiping the Son is permitted since the Son is also Deity. (John 5:22,23) Moreover, no one comes to know the truth about the Father without first coming to know the truth about Jesus. (John 14:6) This brings us to the next text.

John 1:1,3 **"In the beginning was the Word, and the Word was with God, and the Word was God. He was with God in the begin-**

ning.... **The Word became flesh and made his dwelling among us. We have seen his glory, the glory of the One and Only, who came from the Father, full of grace and truth ... Through Him** [the Word] **all things were made; without Him nothing was made that has been made."**

> Comment: If we allow the Bible to speak for itself, we can see John declares that Jesus created everything and He is a separate God independent of the Father. John says Jesus was with God and Jesus was God before anything was made. This indicates more than one Deity was present in the beginning – polytheism. Jesus is given the title, "the Word," in John 1 because Jesus is the voice of the Godhead. When the Godhead has something to say, Jesus speaks it.

Genesis 1:1 **"In the beginning God created the Heavens and the Earth."**

> Comment: The first verse in the Bible gives us a clue about whether to believe in monotheism or polytheism. The Hebrew word *elohiym* is used for God in Genesis 1:1 which is the plural form of *elowahh* which means Deity. Three deities (plural) were present when Earth was created. The Father commissioned Jesus to create the Earth. (Hebrews 1:2) As the creative agent of the Godhead, Jesus created the Earth (John 1:3,10) and at the same time, the Holy Spirit was hovering over the waters. Wherever the Father and/or Jesus go, the Holy Spirit is already there because the Holy Spirit is everywhere; He is omnipresent. (Genesis 1:2; Acts 5:31,32; 2 Timothy 1:14).

Genesis 1:26 **"Then God said, 'Let *us* make man in *our* image, in *our* likeness, and let them rule over the fish of the sea and the birds of the air.'"** (italics mine)

> Comment: The plurality of God cannot be overlooked or ignored in the first chapters of Genesis. At Creation, Jesus said to the Father and the Holy Spirit, **"Let us make man in our image, in our likeness."** This passage and Genesis 1:1 indicates polytheism existed before the creation of Earth and John 1:1 affirms this is the case. All of God's children are created in His image, after His likeness. Every child of God has a separate, distinct will because each member of the Godhead has a separate, distinct will. Every child of God can know and understand the principles of love because each member of the Godhead is a God of love. When Jesus created Adam and Eve, He gave them a number of characteristics that mirror the

Appendix A – Monotheism Versus Tritheism

characteristics of the Godhead. Because the Godhead lives together as one Deity, a husband and wife can live together as one flesh.

Deuteronomy 6:4 **"Hear, O Israel: The Lord our God, the Lord is one."**

Comment: The English translation of this verse appears to support monotheism (one God). However, when we look into the Hebrew language, Moses used the word *elohiym* for God to indicate that God is plural. A literal translation of this verse means: Hear, O Israel: Our God is plural and Jehovah (Jesus) is the One [who represents them]. Incidentally, about 98% of the references to Jehovah in the Bible refer to the God we call Jesus! The Father also uses the title Jehovah which means eternal God. See Psalms 2:7 and 45:7.

Isaiah 45:5 **"I am the Lord, and there is none else, there is no God beside me."**

Comment: At first glance, the English translation of this verse supports monotheism. However, if we look again into the Hebrew language, Jesus Himself used the plural form of Deity (*elohiym*) in this declaration. A literal translation of this verse means: "I am Jehovah (Jesus). I speak for the Godhead. What I say is from Us." This truth is affirmed in John 1 where Jesus is called "the Word." Jesus is called "the Word" or "the Word of God" (Revelation 19:13) because He alone speaks for the Godhead.

Jesus Is an Almighty God!

Before we leave this discussion on monotheism versus polytheism, I need to address a number of things that have been postponed in previous paragraphs.

Look at this text: **"This is what the Lord says – Israel's King and Redeemer, the Lord Almighty: I am the first and I am the last; apart from Me there is no God** [elohiym]**."** (Isaiah 44:6, insertion mine) Let us study who made this declaration, Jesus or the Father. Open your Bible and thoughtfully compare Isaiah 44:6 with Revelation 2:8, then compare Revelation 22:13 with Revelation 1:8. Exchange the terms used in these four verses and you will discover four facts: (a) Jesus declared that He is the first and the last, (b) Jesus declared that He is the Lord Almighty, (c) Jesus declared that He is Israel's King and Redeemer (Pilate's sign on the cross was correct – compare Luke 23:3

with John 19:19-22), and finally (d) Jesus declared that He is the Alpha and the Omega. Please review these verses until they make sense, just as they read. Jesus revealed many characteristics about Himself in these verses that separate Him from the Father.

When Jesus said that He is the First and the Last, the Alpha and the Omega, He was not saying that chronologically speaking, He was the first God to exist. Rather, Jesus was saying that from the cosmic beginning (before anything existed), He has been the voice of the Godhead. He does not speak on His own behalf. Therefore, as the Word of God, His words are first and they are final (the beginning and the end). When Jesus said that He is the Lord Almighty, He declared that He is an Almighty God, Israel's interface with an Almighty Godhead. Worshiping Jesus is the same as worshiping the Father because they are one and they are equals! (John 5:22,23; Colossians 2:9)

Three Are One or Three Function as One?

The Bible does not explicitly answer how the Godhead came about. However, the Bible contains insight on this topic and when the evidence is carefully put together, a wonderful story unfolds. The following scenario is supported by a variety of texts although some details are my own creation. For purposes of discussion, please consider the following:

The Bible indicates there was time in eternity past, before anything was created, that can be called "the beginning." (John 1:1) Let us assume in the beginning three separate, distinct, coeternal Gods came together for a meeting. According to infinite wisdom and loving kindness, they agreed to unite and unify to create a family that would fill an ever expanding universe. As equal, coeternal Gods, having the same powers and prerogatives, there could be endless competition and warfare or there could be submission to each other. They knew there is not enough space in the universe for three equal, independent, free-will, infinite Gods to live if there was no interest in unity and cooperation! Therefore, if they could not unite as one Godhead, they knew that all creation would get caught in a conflict of loyalties between opposing deities. Because each Deity had a kind heart, their first act as the Godhead was a solemn declaration of submission to each other (comparable to a marriage). This submission involved separate components and with each submission, each God accepted a specific power and a specific limitation. In other words, to live together as one, each God had to relinquish certain powers and prerogatives to the other two so

Appendix A – Monotheism Versus Tritheism

that all three could function as one Deity – their eternal commitment to each other was oneness in purpose, plan, and action.

For example, two Gods (the Father and Holy Spirit) agreed that the other God (the God the angels call Michael and we call Jesus) should serve as the voice of the Godhead. They did this so that everything and anything the Godhead might say to their creation would come from one mouth. This submission on the part of two Gods explains why Jesus is called "The Word" in John 1 and "The Word of God" in Revelation 19:13. In today's vernacular, we would say that Jesus was appointed, "The Speaker of the House." Speaking for the Godhead was not the only submission that Jesus accepted. The Father and the Holy Spirit also relinquished their creative powers to Jesus and He was appointed as "The Creative Agent of the Godhead." Jesus is the only God who creates and He alone created everything that exists in Heaven, on Earth and throughout the universe. (Colossians 1:16,17) Because the Father and Holy Spirit have no voice (that is, neither can speak for the Godhead) and because the Father and Holy Spirit cannot create anything having substance, these two submissions are profoundly important to understand. Look again at John 1 and Colossians 1:16,17:

"In the beginning [before anything existed] **was the Word** [Jesus is called "the Word" because He speaks for the Godhead]**, and the Word was with God** [Jesus was with the Father and the Holy Spirit]**, and the Word was God** [Jesus is a distinct and separate Deity just like the Father and the Holy Spirit are separate and distinct deities]. . . . **Through him** [the Word] **all things were made; without him nothing was made that has been made."** (John 1:1,3, insertions mine)

"For by Him [Jesus] **all things were created: things in Heaven** [the angels were created by Him] **and on Earth** [He created mankind]**, visible and invisible, whether thrones or powers or rulers or authorities; all things were created by Him and for Him. He** [Jesus] **is before all things, and in Him all things** [the whole universe] **hold together."** (Colossians 1:16,17)

The mutual submission of the Father and the Holy Spirit to Jesus encompasses some issues we need to consider. For example, two Gods (Jesus and the Holy Spirit) relinquished their rights to sovereign authority to the Father so the Father rules over Jesus and the Holy Spirit unopposed. As King of kings and Lord of lords (until 1798), the Father was free to exercise His authority according to His infinite wisdom.

Jesus and the Holy Spirit are not only supportive; they are 100% committed to whatever the will of the Father might be! This awesome love and faith cannot be described in words.

The encompassing issue of mutual submission between members of Deity is important to understand because it explains elements which would otherwise be impossible to understand. Another example of submission is when the Father and Jesus surrendered their ability to be omnipresent to the Holy Spirit. Prior to their union, all three Gods had the ability to be everywhere at once. However, the Father and Jesus relinquished this ability to the Holy Spirit so that the Godhead would have one set of universal eyes and ears. This exhibits their complete faith in each other and provides an example of how God's subjects should have faith in the Godhead. What a wonderful concept!

Since the Holy Spirit is the only member of the Godhead who can be everywhere at the same time, He serves as a two-way conduit between the Godhead and all creation. The Holy Spirit sees and hears everything as it happens in real time throughout the whole universe and He conveys this information to the Father and Jesus as it happens. On the other side of the coin, the Holy Spirit is the only member of the Godhead that connects one or all of God's saints with the Godhead without the necessity of an appointment! According to Apostle Paul, the Holy Spirit intercedes for God's saints. He also reports to the Father the contents and desire of every contrite sinner. (Romans 8:26,27) As you might expect, the Holy Spirit is a very busy and active God!

Think this through: Because of their perfect union and submission to each other, we actually serve three Gods. We have God above us (the Father who served as the supreme Ruler of the Universe (until 1798) whose government is righteous and true). We also have God beside us (Jesus, the Creative Agent of the Godhead, who lives among His created beings as one of us showing us what Deity would do if the Father lived within our limitations). Finally, we have a God within us (the Holy Spirit is present within every heart, nurturing us, guiding us, comforting us, edifying us, and bringing God's joy and presence to us).

Is the Holy Spirit a Separate God?

Now that we have discussed how and why the Father and Jesus are distinct, separate, coeternal members of Deity, we need to discuss the nature and identity of the Holy Spirit. I believe the Holy Spirit is a separate, distinct, coeternal member of the Godhead. The Holy Spirit

Appendix A – Monotheism Versus Tritheism

is not the Father. The Holy Spirit is not Jesus. The Holy Spirit is not "an influence" that emanates from the Father (as Catholics and many Protestants teach) like a perfume. The Holy Spirit is a Deity; a being that can speak on His own. He does not speak independently of the Godhead, no member of the Godhead speaks independently, but He does hear and respond in accordance with the wisdom and will of the Godhead! (John 16:13) Seven times in the book of Revelation Jesus said, **"He who has an ear, let him hear what the Spirit says to the churches."**

Please consider four considerations that lead to the conclusion that the Holy Spirit is a Deity, a separate God, and a member of the Godhead:

The first consideration concerns the timeless and universal presence of an unpardonable sin. Have you ever wondered why the unpardonable sin is blasphemy against the Holy Spirit and not blasphemy against the Father or Jesus? Jesus said that blasphemy against the Holy Spirit is unpardonable "in this age and in the age to come!" (Matthew 12:31,32) This means the unpardonable sin is timeless because "the age to come" is everlasting. How does blasphemy against the Holy Spirit occur and why is sinning against the Holy Spirit the only sin which cannot be forgiven?

Blasphemy against the Holy Spirit occurs when a person defies an internal conviction from the Holy Spirit. Suppose the Father directs the Holy Spirit to convict a specific person about something which the Father wants that person to do. For example, the Holy Spirit convicted Noah to build an ark and out of faith he did so. (Hebrews 11:7) Remember the note that Pilate's wife sent to her husband when Jesus was in his court. (Matthew 27:19) Remember King Agrippa's response to Paul that he was "almost persuaded" to become a Christian. (Acts 26:28) Suppose a person rejects the conviction of the Holy Spirit, not once, not five times, but like Pharaoh, he becomes more stubborn with the many times the Holy Spirit attempts to reach the person. Eventually, rebellion will mute all conviction and the internal struggle within will end because the Holy Spirit respects our free will and the only thing He can do is leave. When the Holy Spirit determines there is nothing further He can do within a person's heart, the unpardonable sin occurs.

The Holy Spirit, like the other two Gods, is a God of love. He loves and respects the will of each sinner for whom Jesus has died and He will only leave a person if that person insists on *continued* rebellion. When the Holy Spirit detects that defiance has taken a person beyond the point of repentance, that person's rebellion becomes unpardonable. After every effort had been made to bring them to repentance, God cast Lucifer and his followers out of Heaven because they blasphemed the Holy Spirit. What makes defiance against the Holy Spirit unpardonable? *The only God who can enter our hearts and convey the will of the Father is the God who is omnipresent.* Jesus cannot do this. The Father cannot do this. Neither of them has omnipresence. If we shut out the Holy Spirit, we shut off all communion with God and this is unforgivable. (1 Corinthians 2:14; Romans 8:6-9;8:14)

The second factor that indicates the Holy Spirit is a separate member of the Godhead is that when a sinner is baptized into Christ, he becomes a participant in God's redemption. Therefore, Jesus commanded that such a person be baptized into three distinct, separate, coeternal members of the Godhead, uniquely named and identified as The Father, The Son, and The Holy Spirit. (Matthew 28:10,20) I believe that Jesus commanded this because redemption requires the efforts of all three Gods.

The final factor indicating the Holy Spirit is a separate, distinct member of the Godhead is that the Holy Spirit has relinquished His prerogative and privilege to speak independently. Carefully study this truth that Jesus spoke: **"But when He, the Spirit of Truth, comes, He will guide you into all truth.** [Even though He can,] **He will not speak on his own; He will speak only what He hears** [from the Father and Me]**, and He will tell you what is yet to come."** (John 16:13, insertions mine) Why did Jesus say the Holy Spirit will not speak on His own? Why did Jesus say the Holy Spirit would speak only what He hears? Why did Jesus say the Holy Spirit will tell you what is yet to come?

Jesus used these phrases to indicate that like Himself, the Holy Spirit is a God who hears and speaks. However, the Spirit only speaks what He hears from the Father or the Son. If we treat the Holy Spirit as a separate member of the Godhead, the Bible will make sense *just as it reads*. The next paragraph will demonstrate a sample of this.

Jesus said to His disciples, **"It is for your good that I am going away. Unless I go away, the Counselor will not come to you; but if I go, I will send him to you."** (John 16:7) When Jesus spoke these words, He knew three things. First, Jesus knew that Jerusalem would

Appendix A – Monotheism Versus Tritheism

be destroyed in A.D. 70 and the disciples would be scattered everywhere. (Matthew 24) Second, Jesus knew that the Father's original plan (Plan A) to implement the kingdom of God on Earth during the seventieth week would not be fulfilled. Third, Jesus knew that He would be leaving Earth and returning to Heaven within a few days. (John 14:1-3) When we understand that Jesus does not have the ability to be omnipresent, His words concerning the Holy Spirit make perfect sense just as they read! In essence, Jesus told His disciples that through the ministry of the Holy Spirit, He would be closer and nearer to each of them, no matter where they went after Jerusalem was destroyed. This is why it was for their good that He left Earth. The Holy Spirit would be sent to them and through the Spirit, Jesus would be able to be with all of them no matter where they went. This is how Jesus could say, **"And surely I am with you always, to the very end of the age."** (Matthew 28:20) (For a discussion on Plan A and Plan B and the profound implications of each plan, please see Appendices B & D in my book, *Jesus' Final Victory*.)

Jesus also said, **"Unless I go away, the Counselor will not come to you; but if I go, I will send Him to you."** Jesus meant that on resurrection Sunday, He would ascend to the Father. The Father was very pleased with all that Jesus had done to redeem mankind, but the Father was not pleased with the way Israel had treated Jesus. Because the kingdom of God could not be established on Earth as planned (Plan A), the Father gave Jesus "all authority" to establish His church on Earth. (Matthew 28:18)

Jesus knew that Lucifer and his demons would do everything possible to destroy His church. Therefore, a few days after ascending to Heaven, Jesus sent the Holy Spirit to Earth on a mission. Jesus knew the most convincing way to overcome the religious paradigms of the Jews and establish His church throughout the Roman Empire was through miracles and evidence of divine power. (See Acts 14:3.) Jesus also knew that His believers would not have sufficient wisdom and insight on managing and directing His church. Therefore, He promised to send "the Counselor" or "The Advisor" to them. Through the power and ministry of the Holy Spirit, a new religious body would not only begin, it would manage, against all odds and demonic assaults, to endure persecution and apostasy for centuries to come. The book of Acts tells a compelling story, how the power and ministry of the Holy Spirit enabled a few humble fishermen to change the course of human history. The Holy

Spirit could do things for the church that Jesus Himself could not do if He remained on Earth. This is why Jesus was taken from Earth and the Holy Spirit was sent!

Was the Holy Spirit Held Back Until Pentecost?

Often people wonder if the Holy Spirit has always existed, why God waited thousands of years to pour out the Holy Spirit at Pentecost. The outpouring of the Holy Spirit during the first century A.D. was a special manifestation of divine power designed to achieve a special outcome. However, the work of the Holy Spirit within the hearts of individuals *prior* to Pentecost and *after* Pentecost did not change.

Here is the story: Because religion is a powerful paradigm, it controls what most people will consider about God. Remember, Jesus knew "the most convincing way to establish His church in Jerusalem and elsewhere in the Roman Empire was through a display of divine power." People in Bible times did not know much about Earth sciences and they did not have a thousand explanations which technology has provided for us today. Therefore, the ancients were prone to superstition and fear of "the unexplained." When the Holy Spirit descended at Pentecost, there was a great wind (intimidation), tongues of fire appeared on the heads of the disciples (the anointing of chosen people), and the gospel was heard in many languages (the gift of tongues). This phenomenon was instantly deemed "an act of God" and 3,000 souls were baptized into Christ on the basis of what they saw and heard. This show of divine power gave the gospel of Jesus a huge dose of credibility which gave the church of Christ a huge boost in membership. The rest of the story, recorded in Acts, is church history. Early Christians regarded Pentecost as the birthplace of Christ's church. (Acts 7:39)

Unfortunately, early Christians poorly understood their new religion. They knew just enough to abandon some of their former ways. Therefore, the first century A.D. was marked by Holy Spirit power much like the Great Tribulation will be marked by Holy Spirit power for 1,260 days. (Revelation 11:3) Through the ages, the Holy Spirit has been "poured out" on various people. For example, the Holy Spirit came upon Saul (1 Samuel 19:23), David (1 Samuel 16 & 17), Gideon (Judges 6:34), and Philip (Acts 8:39). In each case, Jesus wanted people to know that He had chosen certain people to do or say certain things. Do not forget, the Holy Spirit is omnipresent. He is at work at all times and in all places, edifying (building up) the body of Christ with gifts of all

Appendix A – Monotheism Versus Tritheism

kinds. (1 Corinthians 12-14). He is also at work in every human heart as long as we permit Him to dwell within.

Special events and manifestations of the Holy Spirit (such as those at Pentecost) are not to be confused with the still small voice of the Holy Spirit calling us to intimately walk with God. Look closely at this text: **"Then the Lord said** [to Noah]**, 'My Spirit will not contend with man forever, for he is mortal; his days will be a hundred and twenty years.' "** (Genesis 6:3) The Lord indicated the Holy Spirit would not endlessly contend with the antediluvians. **"The Lord saw how great man's wickedness on the Earth had become, and that every inclination of the thoughts of his heart was only evil all the time. The Lord was grieved that he had made man on the Earth, and his heart was filled with pain."** (Genesis 6:5,6) Corporately speaking, a majority of the people in Noah's day had committed or was in the process of committing the unpardonable sin. The Holy Spirit could not soften the rebellious hearts of the antediluvians. Therefore, God had to destroy the whole world for the benefit of oncoming generations. The same is true of the world today. All signs indicate we have passed the point of no return. Our world (corporately speaking) will not repent and reform. According to the books of Daniel and Revelation, God's wrath will come just as He said it would.

Finally, there is a fourth issue which indicates the Holy Spirit is a separate member of the Godhead. Chapter 8 in this book gives reasons why the four living creatures in Revelation 4 and 5 represent the Holy Spirit. A summary of those reasons is presented here:

1. The four living creatures are identical; four clones of the same entity. They stand closest to God and His throne. This representation suggests there is an omnipresent being who can take any form and remain alive! They are called "the four living creatures" because the power to give life is within them. The 24 elders are not called, "the 24 living elders" and the angels are not called "the living angels." The four living creatures are "living creatures" because the power of life is within them. Additionally, the four living creatures are present in the north, south, east, and west, the four points of a compass, all at the same time.

2. The four living creatures are covered with eyes. This indicates the Holy Spirit instantly sees everything occurring in the universe. The eyes, signifying the Holy Spirit's omnipresence, indicate Deity

because the Holy Spirit serves as the eyes and ears of Jesus and the Father. The Holy Spirit sees everything in the universe instantly and reported in real time. The amount of data that flows from the Holy Spirit every millisecond is unimaginable.

3. Ezekiel and John saw the same four faces on each living creature. Each face describes certain challenges which the Holy Spirit "faces." For example, the Holy Spirit has intelligence. He knows God's ways and will as well as mankind's thoughts, motives, words, and deeds (this ability is represented by the face of a man – Ecclesiastes 8:1). The Holy Spirit has divine strength (represented by the face of an ox – Numbers 23:22). The Holy Spirit is deadly and can destroy anything that has been created (represented by the prowess of a lion – Numbers 23:24). The Holy Spirit travels at warp speed, much faster than light (represented by six wings). When necessary, the Holy Spirit can swoop down and catch any prey wherever or whatever it may be (represented by the face of an eagle – Deuteronomy 28:49).

4. The Holy Spirit is as selfless and humble as Jesus and the Father. The Holy Spirit extolls the Father's majesty, generosity, wisdom, love, goodness, and grace perpetually. The Holy Spirit's highest work is to bond God's children with the Father and Jesus in spirit and in truth. The Holy Spirit constantly brings glory to the Father and Jesus by exalting them. (John 16:14) The Holy Spirit also serves as a conduit between God and His children. He takes God's happiness, joy, and goodness and shares it with everyone willing to receive it producing "the fruit of the Spirit." (Galatians 5:22-24)

When we factor all of the attributes that Ezekiel and John mention, the four living creatures point to one person, the Holy Spirit. The most impressive element about the Holy Spirit is if it was not for His ministry, no one would ever know God! The Holy Spirit's job is to reveal the other two Gods. He is fulfilling His job perfectly because He is just like them, a selfless member of Deity like the Father and Jesus.

If you would like to prove to yourself that the Father, Jesus, and the Holy Spirit are separate, distinct, coeternal members of the Godhead, try this simple experiment. In mathematics, we say that if a, b, and c have the same value, any of these three variables can be substituted at any time. Using this approach, if we say that the Father, Son, and Holy Spirit are the same God (expressing Himself in three different

Appendix A – Monotheism Versus Tritheism

ways), we should be able to go through the Bible and substitute any mention of God with any title for God and the result should be the same. Obviously, this approach does not make any sense. For example, Jesus did not find the Father worthy in Revelation 5 and then give the book sealed with seven seals to the Holy Spirit.

I hope this study has been helpful. I hope you will read through it a couple times and pray about it. At first, you may think this topic is not very important. Understanding this topic is not required for salvation, but if you wish to understand the Bible in general and apocalyptic prophecy in particular, you need to understand this topic. We have looked at monotheism (one God), polytheism (more than one God), and tritheism (three Gods). The fullness of Deity is within Jesus just as the Father has the fullness of Deity within Himself. (Colossians 2:9) Jesus is not the Father and the Father is not Jesus or the Holy Spirit. I believe there are three separate, distinct, coeternal deities which function as One. One in purpose, plan, and action and they are forever committed to this arrangement. What an amazing demonstration of love for eternity to come!

Appendix B
The Physical Appearing of Lucifer

I would have never believed that the world's religions and nations would be abolished before Jesus returns, but Revelation 13:14 and Revelation 17:12 makes this prediction. Since this may be the first time you have ever considered such a prediction, I am sure you are wondering how these things can happen.

Apocalyptic prophecy predicts a series of coming events which are stranger than fiction. The world during the Great Tribulation will be a very different place than the world we know today. The Bible predicts a coming world order unlike anything people are anticipating. In a parallel way, the same thing happened in Noah's day. No one believed tomorrow could be so vastly different from today. This is why we have "the more sure word of prophecy." God wants His children to study and understand His Word so that when He steps into the affairs of mankind and alters everything we know, we will not be overwhelmed, discouraged, or deceived.

Revelation 9 indicates a time is coming when God will permit Lucifer (the devil, the Antichrist) and his demons to physically appear on Earth. As I understand this subject, Jesus will only permit the devil and his angels to exit from the spirit realm (the Abyss) when two-thirds of the time allotted for the Great Tribulation has expired. If this is so, Jesus will hold the devil and his angels back until the 891st day of the Great Tribulation arrives. Then, He will release these supernatural beings from the spirit realm and give them physical bodies. When the appointed time arrives, the devil and his angels will descend to Earth from the sky. (Revelation 9:3) This appearing will be brilliant and highly intimidating. So many angels will appear with Lucifer that they will fill the sky from horizon to horizon, like a swarm of locusts. At first, the people of Earth will run for shelter to escape their commanding presence. Then, hundreds of millions will go out and participate in "the greatest deception" to ever occur on Earth.

The Bible tells us that God is love and He is not willing that anyone should perish. This may seem strange, but God intends to use the devil's physical appearing to save people that would not otherwise choose salvation! Please consider some of God's objectives during the fifth and sixth trumpets (described in Revelation 9).

Appendix B – The Physical Appearing of Lucifer

Searching Among the Wicked for Precious Souls

Long ago, God thoughtfully and deliberately designed the Great Tribulation to accomplish several objectives. One of God's objectives is to save as many people as possible during the 1,260 days allotted to the Two Witnesses. (Revelation 11:3) There are two problems with this objective: First, from God's point of view, all of the religions of the world are blasphemous (insulting) and in darkness (ignorance). Mankind is basically ignorant of God and His truth. Second, God has given each person on Earth the power of choice. Therefore, God intends to use His 144,000 servants to enlighten the world with His truth and judge the living to determine who will and will not be saved. Each person will hear and understand the properties of sin and how to be saved from sin. Once a person receives this knowledge, that person will be in a position to make an informed and intelligent decision about his eternal destiny.

The first two and a half years of the Great Tribulation will be agonizing. God's first four judgments (Revelation 8:7-13) will devastate Earth and reduce its population by 25%. Overwhelmed with apocalyptic destruction, the nations of Earth will have to implement martial law shortly after the Great Tribulation begins. To appease God's wrath, the religious and political leaders of the world will create a crisis government. The book of Revelation calls this government Babylon. It will create and enforce many laws trying to change people's behavior. Babylon will persecute everyone who refuses to obey its laws. Given the dire consequences of God's judgments, survival will be questionable and the necessities of life will be few. I believe that for 890 days, the survivors of God's judgments will hear the 144,000 present the gospel of Jesus. Most people will have made their decision by the 891st day.

I believe that God will continue to keep the devil and his angels in the spirit realm (where they now live) for two-thirds of the 1,335 days allotted for the Great Tribulation. Lucifer and his demons will only be released for the final one-third of the days (day 891) when people are no longer willing to consider the testimony of the 144,000. When God releases the devil and his angels, it will be a powerful "game changer." The devil's physical appearing along with millions of angels will produce a situation which the world has never seen.

When the devil appears, he will masquerade as Almighty God. Claiming to be God, he will travel the world for five months, winning the confidence of billions through signs and wonders and *appearing* to be

Appendix B – The Physical Appearing of Lucifer

holy, righteous, generous, forgiving, and gracious. His appearance and actions will deceive a large portion of the world. Pretending to be Almighty God, the devil will perform amazing miracles, even calling fire down out of Heaven to prove his assumed divinity. He will quickly grow in popularity and most of the world's population will admire, adore, and worship him. Millions of wicked people will bow down before him in humble obedience.

Currently, many nonreligious people on Earth (atheists, agnostics, etc.) do not believe there is a God and they will continue to deny there is a God even when Lucifer walks on the Earth! During the five months allotted to the fifth trumpet, Lucifer's demons will have a specific task to eliminate the "infidels." The demons will find and torture the "infidels" with indescribable pain. Thus, during the fifth trumpet, a large percentage of nonreligious people will capitulate and join those who "believe" that Lucifer is Almighty God. There will be only one antidote for this demonic torture. If a person surrenders to the gospel of Jesus, Jesus will not permit the devil's demons to torture him any further. The demons will torture and eliminate many infidels during the fifth trumpet. Millions of infidels will join forces with Lucifer (to escape demonic torture), but a few will wake up, surrender to Jesus Christ, and be saved!

Notice Paul's comment about this coming event. Paul describes Lucifer as the "lawless one" (or KJV, "man of sin") because Lucifer will not be subject to any laws but his own. He will do as he pleases and given his incredible powers, no one will be able to obstruct or thwart his actions:

"The coming of the lawless one [will appear to be a divine event, but the devil's actions] **will be in accordance with the work of Satan** [who he really is] **displayed in all kinds of counterfeit miracles, signs and wonders, and in every sort of evil that deceives those who are perishing. They perish because they refused to love the truth and so be saved.** *For this reason God sends them a powerful delusion* **so that they will believe the lie and so that all will be condemned who have not believed the truth but have delighted in wickedness."** (2 Thessalonians 9:9-12, insertion and italics mine)

We will consider two matters from this passage. First, Paul says the wicked **"refused to love the truth and so be saved."** His language indicates an element that many people overlook. The appearing of the lawless one occurs *for a specific reason*. Before Lucifer can appear, the world will hear the gospel and reject it. We know the world will hear the gospel and rebel against it because God does not assign guilt to a person for something that he does not know and has not heard. (See James 4:17.)

Second, because the wicked refused to accept the truth and be saved, God sends a "game changer," a powerful delusion so that all wicked people will believe the lie and be condemned. From the beginning God predetermined that the living would be thoroughly tested during the Great Tribulation to see who will choose to live by faith and be saved. Because every person has the power of choice, each person will have to make a choice. The response to the testimony of Jesus spoken through the lips of the 144,000 will determine the eternal destiny of each person.

After two and one half years of dealing with hardship and survival, many wicked people will shrug off and ignore the testimony of the 144,000. When the distribution of the gospel stalls, Jesus will release the devil. The world's population will see and feel the devil's brilliant presence and counterfeit miracles. Masquerading as Almighty God, the devil will solicit adoration and worship. Those who love wickedness will receive the devil as their savior. Meanwhile, the devil's demons will seek out infidels and torture them into submission. However, many infidels will realize their need of the Savior allowing Jesus to rescue many precious people during the fifth trumpet.

Abolishing the Religions and Nations of the World

When the five months allotted to the fifth trumpet ends, the devil's deceit will be over and he will suddenly change behavior and character. The primary change is that during the sixth trumpet, the devil and his forces will be permitted to kill people. In fact, the Bible indicates Lucifer's forces will kill one-third of mankind. (Revelation 9:15) The devil will kill His opposition which includes many saints, the remaining "infidels" and many wicked people! The saints will defy the devil's authority and blasphemous claims. They know Lucifer is the devil, the Antichrist. The infidels will defy Lucifer's ambition to establish a global church/state. In addition, many religious people who rejected the 144,000 and their testimony for Jesus will defy Lucifer's declaration that abolishes the religions of the world.

Lucifer will give orders to abolish the religions and governments of the world at the sixth trumpet for two simple reasons. First, when God Himself lives among men, there is no room for religious plural-

Appendix B – The Physical Appearing of Lucifer

ity (people having different views about God's will). Second, because Lucifer intends to rule over mankind as Almighty God, he is opposed to religious diversity. (2 Thessalonians 2:4) Lucifer will demand that everyone worship and obey him or die. The image to the beast mentioned in Revelation 13:14 is Lucifer's one world church state. He will rule over the world as "King of kings (ruler over political matters) and Lord of lords" (ruler over spiritual matters). There will be one lord, one faith and one baptism. Anyone resisting membership in Lucifer's one world church state will be considered part of the opposition and will be killed. (Revelation 13:15)

A one world government cannot exist when governments and national boundaries exist. Therefore, Lucifer will eliminate the governments of the world by dividing the world into ten sectors and appoint ten puppet kings over these ten sectors.

The first four trumpets (Revelation 8:7-13) will destroy much of the world's infrastructure. Communication, travel, banking, manufacturing, and energy will become nonexistent. When the devil appears on Earth at the fifth trumpet, his agenda will be to destroy the world in general and God's saints in particular. This is why in John's vision he is given the titles, Abaddon and Apollyon in Revelation 9:11. These titles mean "the destroyer."

God permits the devil to abolish the religions and nations of the world to fulfill God's objective for the Great Tribulation to save the largest possible number of people. During the fifth trumpet, Jesus permits the devil to torture the infidels so that this group of people will realize their need of a Savior. During the sixth trumpet, Jesus permits the devil to abolish all of the religions and nations of the world so that there can be no impediment to accepting the gospel of Christ. One of the greatest impediments to receiving a new gospel is the existence of an old gospel, or as some people might call it, "old time religion." Many good-hearted people would rather cling to their "old time religion" than to embrace God's advancing truth. When Lucifer abolishes and outlaws all of the "old time religions," a huge obstacle for accepting God's "present gospel truth" will be removed. People will find themselves having to choose between God's truth and the devil's lies. Lucifer will not permit past traditions and the practice of "old time religion!"

Because the first four trumpets will destroy a large part of each nation, all governments will be in disarray and ineffective during the Great

Tribulation. So, the devil will dictate that all governments be abolished. He will establish his one world church state by dividing the world into groups of one thousand people and he will place captains over each group that are loyal to him. (Dividing people into groups of a thousand was a common practice in ancient times. It is an efficient way to logistically manage a multitude of people and also keeps any one group from becoming powerful. See Exodus 18:21,25; Numbers 31:14; 1 Samuel 22:7 and 1 Samuel 29:2.) There will be no constitution. There will be no Bill of Rights, no Congress, and no court of appeal. The devil will have total control over the people of the world at the micro level, down to groups of one-thousand people. When the devil has implemented this control mechanism, he will offer survival to everyone who swears total loyalty to him and his government. Those refusing to go along will be killed. Thus, one-third of each group will be killed and the remaining 666 people in each group will wear a tattoo on their right hand showing the number "666." This means they have declared their loyalty to Lucifer and they will be permitted to live. They will be considered Lucifer's property.

The good news is that during this final hour of salvation, a few people will give up their "old time religion." They will wake up and realize their desperate need of a Savior; a God whose ways are righteous and whose eternal government is based on principles of love. When these last few sheep come out of Babylon, God's offer of mercy will end. The seven bowls will then fall and Jesus will appear. He will return Lucifer and his angels to the Abyss and destroy the wicked by the breath of His mouth (a command that comes out of His mouth, represented in Revelation as a doubled edged sword). Then, He will resurrect the righteous dead and gather the remaining saints. They will meet the Lord in the air and return with Jesus to the Holy City for 1,000 years. At the end of the 1,000 years, Jesus will break the seventh seal and every living being will see the final revelation of Jesus!

Bible Cross Reference

Gen 1:1 31,208	Lev 25 70	2 Chr 36:22 106
Gen 1:2 208	Lev 26 94	2 Chr 36:22 107
Gen 1:26 31,208	Lev 26:12-39 92	
Gen 2:16,17 32	Lev 26:14-16 158	Ezr 1:1 100
Gen 2:17 126,157		
Gen 2:24 198	Num 4 81	Est 3:9-11 104
Gen 3:15 166	Num 14:34 70	Est 8 105
Gen 3:21 166	Num 22 98	Est 8:10-14 104
Gen 4:8-10 173	Num 23:22 99,218	
Gen 4:11-16 173	Num 23:24 99,218	Job 1 42
Gen 6:3 207,217	Num 26:53,54 81	Job 38:7 31,51
Gen 6:5 94	Num 31:14 226	
Gen 6:5,6 217		Psa 2 37
Gen 15:16 94	Deu 6:4 209	Psa 2:7 209
Gen 18:19 94	Deu 8:11-14 68	Psa 2:7-12 37
Gen 19 94	Deu 12:27 170	Psa 18:2 24,74
Gen 22:11-18 43	Deu 23:2 81	Psa 18:7-12 181
Gen 49:24 120	Deu 25:5,6 81	Psa 18:31 120
	Deu 28:49 99,218	Psa 24:10 186
Exo 3 29	Deu 32:4,15 120	Psa 45:7 28,204,209
Exo 3:2-6 43	Deu 32:15-25 92,93	Psa 69:28 84
Exo 3:14 120		Psa 78:35 74
Exo 6:3 28,207	Jos 2:1-5 43	Psa 91:8 183
Exo 12:1 70	Jos 14:5 81	Psa 109:1-17 81
Exo 18:21,25 226		Psa 110:1 41
Exo 20:2,3 206,207	Jud 2 29	Psa 139:15,16 28
Exo 20:2,8-11 32	Jud 6:34 216	Psa 139:15-17 5
Exo 20:3 197	Jud 14:6 154	Psa 139:16 81,84
Exo 20:7 39	Jud 14:19 154	Psa 145:21 25
Exo 20:8-11 161	Jud 16:30 121	
Exo 20:18,19 182		Ecc 8:1 99
Exo 32:1 206	1 Sam 2:2 120	Ecc 8:2 218
Exo 32:32 84	1 Sam 16 & 17 216	Ecc 9:5 143
Exo 32:32,33 84	1 Sam 19:23 216	Ecc 12:14 . 80,83,84,140,190
Exo 40 81	1 Sam 22:7 226	Ecc 14:12 9
Exo 40:5 170	1 Sam 28:6 29	
Exo 40:6 170	1 Sam 29:2 226	Isa 1:4 74
		Isa 1-4 169
Lev 5:9 170	2 Sam 22:3 24	Isa 9:6 186
Lev 8:15 170		Isa 13:9-11 185
Lev 16 148	1 Kgs 9:5 74	Isa 22:20-23 121
Lev 16:12 170	1 Kgs 18:21 174	Isa 25:9 180
Lev 18 94		Isa 37:36 34
Lev 18:24 94	1 Chr 21 94	Isa 44:6 28,197,209
Lev 19:31 143		Isa 45:5 209
Lev 20:6 143	2 Chr 2:10 144	Isa 45:18 31

Isa 45:23-25 10	Dan 7	Mal 4:1-3 195
Isa 45:24 191	. . . 59,61,62,64,65,67	
Isa 53 145	. . 71,72,77,78,79,198	Mat 1:20-21 37
Isa 53:2 27,186	Dan 7:7,8,19,2 63	Mat 3:4 38
Isa 53:2,3 39	Dan 7:9 72,76	Mat 3:16 98
Isa 53:7 24	Dan 7:9,10 . . 73,76,79,80,83	Mat 4:7 40
	Dan 7:9,10,13, ... 87	Mat 5:6 164
Jer 1:5 38	Dan 7:10 76,80,140	Mat 6:9 39
Jer 13:23 127	Dan 7:13 77	Mat 7:2 191
Jer 14 94	Dan 7:13,14	Mat 7:13 177
Jer 25:9 106,107	. . . 24,25,55,57,73,78	Mat 7:14 190
Jer 27 94	Dan 7:14 77	Mat 10:34 131
Jer 44 94	Dan 7:20 71	Mat 11:9-11 38
Jer 48:40 153	Dan 7:21,22 71	Mat 11:11 132
	Dan 7:22 124	Mat 12:31 33
Eze 1 97	Dan 7:25 . . . 65,68,69,70,71	Mat 12:31,32
Eze 1:5 97	Dan 8 79	. . . 29,100,191,198,213
Eze 1:6,7 97	Dan 8:14	Mat 16:13-19 119
Eze 1:10 97	. . .57,80,147,148,149	Mat 16:18 74
Eze 1:13 97	Dan 8:19 58	Mat 17:2 167
Eze 1:14 97	Dan 9 71	Mat 17:5 30
Eze 1:15,16 98	Dan 9:24 74	Mat 19:24 190
Eze 1:20 98	Dan 9:24-27 57	Mat 19:6 198
Eze 1:22 97	Dan 10:13 41	Mat 23:9 39
Eze 1:26 97	Dan 10:21 79	Mat 23:11 42
Eze 4:5,6 70	Dan 12:1 57,79,175	Mat 23:16 150
Eze 5 94	Dan 12:1,2 41	Mat 23:27 177
Eze 6 94	Dan 12:4,9 58	Mat 24 215
Eze 10 97	Dan 12:9 207	Mat 24:27 180
Eze 10:12 97	Dan 12:12 156,181	Mat 24:30 181
Eze 10:16 98	Dan 12:12 181	Mat 24:36 184
Eze 10:16,17 98	Dan 12:12,13 183	Mat 24:37-39 58
Eze 10:17 98		Mat 24:38,39 162
Eze 14:12-21 92,93	Joe 2:11 181	Mat 25:31 40
Eze 14:21,22 158		Mat 26:63,64 181
Eze 18:4 136,172	Zec 1:8-10 24	Mat 26:64 182
Eze 21:7 180	Zec 1:18-21 106	Mat 27 176
Eze 28:12-14 27	Zec 3:2 40	Mat 27:19 213
Eze 28:12-19 45	Zec 4:6,7 107	Mat 27:52 87
	Zec 6 105,106	Mat 28:10,20 214
Dan 2 . . 59,61,62,77,79,187	Zec 6:1-5 24	Mat 28:18 215
Dan 2:42 60	Zec 6:1-8 105	Mat 28:19 198
Dan 2:44 61	Zec 6:5 103	Mat 28:19,20 . . . 74,121,171
Dan 4:34-37 107		Mat 28:20 215
Dan 5:18,19 107	Mal 3:16 83	
Dan 5:27 139	Mal 3:16 80	Mar 1:15 74

Bible Cross Reference

Mar 2:27,28 32	Joh 14:6 207	Rom 16:25,26 207
Mar 5:37 38	Joh 14:9 29,203	
Mar 6:18 132	Joh 14:24 30	1 Cor 2:14 214
Mar 9:7 200	Joh 15:5 120	1 Cor 5:7 120
Mar 15:34 201	Joh 15:20,21 172	1 Cor 6:2,3 191
	Joh 16:1-4 131,171	1 Cor 10:4 44,120
Luk 1:13 37	Joh 16:7 215	1 Cor 12-14 217
Luk 1:15,35 38	Joh 16:8 164	1 Cor 15:24-26 195
Luk 1:69 24	Joh 16:13 . . 29,135,213,214	1 Cor 15:24-28 72,73
Luk 2:25-27 100	Joh 16:13 214	1 Cor 15:25-28 202
Luk 3 81	Joh 16:14 25,99,218	
Luk 3:22 30	Joh 17 177	\2 Cor 3:17 68
Luk 10:20 85	Joh 17:8 30	2 Cor 5:10
Luk 18:8 129	Joh 19:19-22 210	 9,80,83,84,121
Luk 22:42 129,200		 140,149,191
Luk 23:3 209	Act 2 199	2 Cor 12:2-7 72
	Act 4:10-12 38	2 Cor 12:9 177
Joh 1 208,209,211	Act 5 98	
Joh 1:1 208,210	Act 5:1-11 154	Gal 1:1 201
Joh 1:1-3,14 30	Act 5:31,32 208	Gal 1:19 120
Joh 1:1,3 207,211	Act 6:15 168	Gal 2:11 120
Joh 1:3,10 208	Act 7:39 216	Gal 5:22 29
Joh 1:9-2:1 126	Act 8:39 216	Gal 5:22,23 154
Joh 1:10 32	Act 12:17 120	Gal 5:22-24 99,218
Joh 1:10,14 31	Act 13:6 38	Gal 6:7,8 157
Joh 1:11 186	Act 14:3 215	
Joh 1:14 32	Act 15 121	Eph 1:9,10
Joh 1:29 37	Act 15:13 120	. . . 24,25,72,77,78,186
Joh 2:16-19 151	Act 15:37 38	Eph 4:8 88
Joh 3:16 168	Act 17:31 121,155	Eph 6:17 132
Joh 3:16,17 175	Act 21:18 120	
Joh 3:19-21 133	Act 26:28 213	Phi 2:5-11 197
Joh 3:21 163		Phi 2:6 204
Joh 4:23 63	Rom 1:16-17 177	Phi 2:8 36
Joh 5:18 198,205	Rom 1:17 123,149,165	Phi 2:8-11 27
Joh 5:22 9	Rom 3:4 201	Phi 2:9,10 28
Joh 5:22,23	Rom 4:15 157	Phi 4:3 85
. . . 121,198,205,207,210	Rom 5:9 157	Phi 4:13 177
Joh 5:25 40	Rom 5:10 176	
Joh 6:38 88,197,200	Rom 6:14 126	Col 1:16 171
Joh 6:39,40 172	Rom 7 and 8 127	Col 1:16,17 32,211
Joh 6:40 40	Rom 8:5-8 133	Col 2:9 29,204,210,219
Joh 6:46 29	Rom 8:6-9;8:14 214	Col 3:5,6 94
Joh 6:63 154	Rom 8:26,27 212	Col 4:11 38
Joh 12:28 30	Rom 8:28 126	
Joh 14:1-3 215	Rom 12:19 191	1 The 2:14,15 158

1 The 4:16 41	1 Joh 5:4,5 177	Rev 6:10 176
1 The 4:16,17 . . . 136,143,183		Rev 6:10,11 173
1 The 4:16-18 172	Jud 1:9 29,39,40	Rev 6:11 167,176
1 The 5:3 153		Rev 6:12 147,181
1 The 5:9 157	Rev 1:7 180,182	Rev 6:12-14 147
	Rev 1:8 209	Rev 6:12-17 179
2 The 2:4 225	Rev 1:17 28	Rev 6:13 147
2 The 2:10-12 174	Rev 1:18 40,201	Rev 6:14 147
2 The 9:9-12 223	Rev 2:8 209	Rev 6:15 180
	Rev 3:5 79	Rev 6:16,17 182
1 Tim 1:17 29	Rev 3:7 121	Rev 6:17 187
1 Tim 6:15 202	Rev 3:10 157,160	Rev 7 187,188
1 Tim 6:15,16 135	Rev 3:17-21 166	Rev 7:1 187,188
1 Tim 6:16 29	Rev 4 139	Rev 7:1-4 164,189
	Rev 4 and 5 96,217	Rev 7:9,13,14 189
2 Tim 1:14 208	Rev 4-6 87,91	Rev 7:9-14 164,189
2 Tim 4:8 117	Rev 4:1 187	Rev 8 187,188
	Rev 4:2,4 76	Rev 8:1 187,189
Heb 1:1,2 31	Rev 4:3,4 76	Rev 8:2 21,24,188
Heb 1:2 193,208	Rev 4:5 76	Rev 8:3 170
Heb 1:8-11 197,204	Rev 4:6 91	Rev 8:5 184
Heb 1:9 28,186	Rev 4:7 . . . 118,131,139,153	Rev 8:7-13 222,225
Heb 1:13 41	Rev 4:8 91	Rev 9 221
Heb 1:14 24	Rev 5	Rev 9:1-3 179
Heb 2:7 29	. 55,56,57,58,59,62,65,76	Rev 9:1,11 174
Heb 4:12 132	 77,78,80,81,201,219	Rev 9:3 221
Heb 4:15 177	Rev 5:1-3 21	Rev 9:5,6 174
Heb 5:7 36	Rev 5:3 80	Rev 9:11 225
Heb 5:7-10 88	Rev 5:6 21,24,91	Rev 9:15 224
Heb 8 and 9 148	Rev 5:7 77	Rev 9:15,16 175
Heb 8:1,2 41	Rev 5:9 76,88,121	Rev 11:3 216,222
Heb 8:1-5 140,170	Rev 5:9,12 77	Rev 11:15-19 41
Heb 11 126,162	Rev 5:11 76	Rev 11:17 41
Heb 11:7 213	Rev 5:12 78	Rev 11:19 184
Heb 12:17 191	Rev 5:12-14 25	Rev 12:6 70,72
	Rev 6	Rev 12:7 29
Jam 2:19 171	. . . 101,105,106,107	Rev 12:7,8 42
Jam 4:17 224	. . . 117,164,187,188	Rev 12:7-9 57
	Rev 6:1 87	Rev 12:11 165
1 Pet 1:20 31,207	Rev 6:1,2 103,117,118	Rev 12:14 70,72
1 Pet 4:4 133	Rev 6:3,4 103,131	Rev 12:16 124
	Rev 6:5,6 103,139	Rev 13:1 179
2 Pet 3:9 156	Rev 6:7,8 92,103,153	Rev 13:5 68
2 Pet 3:16 127	Rev 6:9 132	Rev 13:5-7 132
	Rev 6:9 169	Rev 13:6,7 162
1 Joh 1:9-2:1 126	Rev 6:9-11 132,165	Rev 13:7 159
1 Joh 2:4-6 127		

Bible Cross Reference

Rev 13:8 80,91
Rev 13:10 167,169,177
Rev 13:14 221,225
Rev 13:15 132,171,225
Rev 13:18 28
Rev 14:6,7 163
Rev 14:11 164
Rev 14:13 166
Rev 15 41
Rev 15:2-4 183
Rev 15:3 92
Rev 16:4-7 133
Rev 16 41,57
Rev 16:12 180,182
Rev 16:18 184
Rev 16:18,20 181
Rev 17:6 132,159
Rev 17:8 28,84
Rev 17:12 60,221
Rev 18 94
Rev 18:6 176
Rev 19:13 209,211
Rev 19:16 202
Rev 19:19-21 136
Rev 19:20 179
Rev 19:21 180
Rev 20 94,127,136
Rev 20:1-3 179
Rev 20:4 191
Rev 20:5 172,190
Rev 20:5 190
Rev 20:5,6 143
Rev 20:9,10 195
Rev 20:12
 ...79,80,83,136,189
Rev 20:15 80,190
Rev 21:2 190
Rev 21:5 195
Rev 21:8 195
Rev 21:27 28,80
Rev 22:11 175
Rev 22:12 83
Rev 22:13 209

About the Author

Larry Wilson, Director of Wake Up America Seminars, became a born again Christian after returning from a tour of duty in Vietnam. The understanding of the gospel, the plan of salvation, and the atonement of Jesus Christ has thrilled his soul for the past 35 years. Since his conversion, he has spent over 30 years intensely studying the prophecies of Daniel and Revelation.

In 1988, he published the book *Warning! Revelation is about to be fulfilled* and since then, has written several books (over 750,000 books in circulation throughout the world in more than 60 countries). He also writes a feature Bible study in the *Day Star* (a monthly publication produced by Wake Up America Seminars). He gives seminar presentations, produces video programs which have been broadcast from various locations throughout the United States, and is a frequent guest on radio talk shows.

About the Organization

Wake Up America Seminars (WUAS) is both a non-profit and a non-denominational organization. With God's blessings and the generosity of many people, WUAS has distributed millions of pamphlets, books and tapes around the world since it began in 1988. WUAS is not a church, nor is it affiliated or sponsored by any religious organization. WUAS does not offer membership of any kind. Its mission is not to convert the world to a point of view. Although WUAS has well defined views on certain biblical matters, its mission is primarily "seed sowing." It promotes the primacy of salvation through faith in Jesus Christ, His imminent return, and is doing its best to encourage people with the good news of the gospel. People of all faiths are invited to study the materials produced by WUAS.

Wake Up America Seminars, Inc.
P.O. Box 273
Bellbrook, OH   45305

http://www.wake-up.org
email: *wuas@wake-up.org*